FOREIGN POLICY
AND REGIONALISM
IN THE AMERICAS

FOREIGN POLICY
AND
REGIONALISM
IN THE AMERICAS

edited by

Gordon Mace
Jean-Philippe Thérien

LYNNE
RIENNER
PUBLISHERS

BOULDER
LONDON

Published in the United States of America in 1996 by
Lynne Rienner Publishers, Inc.
1800 30th Street, Boulder, Colorado 80301

and in the United Kingdom by
Lynne Rienner Publishers, Inc.
3 Henrietta Street, Covent Garden, London WC2E 8LU

Library of Congress Cataloging-in-Publication Data
Foreign policy and regionalism in the Americas/edited by Gordon
    Mace, Jean-Philippe Thérien.
        p.   cm.
    Includes bibliographical references and index.
    ISBN 1-55587-513-0 (hc: alk. paper)
    ISBN 1-55587-637-4 (pb: alk. paper)
    1. America—Foreign relations—20th century. I. Mace, Gordon.
II. Thérien, Jean-Philippe.
E18.85.F67   1996
327.7—dc20   95-41106
                                                            CIP

British Cataloguing in Publication Data
A Cataloguing in Publication record for this book
is available from the British Library.

Printed and bound in the United States of America

         The paper used in this publication meets the requirements
  ∞   of the American National Standard for Permanence of
         Paper for Printed Library Materials Z39.48-1984.

    5 4 3 2 1

To Nicolas, Michaël,
and the children of the Americas

CONTENTS

ACKNOWLEDGMENTS

◆

This book has benefited from the collaboration and support of a great number of people. We would first like to thank all the contributors who have participated in this collective effort. Their expertise and professionalism have greatly facilitated our work.

We also gratefully acknowledge the support offered by the Institut québécois des hautes études internationales and the Department of Political Science at Laval University throughout the preparation of the manuscript. Marie-Pierre Ashby and Élise Lapalme played a key role by diligently attending to the word processing. Martin Roy provided a valuable helping hand in finalizing the bibliography. We especially thank Louis Bélanger for his assistance, which was constant and took many forms.

Lazer Lederhendler, Siobhan Harty, and Richard Keswick allowed us to overcome the language barriers encountered with contributors whose native languages are Spanish, Portuguese, or French. To all three, our thanks.

Financial support for this project was generously provided by the FCAR Fund of the Government of Québec and by the Social Sciences and Humanities Research Council of Canada. We are grateful to both institutions for their confidence in our project.

We express special gratitude to Lynne Rienner for her personal encouragement in this endeavor, to Bridget Julian for her efficiency and helpful suggestions, and to Michelle Welsh-Horst and Laurie Rogers, without whom the quality of this book would not have been as high. Naturally, we take sole responsibility for any remaining errors in the pages that follow.

G. M.
J.-P. T.

Introduction:
Foreign Policy and
Regionalism in the Americas

◆

Gordon Mace & Jean-Philippe Thérien

> For the first time in history, the Americas are a community of
> democratic societies.
>
> —*Summit of the Americas*
> *Declaration of Principles*
> *December 1994*

> Our aim is to strengthen mutual confidence that contributes to the
> economic and social integration of our peoples.
>
> —*Summit of the Americas*
> *Plan of Action*
> *December 1994*

Recent developments seem to have created a particularly favorable environment for the establishment of a new regional system of the Americas and, eventually, a true community of American nations. Some
Latin American commentators have even gone so far as to say that the
1994 Summit of the Americas could perhaps prove as important for region building as Europe's decision to form its Common Market (Summit 1994: 5). Of course it is still much too early to determine the exact
nature and scope of the new regional environment in the Western
Hemisphere. Nevertheless, it is almost impossible to ignore the chain
of events beginning in the early 1980s that seems to point to a new
configuration of international relations on the American continent.

It is clear that this expansion of regional cooperation is not limited only to the Americas. For some years now, the terms "triad,"
"trading bloc," "commercial zone," and "open regionalism" have
been used to describe a new pattern of international interactions. In
one way or another, the literature identifies a "new regionalism" as a
major feature of the post–Cold War international system (Rostow
1990; Belous and Hartley 1990; Rosecrance 1991; Brand 1992; Buelens 1992; Oman 1994).

1

This new regionalism is centered primarily in the industrialized world. The triad is composed of Western Europe, North America, and part of Asia, with Germany, the United States, and Japan as bloc leaders. There are indications that these industrial and technical centers of gravity may possibly extend to even larger economic, if not political, regional groupings such as Europe, the Americas, and the Asia-Pacific.

Despite a growing literature discussing regionalism or a new regionalism, the concept is still rather vague and imprecise as Tokatlian and Tickner point out in Chapter 6. As was the case with the concept of regional integration some thirty years ago (Rogers 1995), there are competing visions of what regionalism is or should be. Some scholars have used the term "strategic regionalism," which they apply to region building that is a reaction to the globalization of production, markets, and ideas (Deblock and Brunelle 1993: 597–611). Other scholars consider regionalism as a set of states' policies "designed to promote the emergence of a cohesive regional unit" (Hurrel 1992: 123). Still others look at it as a multidimensional process leading to stronger interdependence (Tokatlian and Tickner, this volume).

We tend to agree with the last point of view, although we do not exclude the idea that regionalism is, to a certain extent, a reaction to external processes. This view of regionalism has been subscribed to as far back as the 1950s with the creation of the European Communities, the only difference being in the nature of the external processes at the time. Consequently, we would define regionalism as a process occurring in a given geographical region by which different types of actors (states, regional institutions, societal organizations) come to share certain fundamental values. These actors also participate in a growing network of economic, cultural, scientific, diplomatic, political, and even military interactions. Although the progression may not be automatic and may vary in speed from sector to sector, the combination of increasing interactions and shared values should produce not necessarily a new political unit but rather a stronger and more diversified capacity for regional management of regional problems. This regional management may occur through formal multilateral organizations, such as the Organization of American States (OAS) in the Americas, or in an ad hoc fashion through meetings of ministers or civil servants, such as the inter-American meeting of the ministers of defense that was convened for the first time in Williamsburg, Virginia, in July 1995.

Thus, from our point of view, the concept of regionalism is not altogether different from the concept of regional integration proposed some thirty years ago by pioneers such as Ernst Haas, Karl Deustch, and Leon Lindberg. But as used today, "regionalism" refers to a phenomenon that is less institutional, less automatic, more diffuse, and more imprecise with regard to the dependent variable than what was envisaged in prior analytic models and theoretical constructions.

Consequently, it seems that we are now witnessing, in the Americas and in other parts of the world, the emergence of a new regionalism. We should not forget, however, that regionalism is not something new in the Americas. It has been present in various guises in the hemisphere for almost 200 years. In fact, until very recently, there were two competing visions of the regional system of the Americas, one originating in the North, the other in the South.

TWO COMPETING VISIONS OF THE AMERICAS

The first of these visions was developed in the United States and included two aspects: the Western Hemisphere idea and the commercial zone or free trade area of the Americas.

The U.S. Vision

The first element of what we will call the U.S. vision of a regional system of the Americas involved the twin concepts of the Western Hemisphere idea and the commercial zone (Molineu 1986: 15–51). It was essentially a view of how overall relations in the Americas should be conducted, and it implied an American continent free from the influences of nation-states in other parts of the world and dominated by the United States.

This image has been present in the minds of many U.S. policymakers since the birth of the U.S. republic. It appears, for example, in the writings of Thomas Jefferson, who penned the following as early as 1786: "Our Confederation must be considered the nucleus from which the settlers of the north and south of the Americas will come forth" (Aguilar 1968: 25–26). It was also a major preoccupation of President James Monroe and his secretary of state, John Quincy Adams, who by 1822 had become more favorable to Henry Clay's concept of a "system embracing the United States and Latin America" (Connell-Smith 1974: 52). The President's Message to the U.S. Congress of December 2, 1823, did not constitute a major policy statement concerning the future of the American continent at the time. As Connell-Smith rightfully argues: "The Monroe Doctrine is vastly more important for what it was to become than for what Monroe actually said in 1823" (Connell-Smith 1974: 62). What the message essentially did was to declare the Americas free of further European colonization while proclaiming U.S. neutrality in the wars of

Spanish-American independence. However, Monroe's words would be variously interpreted in later years.

One subsequent interpretation was that the affairs of the American continent were the concern of the United States, thus according the U.S. government the right to interfere in regional affairs to maintain law and order, as well as to create or restore a climate favorable to business and investment. It was in this sense that President Monroe's message to Congress became the Monroe Doctrine, which in turn became the underlying rationale for U.S. policy in the hemisphere.

Thereafter, the Monroe Doctrine was regularly alluded to in U.S.–Latin American relations and grew more precise in terms of its content. President Theodore Roosevelt significantly clarified the meaning of the doctrine on December 6, 1904, when he made this now famous statement in his annual message to Congress:

> Chronic wrongdoing, or an impotence which results in a general loosening of the ties of civilized society, may in America, as elsewhere, ultimately require intervention by some civilized nation, and in the Western Hemisphere the adherence of the United States to the Monroe Doctrine may force the United States, however reluctantly, in flagrant cases of such wrongdoing or impotence, to the exercise of an international police power. (Connell-Smith 1974: 115)

The Roosevelt Corollary to the Monroe Doctrine, as it was later dubbed, reinforced the image of an American system dominated by the United States. No U.S. president since Roosevelt has been as blunt in his discourse on U.S. policy toward the hemisphere, but the Monroe Doctrine and the Roosevelt Corollary were often alluded to when justification was needed for U.S. interventions in Latin America throughout the twentieth century.

Therefore, from the 1820s to the 1980s, the idea of a system of political and military interaction free of outside influence and with the United States firmly entrenched as the major regional power at its core was a central element in the U.S. vision of a regional system of the Americas.

The other major aspect of this U.S. vision of a regional system of the Americas was more economic in nature. It goes back to an idea of James G. Blaine, secretary of state under James Garfield, to create a commercial zone or customs union between the United States and the Latin American countries.

Blaine had two principal aims: to increase U.S. trade with Latin America and to propose a mechanism for peaceful settlement of disputes between American states (Connell-Smith 1974: 107). Both would reduce chances for European, and especially British, intervention in the Americas while developing a favorable environment for business relations throughout the hemisphere.

To this end, Washington issued invitations to other American governments in 1881 asking them to participate in a conference in the U.S. capital. President Garfield's assassination put a temporary stop to the project, which finally materialized in 1889 with Blaine's return as secretary of state under Benjamin Harrison. The First International Conference of American States was held in Washington from October 1889 to April 1890 to discuss U.S. proposals concerning peaceful settlement of disputes and the establishment of a customs union. Both concepts were rejected by Latin American governments at the time but were never really abandoned by successive U.S. governments in subsequent Pan-American conferences.

The transformation of the Pan-American Union into the OAS in Bogotá in 1948 was an important step on the road to building a regional system of the Americas, although there were conflicting views on the scope and orientations of the system. The adoption of the Pact of Bogotá, or the American Treaty on Pacific Settlement, was a major victory in terms of U.S. policy objectives, but the fact that the Economic Agreement of Bogotá was never ratified showed that Washington's plans for the establishment of a free trade area were still not looked upon favorably by a majority of Latin American governments. This lack of enthusiasm would not, however, prevent subsequent U.S. governments from trying to push the idea whenever possible.

Events of the past 150 years thus reveal a U.S. vision of a regional system of the Americas built around two major concepts: (1) a political and security system of the Americas with the United States as its core and (2) a commercial zone covering most of the hemisphere in which there were very few barriers to inter-American trade and investment. Using a contemporary expression, some might call this vision the "hub-and-spoke" model.

The Latin American Vision

Alongside the U.S. vision was a rival one dating back to the 1810s that was based on the idea of Latin American unity. Instead of a hub-and-spoke model, it was a bloc-to-bloc configuration.

This alternative vision originates from the writings of Simón Bolívar, whose central idea was to create a union of Latin American states. Bolívar thought Latin American unity was necessary for two reasons: internally, it would foster democracy and put a stop to anarchy in many of the newly independent Latin American countries;

externally, it would consolidate international order in Latin America, thus preventing foreign intervention and allowing the region to play a role in the international system (Tovar Tamayo 1974).

This vision of a united Latin America was already in Bolívar's mind prior to the proclamations of Latin American independence, as is clear in this letter from Jamaica, written in 1815: "It is a noble idea to form one single nation out of the whole new world with a single bond joining the parts to each other and to the whole. Inasmuch as they have the same origin, language, customs, and religion, they must . . . have one government which would join together the various states to be formed" (Aguilar 1968: 26).

The vision of unity was also a recurrent theme in a letter Bolívar sent to his Latin American counterparts in December 1824 inviting them to a congress in Panama in 1826. No invitation was sent to the U.S. government by Bolívar himself because, from the Liberator's point of view, the Panama Congress was to be the launching pad for the unity of Spanish America, complete with the adoption of a Treaty of Union, League, and Confederation.

The treaty was never ratified and Bolívar's dream was subsequently shattered by interstate conflicts and the dismantling of the Republic of Greater Colombia and the United Provinces of Central America. But the idea of Latin American unity was kept alive through regional meetings such as the Lima Conference of 1847–1848 and in the writings of Latin American intellectuals and statesmen such as Roque Sáenz Peña, José Inginieros, Alfredo Palacios, Manuel Ugarte, José Enrique Rodó, Pedro Enrique Ureña, Alfonso Reyes, and others.

The ideas developed by these intellectuals were supported and disseminated through a movement for university reform that originated in Argentina in 1919 and spread throughout Latin America in the early 1920s. They also became one of the driving forces behind the American Popular Revolutionary Alliance (APRA), an important political movement that had a significant impact in many Latin American circles in the 1920s and 1930s. Indeed, before becoming a strictly Peruvian political party, the APRA of Victor Raoul Haya de la Torre played a major role in the promotion of ideas such as Latin American unity, control over foreign investments, and bloc-to-bloc negotiation with the United States (Alexander 1968: 23).

The central theme of Latin American unity was still very much present in the years following World War II, but political concerns yielded to a focus on economics. It was during this period that the concept of economic integration was developed, essentially by members of the Economic Commission for Latin America (ECLA, now ECLAC to include the Caribbean). In essence, ECLA's thinking was that if Latin America wanted to be a significant part of the international system, the countries of the region needed to industrialize and their societies to become more modern. Industrialization, in turn, necessitated a strategy of import substitution. This strategy had been employed previously without much success at the national level, which is why it was now necessary to pursue a strategy of import substitution on a wider level by creating regional markets (Baer 1962; Mitchell 1967).

Among regional integration schemes in Latin America, the Central American Common Market and the Andean Group best represent the strategy favored by the ECLA with regard to economic integration. Both contained measures relating to free trade and a customs union, compensation mechanisms, state intervention in the economy, and, in the case of the Andean Group, control over foreign investments.

* * *

The previous discussion illustrates the two different and competing visions of economic and political relations in the Americas that existed for many decades prior to the 1980s. The U.S. vision, equated in many instances with Pan-Americanism, foresaw a regional system based on a free trade area with the United States, as the leading nation in the hemisphere, at its core. The Latin American vision imagined a community of American nations made up exclusively of former Spanish and Portuguese colonies. Linked by history, culture, and language, these nations would form a community capable of dealing with the United States and, eventually, the rest of the world on an equal basis.

The situation in the 1990s reveals a completely different picture. The Free Trade Agreement (FTA) between Canada and the United States, the North American Free Trade Agreement (NAFTA), the Enterprise for the Americas Initiative, and the Summit of the Americas, with its announcement of negotiations for Chilean entry into NAFTA, all point to a dramatic change in inter-American relations. They represent the milestones of a new regional system in the making and, taken as a whole, imply the possibility of a major departure from past behavior and the superseding of traditional visions about the future of the Americas.

ISSUES REGARDING THE
CHANGING ENVIRONMENT OF FOREIGN POLICY

The central question, then, is how to explain this fundamental departure. What external influences are at work here? What has been the role of domestic factors, and how have they influenced the political agendas of the major countries of the Americas? What combination of domestic and external influences explains the particular attitudes and behaviors of different governments throughout the Americas? And what does all of this imply for the future of regionalism in the Americas?

The main objective of this book is to propose answers to these questions. Clearly, it is difficult to determine precisely the nature and extent of the new regionalism of the Americas. Opinions vary concerning the future direction of events. However, there is a consensus that we are currently witnessing a dramatic change in attitudes and behaviors in many governmental and business circles throughout the Americas and that we are in the midst of a significant period of transition in the structuring of the region.

This volume is concerned with the period of transition covering the past fifteen years. It focuses on the foreign policy of strategically located countries of the region. "Strategically located" is not used here in a military sense but is related to the impact of the external behavior of these countries on the future direction of regionalism. More precisely, the phrase refers to the criteria of size of the economy and/or relevance of a country to a given subregional dynamic. The combination of the two criteria explains the choice made here to study the United States, Canada, Mexico, Brazil, and Argentina, whereas the criterion of relevance for subregional dynamics is at the basis of our selection of countries such as Jamaica, Chile, Peru, Colombia, and Venezuela. The focus on foreign policy results from our belief that in a period of change, such as the one that has been occurring in the Americas since the beginning of the 1980s, the foreign policy domain is one of the best scientific sites from which to understand the complex interplays of domestic and external influences and their impact on the process of region building as a way to adapt to a new environment.

In consequence, the book is first and foremost a comparative study of foreign policy in the Americas. It does not, however, deal only with foreign policy. It is also a study of the relationship between foreign policy and regionalism, and it seeks to analyze the impact of foreign policy on regionalism but not exclude the influence of regionalism on foreign policymaking. In order to do this, the following chapters are structured around three basic questions: First, how has each state been affected by recent transformations in the international environment? Second, how have national governments reacted to these transformations in the general orientation of their economic and foreign policies? Third, what place does regionalism currently occupy in the foreign policy of each country? The responses to these questions reveal significant differences among nations in the Western Hemisphere; however, they also reveal a certain number of common traits that are making the Americas an increasingly integrated political space. Three trends in particular merit attention.

The first trend refers to the new importance accorded to the international environment by all states of the hemisphere. The globalization of production, trade, and capital markets has now come to be seen as a reality that must be considered at nearly all levels of decisionmaking. More and more, the traditional distinction between domestic politics and international politics is tending to fade; as a consequence, isolationism increasingly appears unsustainable as a means of promoting national interests.

The second trend concerns the new consensus—if not perfect, then at least unprecedented—on the best way to achieve economic growth. In short, there appears to be no credible alternative to market economics. This idea breaks sharply with the pattern of previous decades in which the model put forward by Latin American countries, which was founded on state intervention and import substitution policies, countered the free-market model championed by the United States. Combined with the end of the Cold War, the adoption of more liberal economic policies by the vast majority of governments in the hemisphere has notably permitted the establishment of more harmonious relations between the United States and its cluster of partners in North America, South America, and the Caribbean.

A third trend results from the previous two, in that greater attention placed on external factors and the realignment of economic policies have favored an increase in regionalism in the foreign policy of most countries in the hemisphere. Certainly, the nature and the depth of this process remain a subject of intense debate. States do not share a common vision of the region to which they belong. It is in effect paradoxical that, on the one hand, the need to invest more political resources at the regional level is generally recognized by all governments in the Americas and that, on the other hand, each country maintains a distinct regional strategy founded on its geographical situation, its economic power, and its political culture. The fate of regionalism in the Americas is certainly far from being sealed. It is nevertheless remarkable to see how inter-American relations in recent years have been marked by the launching or reactivation of numerous cooperation initiatives of a regional character. This in itself constitutes a major change in the foreign policy of the nations of the Western Hemisphere.

A DIVERSITY OF BEHAVIOR

North America

In his chapter on the United States, Louis Balthazar focuses on how the political and economic upheavals of recent years have modified U.S. foreign policy interests. From a military perspective, the end of the Cold War has anointed the United States with sole superpower status; in economic terms, however, the country has been forced to adapt to the rise of increasingly competitive commercial partners. Although it has become more and more preoccupied with domestic problems, the United States appears condemned to play a leadership role in the international arena.

In his analysis of Washington's regional foreign policy, Balthazar emphasizes the distinct position of Canada. Considered a good neighbor and a faithful ally, Canada has traditionally been excluded from the hemispheric vision of the U.S. government. It is revealing that relations with Canada were long the responsibility of the Division of European Affairs within the U.S. State Department. Since the mid-1980s, however, the climate of Canadian-U.S. relations has changed considerably. The FTA and NAFTA have strongly contributed to institutionalizing the economic integration of the two countries.

Balthazar recalls how U.S. relations with Latin America were marked by Cold War logic. Until the end of the 1980s, Washington's Latin American policy was guided by two objectives: the fight against communism and the promotion of free enterprise. However, the decline of the Soviet Union and the difficulties of the Uruguay Round led the United States to reformulate its approach toward Central and South America. Launched by President George Bush, the project to establish a free trade zone from Alaska to Patagonia—the Enterprise for the Americas Initiative—gave rise to a new optimism in relations between the United States and Latin America. Even though numerous obstacles still confront this project, Balthazar suggests that it could be facilitated by the growing Hispanicization of the United States and by the increasing cultural homogenization of the Americas.

Guadalupe González and Jorge Chabat argue that Mexican foreign policy has recently passed from one of ideological isolationism to one of active pragmatism. They explain this evolution as the concurrent product of the globalization of Mexico's economy and of Mexico's alignment with a liberal model of development. Initiated under Miguel de la Madrid and accelerated under Carlos Salinas de Gortari, the opening of the Mexican economy led to an unprecedented rapprochement with the United States. This rapprochement, which was consecrated through the ratification of NAFTA, does not, strictly speaking, constitute a rupture with the past. Given the strength of the commercial and financial connections that have long bound together the two nations, NAFTA can rather be seen as the institutionalization of a de facto integration.

González and Chabat note that, considering the new context of relations between Mexico and the United States, traditional Mexican nationalism is increasingly confined to the rhetorical domain. For Mexico the desire to join the First World tends to prevail over the government's need to seek increased legitimacy through greater independence from Washington. Mexico maintains multiple relations with the rest of Latin America, as is illustrated by the country's participation in the Contadora Group, the Rio Group, and the Group of Three (G-3). Such diplomatic activism, however, contrasts remarkably with the weakness of commercial exchanges between Mexico and Latin American countries. Moreover, Mexico's mistrust of an eventual enlargement of NAFTA erodes the image of a united and interdependent Latin America.

González and Chabat conclude by suggesting that, despite the current fragmentation of Latin America, in the long term the economic growth to which NAFTA will lead could paradoxically instigate an important expansion of economic relations between Mexico and the other countries within the region.

Regionalism is becoming an increasingly important dimension of Canadian foreign policy, according to Gordon Mace and Jean-Philippe Thérien. Mace and Thérien argue that this evolution can only be properly understood as a result of the gradual erosion of Canada's international power in recent decades. At the outset of the 1970s, Canada reacted to changing conditions in the world environment in two ways: first, by making competitiveness a new priority of its foreign policy and, second, by opting for a diversification of its foreign relations, which had traditionally concentrated heavily on the United States. In spite of having little to do with regionalism as it is understood today, this strategy contributed to a significant development of economic links between Canada and Latin American countries.

The gravity of the worldwide recession of 1981–1982 forced the Canadian government to realign its foreign policy even more closely with the country's economic needs. Forced to adapt to the rise of regional groupings throughout the world, Canada finally concluded a free trade agreement with the United States in 1988. Mace and Thérien suggest that this treaty marks the most important change in Canadian foreign relations in the twentieth century. Canada was also one of the original signatories of NAFTA, along with the United States and Mexico. The authors show that, despite the growing importance of economic matters in Canada, the country's new interest in regionalism is not limited to commercial issues. In addition to being an active participant in the resolution of the Central American and Haitian crises, Canada joined the OAS in 1990.

Mace and Thérien conclude that the implementation and the enlargement of NAFTA are likely to be top priorities for Canadian decisionmakers in the coming years. They also suggest that Canada will probably seek to apply to the whole of the Americas the principle of functionalism and the practice of mediation, two traditional elements characteristic of Canadian foreign policy.

The Caribbean Basin

Anthony Payne notes that Jamaica, like other Caribbean countries, has historically been noteworthy for its status as a "peripheral state" within a double system of North-South relations: the European system, now under the direction of the European Union; and the inter-American system, under the direction of the United States. Payne contends that this position has recently been transformed: the maintenance of European links increasingly appears as a vestige of the past, and the reinforcement of ties with the United States appears to be the only open path for the future. In view of the radical changes they brought to Jamaica's external environment, the Single European Market and NAFTA are two key reasons Jamaican authorities have accorded increased attention to the United States.

Jamaica's recent evolution is well illustrated by the contrast between the economic policies of the two Manley governments. After flirting with socialism during the 1970s, the country finally and unequivocally rallied to the logic of market economics in the 1980s. This reversal in attitude accounts for Jamaica's ability to lead the response of Caribbean nations to the Enterprise for the Americas Initiative.

The future of regionalism in the Caribbean will likely be influenced strongly by the creation of the Association of Caribbean States (ACS), which could comprise not only the members of the Caribbean Community and Common Market (CARICOM) but all the countries of the Caribbean Basin area. It is doubtful whether these countries will be able to develop a common strategy with respect to the enlargement of free trade within the Americas. However, the efforts of recent years to promote broader schemes of subregional cooperation will weigh considerably in the future foreign policy choices of Jamaica and other Caribbean states.

In his chapter on Venezuela, Andrés Serbin highlights the major reorientation of economic policy and foreign policy that occurred in 1989, during the second mandate of President Carlos Andrés Pérez. Serbin views this *gran viraje* as a response to a series of external factors (including the fragmentation of the world economy into trading blocs and the retreat of the superpowers from the Caribbean Basin) and to an unprecedented domestic economic crisis. In terms of economic policy, the gran viraje put forward a new model of development based on private enterprise and the promotion of exports. In terms of foreign policy, the strategy adopted in 1989 gave precedence to economic issues over political issues and proposed that Venezuela's external relations be centered on the Caribbean region.

Insofar as it remains the principal market for exports, the United States continues to be a diplomatic priority for Venezuela. However, because of the great asymmetry in U.S.-Venezuelan relations, subregionalism appears to be the true motor of current Venezuelan international activity. Difficulties in introducing a common external tariff among Andean Group countries have not prevented a spectacular increase in cooperation between Venezuela and Colombia. According to Serbin, the expansion of trade between these two countries is nothing less than a success story. Furthermore, Venezuela is an active member of the G-3. The distinct interests of Mexico, Colombia, and Venezuela hinder the creation of a free trade zone, but the G-3 does allow Venezuela to improve its position for admittance into NAFTA. The G-3 has also vaulted Venezuela into stronger relations with the states of Central America and the Caribbean. Not only did Venezuela conclude a series of commercial agreements with these countries, it was a founder of the ACS as well. Venezuelan foreign policy today appears less ambitious than before; for Serbin, this change is positive to the extent that it reveals a more realistic vision of Venezuela's needs and of international power relations.

Juan Tokatlian and Arlene Tickner interpret the recent evolution of Colombian foreign policy in light of the changing conditions of hegemony in the global system. According to these authors, we have entered into a new era of minimal hegemony where, despite an important reconfiguration of economic power, the center-periphery cleavage remains pivotal. At the domestic level, the administrations of Virgilio Barco and César Gaviria Trujillo followed the hemispheric movement by favoring a liberalization of Colombian policy in the areas of commerce, finance, and labor.

In terms of foreign relations, the United States continues to weigh heavily upon Colombia's policies as a result of the drug problem and NAFTA's attractiveness. However, in accordance with the 1991 constitution, the Colombian government is undertaking a parallel effort to strengthen its relations with Latin American and Caribbean states. Colombia thus participates in a variety of subregional initiatives, the effectiveness of which appears to be inversely related to the number of partners involved. The Rio Group, which comprises the majority of Latin American countries, has increasingly revealed itself to be a "talk shop" unable to generate substantive accords. The G-3, with its more limited membership, has certainly been more effective in managing diplomatic and economic problems in the region. Nevertheless, the specific nature of Mexico's interests with respect to the interests of Venezuela and Colombia, along with

Colombia's failings in policy coordination, limits the benefits so far produced by the group. It is in the even more restrained framework of Colombian-Venezuelan relations that the most important progress has been noted; confirming Serbin's analysis on Venezuela, Tokatlian and Tickner suggest that the two countries have embarked on a process of binational integration that is bound to intensify. Arguing that Colombia's regionalism is a function of its fourfold identity as part of the Andean, the Caribbean, the Pacific, and the Amazonian regions, Tokatlian and Tickner conclude their chapter with the prognosis that Colombia will become increasingly active in inter-American affairs.

Peru and the Southern Cone

Basing his arguments on a detailed historical analysis, Ronald Bruce St John shows that Peru's foreign policy preoccupations have changed little since the country achieved independence. He suggests that, despite continued prointegration government rhetoric, it is unlikely that Peru will engage in an actively regionalist foreign policy. From its involvement in the 1826 Panama Conference to its participation in the Latin American Free Trade Association (LAFTA) and the Andean Group, Peru has always supported Latin American regional cooperation initiatives. However, St John explains that Peru's economic, political, and social problems have consistently impeded the regionalist momentum of Peruvian foreign policy. In the 1980s, Peru found itself in the grasp of its worst economic crisis in the twentieth century as a result of its foreign debt load, the drop in commodity prices, and the rise of the Sendero Luminoso insurrectional movement. Yet in addition to antagonizing the United States, the policies put forward by the administration of Alan Garcia Perez only succeeded in making matters worse.

After taking power in 1990, President Alberto Fujimori eased the crisis by applying a set of liberal measures, including tariff reductions, privatization of public enterprises, and a greater openness to foreign capital. However, Fujimori's proclaimed support for regional cooperation was suddenly placed in doubt with the *autogolpe* of April 1992. Anxious not to legitimate the behavior of the Peruvian president, the members of the Andean Group avoided concluding new economic agreements that included Peru. In the wake of the constitutional crisis, the government in Lima temporarily withdrew from the subregional grouping. Even though Peru was finally able to reintegrate the organization in 1994, this episode illustrates the mitigation of Peru's interest in regional cooperation. As St John stresses, it also demonstrates to what extent Peruvian foreign policy is atypical in relation to that of its neighbors.

In her study of Brazil, Maria Regina Soares de Lima explains that the country's attitude toward regionalism is ultimately determined by the inward orientation of its political culture. From this perspective, she argues that, compared with the majority of Latin American countries, Brazil figures as an exception because it does not consider the current movement toward subregional integration as the onset of an inevitable hemispheric integration.

Despite the importance of endogenous factors in its political decisionmaking process, Brazil has not been impervious to the recent evolution of the international system. Transformations in the world geoeconomic structure, the quasi-universal adoption of more liberal economic policies, the crisis of multilateralism, and the end of the Cold War constitute a series of factors that help explain why, in the past decade, regionalism has occupied a growing place in Brazil's external relations.

Three steps have marked the drive toward regionalism in Brazilian foreign policy since the mid-1980s. First, the Declaration of Iguaçú in 1985 created a dynamic of cooperation in relations with Argentina and paved the way for the signing of the Brazil-Argentina Economic Integration and Cooperation Program in 1986. Second, the creation of the Southern Cone Common Market (MERCOSUR) in 1992 set a deadline for the establishment of a common market between Uruguay, Paraguay, Argentina, and Brazil. Third, the 1993 announcement by the Brazilian government proposing a South American Free Trade Area (SAFTA) vividly confirmed Brazil's penchant for subregional cooperation as opposed to hemispheric cooperation.

Soares de Lima interprets Brazil's regional policies as the product of a twofold desire to avoid isolation in the region and to strengthen its negotiating power in light of the U.S. project for the creation of an inter-American free trade zone. Considering that Brazil is highly preoccupied with the promotion of its global interests, and given that Brazilian public opinion is more interested in domestic issues than in international issues, the place of regionalism on the Brazilian political agenda nonetheless remains uncertain.

Marc Hufty summarizes the spectacular changes Argentina has undergone in recent years by arguing that Argentineans see full and complete participation in the global political economy as the only approach capable of ensuring the country's modernization. This reconceptualization of the national interest represents a transfiguration if one considers the traditional ascendancy of nationalism and corporatism in Argentinean politics.

The turn taken by Argentina during the 1980s may be explained by a particular combination of international and domestic factors. On the international front, the slowing of growth in developed nations and the rise in interest rates rendered the country's debt load insupportable. On the domestic front, the military's loss of credibility and the exhaustion of import substitution as an economic model led to the introduction of important political and economic reforms. After the failure of the heterodox political program proposed by Raúl Alfonsín, the government of Carlos Saúl Menem proceeded with a radical liberalization of the economy, adopting a series of far-reaching measures that included the reduction of trade barriers, the privatization of public enterprises, an opening to foreign capital, and a major monetary reform.

To maximize the chances of success for its new economic policy, the government also strove to define a more active foreign policy and to improve ties with its regional partners. Argentina's participation in the Gulf War led to a notable amelioration in its relations with the United States. The historical competition between Argentina and Brazil for domination of the Southern Cone came to an end with the signing of the MERCOSUR Agreement in 1991. In the same year, a treaty put a term to Argentina's contentious border dispute with Chile, and an economic accord was reached between the two countries. As underscored by Hufty, regionalism is now perceived by Argentinean authorities as an instrument that can foster the economic growth of the country. However, it remains to be seen how well regionalism can contribute to reducing the increasing economic inequalities that characterize the new Argentine model of development.

In his chapter on Chile, Roberto Duran explains that the Chilean government's attitude toward regionalism was transformed when the military regime was replaced by a democratic government in 1990. Since then Chilean foreign policy has reverted to its traditional position, characterized by relatively active participation in multilateral organizations at both the global and regional levels. In Duran's view, such a change must be interpreted as a function of Chile's particular means of internalizing a number of worldwide tendencies, most notably the universalization of the democratic model and the globalization of the economy. During the period of military dictatorship (1973–1990), Chile's foreign policy was characterized by isolationism. On the political front, the Chilean junta was condemned on numerous occasions by the international community for human rights abuses.

On the economic front, a neoliberal strategy led Chile to set itself apart from the rest of Latin America by adopting a much more conciliatory approach toward foreign investors and lenders. Upon taking power, the democratic government attempted to modify Chile's political position by using the regional arena as an instrument to improve the country's international image. It was under these circumstances that Chile joined the Rio Group in 1990. At the same time, the national economy's strong showing in the second half of the 1980s justified the continuation of the military's economic policy of openness. In order to keep all of its options open, Chile has attempted to expand its markets in Europe and Asia, as well as in the Americas. This preoccupation with the diversification of its foreign economic relations explains the country's initial mistrust of membership in MERCOSUR. However, the vigor of its Latin American trade is currently forcing Chile to reconsider the prospect of joining this subregional grouping.

Finally, Duran notes how the new regionalism provides political as well as economic benefits for Chile. Through forums such as the Organization of American States, the new regionalism permits a consolidation of democracy. On the economic front, it offers the possibility of strengthening growth through export promotion.

REGIONAL STRATEGIES IN THE WAKE OF NAFTA

Written by Andrew Axline, the concluding chapter of this volume surveys the recent evolution of regionalism in the Americas. In Axline's view, since the United States is bound to dominate the renewed inter-American order, NAFTA is the institutional entity that will shape interstate cooperation in the region. Three scenarios summarize the options available to the countries of the hemisphere: certain states could attempt to negotiate bilaterally their admittance into NAFTA; others may seek to use subregional integration schemes as a springboard for gaining collective entry into NAFTA; still others could promote subregional integration in order to create an institutional alternative to NAFTA. A comparative analysis of the strengths and weaknesses of the countries studied in this volume casts doubt on the feasibility of building a single hemispheric bloc as well as on the possibility of creating a bipolar structure in which a SAFTA would counterbalance NAFTA. According to Axline, the Americas of tomorrow will more likely be characterized by a complex architecture in which a combination of bilateral and subregional strategies will intertwine in order to respond to NAFTA's power of attraction.

1

Changes in the World System and U.S. Relations with the Americas

◆

Louis Balthazar

On June 27, 1990, President George Bush launched the Enterprise for the Americas Initiative. Coming just a few weeks after the announcement of negotiations between Mexico and the United States on an eventual free trade agreement, and just a year and a half after the beginning of the Free Trade Agreement (FTA) with Canada, this initiative sent the signal that the Bush administration would open a new chapter in the relations of the United States with the Americas.

Does this policy represent a U.S. adjustment to the imperatives of regionalism? Or was the initiative just another way of enhancing the hegemony of the United States in Latin America, as had regularly been the case in the past? Was it just another declaration of good intentions destined to be gradually overshadowed by the pursuit of U.S. interests in the hemisphere? This chapter addresses these questions within the context of the recent systemic changes that have affected U.S. foreign policy. First, I will briefly explore the major structural transformations of the world system since 1960. I will then examine responses to these changes in the United States, particularly as they pertain to Latin America. This should help us understand the meaning of the United States' new hemispheric policy orientation, which is the main purpose of this chapter and its most substantial part.

CHANGES IN THE WORLD SYSTEM

Maturation of Europe and Japan

Certainly the most significant international development of the past thirty years has been the transformation of Western Europe and

Japan into economic competitors of the United States. Oddly enough, when U.S. officials set up the policies that would so successfully contribute to the reconstruction of the industrial countries devastated by World War II, particularly Germany and Japan, they apparently had not evaluated all the implications of the development they were fostering.

They did not seem to be aware that an old European ambition to vie with the United States was one of the factors motivating the building of a new, united Europe. On the contrary, the U.S. architects of a new economic and political Western system tended to think in terms of an all-embracing Atlantic civilization. They saw Europe coming of age in conformity with the U.S. model. It was as though the Europeans would remake the American Revolution on their own continent. According to this new liberal vision, the Atlantic Ocean was becoming a lake in the middle of a democratic and capitalistic area where peoples sharing the same heritage would one day be amalgamated within a single culture (Calleo and Rowland 1973).

Today we can appreciate the futility of this project, which was quite typical of a U.S. tendency to see itself as a universally valid model to be adopted by all, given the proper conditions. Stanley Hoffmann (1968, 1978) and others have elaborated on this ideology (or style) that affects a great many U.S. perceptions and decisions (Dallek 1983; Hunt 1987). It appears to be extremely difficult, even for otherwise sophisticated U.S. officials, to take into account the world's cultural heterogeneity in a realistic and meaningful way.

Thus the evolution of Europe was often quite contrary to what Washington expected. The European economic community organized itself in a manner that would appear protectionist to outsiders and liberal to its own members. In due time, even the British had to give up their special relationship with the United States.

Whenever détente made it less imperative for Europeans to align themselves solidly with their U.S. mentor, they expressed their own autonomous views, especially on economic matters. This became more and more possible as European industry, trade, and standards of living caught up with those of their U.S. counterparts. When the Cold War ended, the trend became stronger than ever, as was aptly illustrated in the extremely arduous Uruguay Round negotiations.

A similar evolution took place in the relations between Japan and the United States. There was, of course, none of the rhetoric concerning the single Western civilization. But it was hoped that the Pacific Rim would become a cooperative economic system ruled by liberal principles. The United States applauded the rapid growth of Japan and the so-called small dragons. Washington's perceptions were very optimistic until the early 1970s, when it became clear that the Japanese were turning into tough economic players, with interests of their own, who would not consistently conform to U.S. rules. Japan developed its own brand of capitalism, one governed by industrial policies that were considered heresy in the United States. Such policies allowed Japan to grow into an economic giant and become a creditor of the United States, for, thanks mainly to their Cold War policies and their reluctance to increase taxes, decisionmakers in Washington had plunged the United States into chronic budgetary deficits that were soon followed by serious trade deficits.

These developments can be seen as normal. Japan and Europe were bound to regain their previous strength and challenge U.S. economic power. However, because of the resiliency of the American dream, this evolution was perceived as malevolent. Given its history of successes, victories, and almost unceasing progress, the United States tended to see its domination of the world economy as a permanent phenomenon. Consequently, the 1950s were considered the golden years, while what followed was seen as a rather unfortunate turn of events.

Hypertrophy of the Soviet Military System

The golden 1950s were also years when Washington could sit atop its military power at a relatively cheap price. By the early 1960s, however, the Soviets had acquired the capacity to threaten the United States with long-range missiles. We can now fully realize how foolish and costly it was for the Kremlin, with its meager economic resources, to maintain such military power just for the sake of confronting the United States.

Détente, however, did not occur in the 1960s for various reasons; in particular, it was delayed by two developments that, because of misguided U.S. policies, were allowed to take on catastrophic proportions.

First, the American hemispheric fortress, thought to be impenetrable, was infiltrated by communism. At the outset, this had nothing to do with the Soviets, since Fidel Castro conducted his revolution in Cuba alone and, according to many observers, could have been assuaged by an open-minded and enlightened U.S. government. But in Washington he met with harsh, inflexible, and suspicious attitudes and the lingering anti-Communist heritage of McCarthyism, which may have induced him to embrace communism. Castro, however, has declared that he was a Communist long before then. Whichever version is correct, it is clear that Washington did very little to tame the new government of the island it had controlled for so long. Confrontation soon became the only affordable policy, which resulted in the disastrous Bay of Pigs invasion and eventually, thanks to Nikita

Khrushchev's gross miscalculation, the 1962 missile crisis. These events considerably hindered progress toward détente. The Kennedy administration did obtain the atmospheric Nuclear Test Ban, the first arms control treaty, concluded, amazingly, less than a year after the height of Cold War confrontation. But the missile crisis cost Khrushchev his power and fostered the acceleration of programs that would bring the USSR up to nuclear parity with the United States.

The other event that contributed to postponing détente was, of course, the Vietnam War, which may be seen as another legacy of misguided anticommunism. As long as U.S. involvement in Vietnam was being maintained and escalated, there could be no rapprochement between Washington and Moscow.

Thus the détente that would have been possible and desirable in the early 1960s did not occur before the early 1970s. It was pursued, first by Richard Nixon and Henry Kissinger, and then by Jimmy Carter, Cyrus Vance, and Zbigniew Brzezinski, until misperceptions, misreadings, and errors on both sides resuscitated a Cold War that was more artificial and unnecessary than ever.

Finally, when Mikhail Gorbachev came to power, he proceeded to conduct the most spectacular peaceful retreat in history. The crumbling of the Soviet empire was seen as a result of U.S. containment policies. But it soon appeared to be a Pyrrhic victory, for the Cold War had somewhat occulted the world's real structural problems: the growing disparity between developed and underdeveloped (or less developed) countries and the competition between the great industrial powers, not to mention the stifled yearnings of a number of peoples for recognition of their various collective identities.

Decline of the United States?

In this context, the United States appeared to many as a declining power. The end of the Cold War did not alter the fundamental parameters of a troubled world economy and of a relatively weaker U.S. power. One of the reasons that has been given for the decline is "imperial overstretch" (Kennedy 1987), that is, the disproportion between military expenditures and other public and private investments.

Imperial overstretch applies much more, of course, to the Soviet Union than to the United States. In the United States, the real decline seems to be mostly a domestic phenomenon, the result of an enormous contradiction between a recurrent budgetary deficit and the escalation of military spending during the Reagan years without an accompanying tax increase. The anomaly is that, in a country having a gross domestic product of more than $5 trillion, a government running a budget of more than $1 trillion, with some $300 billion allocated for defense, has made a point of not asking its population to contribute adequately to the cost of public expenses. Hence, while the U.S. public does not pay its dues, Japanese and European capital is called upon to finance the growing debt of the richest country in the world. While U.S. citizens are consuming, their economic rivals are investing in the United States. The White House has recognized this anomaly, but the Clinton administration has not successfully coped with it up to now.

The world has thus become economically multipolar, while it has moved from military bipolarity to unipolarity. No power may, in the foreseeable future, match the might of the United States. The country's military preponderance is, however, seriously limited by its public's unwillingness to support interventions as well as by financial constraint.

All of this may be understood only if we take into account another important structural development: the progress of transnational relations.

Transnational Relations

The new world order is one between peoples and institutions, as well as between states (Nye 1990). For quite some time, as Keohane and Nye (1977) have shown, the world system could not be grasped without factoring in the various and multiple transactions between persons and nongovernmental organizations.

The system has become too complex to be analyzed on the basis of the old concepts relating to the balance of power. The transitory ideologies of fascism and Marxist socialism are no longer predominant political forces; instead, we are witnessing the forceful return of nationalism. Problems pertaining to the dismantling of the Ottoman and Hapsburg empires are still calling for solutions and serve as a dramatic reminder that we continue to live in a world of nations. Thus, in the words of Nye, our world is marked by "the dialogue between the national and the transnational" (Nye 1992: 86). This is a system that Hoffmann once labeled "asymmetric multipolarity" (Hoffmann 1978) and that Nye has portrayed as consisting of three layers: the military, dominated by the United States; the economic, where three main actors prevail (the United States, Europe, and Japan); and the transnational, where there is a proliferation of actors. Nye refers to these three layers as "multilevel interdependence" (Nye 1992: 88).

Let us now examine U.S. responses to those changes and what they mean for the hemispheric system.

U.S. RESPONSES

During the 1960s, there was a gradual realization that the globalism expressed by John F. Kennedy in his celebrated inaugural address had become unacceptable and impossible.

Lyndon Johnson, however, conducted his Great Society programs and his expensive involvement in Southeast Asia without raising taxes. U.S. citizens were led to believe that they could benefit from welfare policies at home while pursuing military operations abroad, all without incurring any additional expenses. There lies the root of the contemporary economic quandary.

Richard Nixon and Henry Kissinger recognized the limits of U.S. power on military and economic matters, which made détente possible.

Gerald Ford continued in the same vein but was powerless to prevent the protectionist thrust of the 1974 Trade Reform Act. Jimmy Carter was no more successful than Ford in trade matters. In spite of some progress in the Multilateral Trade Negotiations (MTN) and the passage of the 1979 MTN Trade Agreements Act, U.S. trade policy, because of a protectionist Congress, remained quite defensive and restrictive.

But Carter took a fresh, liberal approach toward the détente already under way. In a speech at Notre Dame University in May 1977, he argued that the people of the United States were "now free of that inordinate fear of communism which once led us to embrace any dictator who joined us in that fear" (Hartmann and Wendzel 1985: 258). Thus Carter would not be content with pursuing détente with the Soviet Union and China and acting to achieve a rapprochement between old enemies in the Middle East. He would positively promote human rights whenever possible, particularly among allies.

With a second oil crisis, the reported rise in Soviet armaments and international presence (not only in Cuba and Nicaragua but in Angola, Mozambique, Ethiopia, and Yemen as well), the fall of the so-called friendly regime of the shah of Iran, and, by the end of 1979, the invasion of Afghanistan by Soviet troops, the U.S. population was growing restive, and Carter was forced to abandon his liberal policies.

In the Reagan administration, détente became a bad word, a perverse liberal doctrine contrived to bring about the decline of the United States. Consequently, the Cold War came to be seen as a harsh reality, rising military expenses became a blessing, and the Soviet Union had to be dealt with as a threatening enemy so that the United States would "stand tall again." To facilitate this policy,

Ronald Reagan faced three weakened, aging men in his first term. With a worried and ill Leonid Brezhnev, an uncertain Yuri Andropov, and an old-guard Konstantin Chernenko, it was easy for Reagan to play the role of the "Rough Rider," the reincarnation of Teddy Roosevelt with a magic smile.

Reagan's economic policies were quite simple. Free enterprise would be allowed to take over again and all problems would be solved. Therefore, nothing was done to address domestic issues, social problems, or environmental decay. Moreover, Americans would not have to pay a price for these policies. More weapons, more grandeur, but no "blood, sweat, and tears"! Symbolism was taking the place of policy.

Reagan was lucky enough to be in power when Gorbachev became the head of the Soviet Union. After the three old and dying leaders, here was a younger man obviously intent on bringing about profound reforms in his country and negotiating arms reduction and peace with the United States. Perhaps some of Reagan's policies, particularly the unflinching resolution to counter Soviet intermediate-range missiles in Europe with U.S. ones, led to the softening of the Soviets under Gorbachev. But one has to be blindly partisan to assert that Reagan was the main cause of glasnost, perestroika, and the fall of the iron curtain.

President Bush belonged to the old "realist" school. He was trained in Cold War methods but had to face the end of the Cold War and the complete transformation of the Eastern European system. He received praise for his coolness in the face of the dissolution of the Warsaw Pact, the unification of Germany, the disintegration of the Soviet Union, and the opening of Russia and others to the free market. He did not overplay his hand or do anything to humiliate his former enemies. But he took no new initiative, was rather slow to react to events, and, according to many observers, did not fully exploit new opportunities. In spite of Bush's repeated allusions to a new world order, the United States was left with no new blueprint for its foreign policy and no new vision.

The war in the Persian Gulf turned out to be a great success. It gave a temporary boost to U.S. morale, but the traumas of the relative decline and weakening of the United States in the new world system would soon resurface. Bush did nothing to tackle the issue; he stuck to his old themes, denied there was a structural problem, and ran headlong to his defeat.

Bill Clinton took over the White House largely by capitalizing on his predecessor's mistakes. George Bush's popularity had declined because of his failure to cope with the serious domestic malaise. This laid the basis for Clinton's campaign and successful bid for the presidency. International and foreign policy issues were either sidestepped or subordinated to social and economic issues.

Going to the other extreme, however, did not prove to be a solution. The United States obviously could not afford to forget for very long about foreign affairs. Clinton learned the hard way, confronted as he was from the very start with pressing and complex international problems: the United States' presence in Somalia, the call for intervention in Bosnia, an intolerable regime in Haiti, constant struggle in the former Soviet Union, negotiations in the Middle East, the nuclear threat in Korea. On most of these issues, he showed indecision, procrastination, and a lack of planning. By the summer of 1994, there was still a worrisome absence of clear vision and definite orientation of U.S. foreign policy. The United States' response to the world transformation had not taken shape.

Clinton's best success during his first year in office came at the end of 1993, when he apparently achieved a linkage between his main domestic concerns and a world policy. After obtaining a revision of the North American Free Trade Agreement (NAFTA) in matters of labor standards and environmental protection, he presented the deal as equally conducive to economic progress at home and to better relations with neighbors. After winning in November a hard-fought battle in Congress to have the agreement sanctioned, Clinton was able to present the United States as an outward-looking champion of trade liberalization at the Asia-Pacific Economic Cooperation (APEC) meeting in Seattle. He would do so again in the General Agreement on Tariffs and Trade (GATT) negotiations when the Uruguay Round was successfully concluded in December 1993.

Thus Washington appeared to be turned simultaneously toward the hemisphere and the world at large. Regionalism appeared reconciled with globalism. In fact, it could not be that simple. To underscore the complexity of the relationship between the United States' responses to world trends and its attitudes toward the hemisphere, let us look now at the recent evolution of Washington's policies in the Americas.

THE UNITED STATES AND THE AMERICAS

Canada

Until recently, what was referred to as "the hemisphere" by U.S. officials and policy analysts generally did not include Canada. Although the northern neighbor is an obvious part of the American continent, for historical reasons it was always considered entirely different from the Americas, to the point of being included in the U.S. State Department's European Affairs division. For a long time, actually, Canada meant a British presence in North America. Ironically, after 1814, this presence was never seen as a major threat by the country whose very existence was founded on the struggle against Great Britain. But the American Revolution was strictly political; it did not preclude that, less than forty years after it was fought, a special relationship would arise between the United States and what, in the minds of most U.S. citizens, was still the mother country.

Thus the Monroe Doctrine, which coincided with British as well as U.S. policy, was not directed toward Canada. Consequently, Washington adopted one general policy for the southern part of the hemisphere, Central America, and Mexico—in sum, Latin America—and another for Canada. For that reason, the United States was never eager to include Canada in any hemispheric organization such as the Pan-American Union or the Organization of American States (OAS). Canadians were not always happy with their European label. From at least the middle of the twentieth century, they tended to consider themselves more North American than British. But, at the same time, they certainly felt enough distance between Canada and Latin America not to want to become part of the OAS.

As Canada's economy and defense became inextricably woven with those of its southern neighbor, it saw itself more and more as a part of North America and had to give up its old ideal of being a bridge between Europe and the United States. Its ties to the United States were reinforced with the signing of the North American Air Defense Agreement (NORAD) in 1958, the passage of the Auto Pact in 1965, and Great Britain's entry into the European Economic Community in 1973.

But politically speaking, Canada continued to be perceived mainly as a loyal ally within the North Atlantic Treaty Organization (NATO) and other transatlantic organizations; a very special and reliable neighbor, indeed, but not part of a great hemispheric region. There was even a tendency to forget that Canada was a distinct country.

Richard Nixon went to Ottawa in 1972 to apply his doctrine to Canada, recognizing that the country had a distinct national interest and thus bringing grist to Canadian nationalism. But in one memorable speech, the same Nixon forgot that Canada was the United States' first trading partner, assigning that position to Japan.

Jimmy Carter paid more attention to Canada. It was agreed, under his administration, that he and the Canadian prime minister would meet at least once a year, and other members of the two governments more frequently. The Reagan administration, although at first quite hostile to Canadian nationalist interventions such as the National Energy Program and the Foreign Investment Review Agency, developed a special policy toward the friendly neighbor. At the end of the Trudeau mandate (1968–1979; 1980–1984), sectorial free trade agreements were considered. With the advent of Brian Mulroney in 1984 and the spectacular Shamrock Summit of 1985, the ground was set for free trade negotiations. The agreement was concluded in 1987 and endorsed with relative ease by Congress in 1988.

In a situation of growing trade, a current accounts deficit, and related protectionist sentiments in Congress, the FTA took on special importance for Washington. It certainly was not conceived as a new regionalist posture or the consolidation of a closed North American market. In fact, by making frequent use of all the nontariff barriers at their disposal, in spite of FTA, the U.S. Congress and the International Trade Commission treated Canada as a distinct country more than they had in previous years. Nonetheless, FTA was heralded as a great advance in trade liberalization and would be, for Washington as well as for Ottawa, a springboard to a better position at the GATT talks. Far from being a substitute to GATT, FTA was seen as "a reaffirmation of the open trade policy that underpins the GATT" (Schott 1988: 31).

With the launching of NAFTA, Canada was invited to be part of a larger free trade zone and to embrace the dream of a market of 360 million people from the Yukon to the Yucatán. Thus, it was finally recognized as part of the hemisphere, part of the Americas and the new, grand, regional schemes. In Washington Canada's position as northern neighbor has taken on new relevance, especially with its entry into the OAS in 1990. In the meantime, Washington clings to its natural leadership in the region, while the "hub and spoke" conception of NAFTA and its eventual extensions prevails. U.S. hegemony may take new forms, but it remains a fact of life. And it is particularly in relation to Latin America that Washington has always found it difficult to develop a policy of genuine recognition and partnership.

Latin America

The Kennedy administration's much publicized Alliance for Progress is a good example of a regionalist policy submitted to globalist criteria. It was supposed to address the social and economic ills of Latin America by dealing with its roots. The United States' sense of "good neighborhood" and compassion were most evident when Treasury Secretary Douglas Dillon committed $1 billion to various local projects at Punta del Este, Uruguay, in the summer of 1961. In sharp contrast to the unfortunate Bay of Pigs operation, in Uruguay the fight against communism was to be waged with dollars and social programs, not weapons.

But Cold War imperatives soon overcame this liberal policy. The response to the grand scheme announced by President Kennedy was not the expected one. Instead, Communist guerrillas spread across Latin America, and the Alliance for Progress gave way to the call for counterinsurgency. Consequently, more energy and money were poured into training repressive forces than into sponsoring reforms. President Johnson pursued this course of action and exhibited nothing but a patronizing attitude toward Latin America. His show of force in the Dominican Republic, carried out for dubious reasons, reminded Latin Americans of the worst days of U.S. domination.

It was obvious that U.S.–Latin American relations were "simply some of the threads in a larger global fabric" (Poitras 1990: 33) and could not be kept separate from larger concerns. The United States was acting like a global power even in its supposedly privileged and protected backyard. This behavior continued with the Nixon administration, even at a time when Washington was coming to terms with major changes in the world system.

The Nixon doctrine was applied in Latin America as elsewhere. The message to Latin Americans was that they should rely on themselves and on private investment from the United States. The growth of anti-U.S. feelings among Latin Americans was evident when New York governor Nelson Rockefeller was sent to the region, along with a study commission, to report on ways to improve the relationship; the governor could hardly appear in public without encountering demonstrations (Kryzanek 1985: 62). The Rockefeller report urged the U.S. government to recognize the poor economic conditions of Latin America, but Nixon's way of doing so was to rely mainly on private enterprise and to recommend the breakdown of economic barriers.

The U.S. government did not hesitate to intervene, however, when its national interest as a global power was believed to be at stake. Consequently, all anti-Communist activities were encouraged, even if a "Communist threat" was more or less mythical or far from immediate. In particular, the U.S. government took measures to prevent Salvador Allende from gaining power in Chile and to destabilize his government after his electoral victory in 1970. Kissinger summed up the United States' policy toward Chile when he said bluntly: "I don't see why we have to let a country go Marxist just because its people are irresponsible" (Hunt 1987: 184). So while Nixon was embracing Mao, he was fighting Allende. Latin America was very special indeed.

Gerald Ford did not improve relations with Latin American nations. Perhaps because he saw them becoming more and more impervious to U.S. influence, notably in their attitude toward Cuba (which was included in SELA, the Latin American Economic System, whereas the United States was not), Ford tried to resume normal relations with Cuba but had to withdraw when Castro sent troops to Angola and other African countries (Kryzanek 1985: 66).

Jimmy Carter's human rights policy was nowhere more active than in Latin America. Carter suspended aid to such countries as Argentina, Brazil, Chile, and others where human rights were known to be violated. This was received, of course, very negatively by the concerned governments, which considered the policy unduly patronizing and contrary to the tenets of self-determination. Right-wing elites in the United States (particularly presidential contender Ronald Reagan) also lamented the loss of "friends" while "enemies" were left untouched. However, this policy was applauded in Latin America's progressive and democratic circles.

President Carter also acted to return the control of the Panama Canal to the Panamanians and, faithful to his rejection of dictators, did not act to prevent the downfall of the Somoza regime in Nicaragua in 1979. However, 1979 also marked the passing of this short period of "liberal détente." The fruits of liberalism had not been reaped. In Latin America, Marxism was not declining; it was getting stronger. The Sandinistas replaced Anastasio Somoza Debayle and moved closer to Cuba and the Soviet Union than to the United States. This move lent a good deal of legitimacy to Ronald Reagan's policies.

The two major tenets of the Reagan doctrine were consistently applied to Latin America. First, the fight against communism was a top priority. So, contrary to the Carter prescription, the "inordinate fear of communism" made the United States embrace all available "dictators" and act mainly to oppose Communist "totalitarian" governments, particularly in Central America. The quick and easy invasion of Grenada in the fall of 1983 (a timely opportunity to offset the deaths of nearly 300 Marines in Lebanon) made Reagan boast that his government was committed to see that "not an inch" of land would fall to the enemies.

Second, on other issues, private enterprise was supposed to do the job as it had during the Nixon years; it did not. On the contrary, because of the strains of the deficit and financing problems, U.S. private capital became scarcer than ever in Latin America. The Caribbean Basin Initiative of 1981 did not bear fruit, partly because of investor reluctance and partly because of the opposition of a protectionist

Congress. Also, largely because of Reagan's policies, "from 1981 to 1986, debt interest remittances swallowed $130 billion of Latin America's productivity" (Langley 1989: 251). Latin American borrowers turned more and more to the Germans and the Japanese, thereby greatly eroding the hegemony of the United States. They realized "that the Americans may have the development schemes, but the Japanese have the money" (Langley 1989: 253).

George Bush did not seem to depart from Reagan's policy in the beginning. But as the Cold War ended, and with it the need to contain communism, he was free to deal with other matters. He could end support to the Contras and accept a free election in Nicaragua, commit the United States more strongly to the OAS, and promote the so-called Brady Plan to assist countries facing impossible debt remission.

But apart from waging a war on drugs that put an unfair burden on drug-producing countries instead of dealing with consumer demand in the United States, Bush did not seem to espouse any long-term purpose regarding Latin America. According to Abraham Lowenthal, his aim "seemed to be to remove Latin America from the front pages, rather than to develop a long-term strategy for confronting the region's underlying problems" (Lowenthal 1990: 32). Moreover, the invasion of Panama, although applauded in the United States, reminded Latin Americans of the old U.S. interventionism and was not supported by the elites and main organizations in the hemisphere.

By June 1990, however, President Bush would completely change this image and launch a policy that seemed very promising. The Enterprise for the Americas Initiative cannot be analyzed in isolation from NAFTA. It is no coincidence that President Bush announced the initiative two weeks after he and President Carlos Salinas de Gortari of Mexico had expressed their intention to negotiate a free trade agreement. The new policy was meant to extend the spirit of rapprochement that existed between Mexico and the United States to the whole hemisphere, as if "Washington wanted to reassure the rest of Latin America that its interests did not stop at Mexico" (Hakim 1992: 95). Of course, NAFTA is something much more concrete, whereas the Enterprise for the Americas Initiative consists of a series of statements and intentions, some specific, some rather vague and fragile. Although Washington's relationship with maturing neighbor Mexico is certainly different from its relationship with the rest of Latin America, its rapprochement with that country may be the first step in a larger undertaking, the most immediately attainable part of a long-term objective involving all of Latin America.

The Enterprise for the Americas Initiative consists of three parts:

1. the forgiving of part of the debt of the Latin American countries to the United States ($12 billion) and the willingness to accept payment of the balance in local currencies;
2. the creation of an investment promotion fund in which the United States would invest $100 million a year for a period of five years. Japan and the European Community were invited to do the same and accepted, meaning the fund would eventually amount to $1.5 billion; and
3. the expression of the hope to see free trade extended to the whole hemisphere.

By itself, the initiative does not represent much. The $12 billion is only part of the debt owed to the United States and represents a meager part of Latin America's global debt of $400 billion. The investment promotion fund "will not do much to help Latin America overcome its capital shortage" (Hakim 1992: 99), and general free trade is a very distant possibility. However, if we look at the initiative in the context of the recent transformation of the world system, it may be seen more as "the consequence of changes already in motion" (Hakim 1992: 96). It may even mean that, for the first time, the United States is looking at Latin America for its own sake and not just as part of its world strategy. Furthermore, the initiative could suggest that U.S. foreign policy is affected more than ever by regional realities. To assess this last possibility, let us look at the policy in connection with the three layers that Joe Nye identifies as the components of the contemporary multilevel interdependence system.

The Political-Military Level

When the Cold War bipolar system was running its course, Latin America could be considered at once closer to and more removed from Washington's preoccupations. It was closer in the sense that what happened in Latin America could make U.S. officials worried and nervous. Since Cuba had aligned itself with Moscow in 1960, the fear of another such incident was always present. Washington's Latin American policy was almost completely monopolized by this fear and the imperatives of fighting communism. Except for the first years of the Alliance for Progress and two or three years of Jimmy Carter's policies, all considerations pertaining to Latin America had to be subordinated to Cold War objectives.

It is in this sense that Latin American problems as such became more removed from Washington's policies, which had the unexpected effect of creating important centrifugal forces and eroding a hegemony that had come to be seen as rather formal. Some large states, such as Mexico, Brazil, and Argentina, became more assertive and did not maintain a strict alignment with Washington. Others defected; such was the case for Chile from 1970 to 1973 and Nicaragua since 1979. Even Lilliputians, as it were, could "stand up against United States power much longer than they ever could in the earlier twentieth century" (Poitras 1990: 22).

Thus, in the 1970s and 1980s, there was an increasing tendency to exclude the United States from cooperative schemes. The creation of SELA may be seen as a response to unilateral and patronizing attitudes on the part of Washington. Similarly, the Contadora and Esquipulas (Central American peace plan) schemes were aimed at finding an alternative (closer to the Latin American people's expectations) to both Washington's intransigence and Marxist revolutionary positions (Poitras 1990: 43ff.).

In the post–Cold War era, these positions have become obsolete. U.S. anticommunism is no longer the main criterion for policy. Conversely, for many Latin Americans, the perception of the United States as an aggressive protagonist has given way to a rediscovery of the U.S. model. But this is not a generalized process. Anti-U.S. sentiment is still alive in many quarters, and the invasion of Panama in 1989 did nothing to project a new image of the gringos. Nonetheless, the days of counterinsurgency, military bases, and searching for unconditional allies are over. The United States arguably looks more like an economic partner now, still undoubtedly domineering but much less arrogant because of its weaker international position.

Washington is now freed from its Cold War security obsession and may turn to Latin America with other considerations in mind. It may, of course, forget about its neighbors and be more concerned with the fate of Eastern Europe. Some observers have discerned benign neglect on the part of Washington in spite of the announcement of new policy, but most tend to emphasize the new relevance of Latin America for the United States, which is manifest at the economic level.

The Economic Level

The United States still appears to be a powerful economic actor, but one that has to compete with two rivals, Europe and Japan. Nowhere was this competition more visible or striking than in the last GATT negotiations, where it was vital for Washington to enhance its trade position vis-à-vis the European Community and Japan. But these negotiations were terribly frustrating, and even after the successful conclusion of the Uruguay Round in December 1993, it is doubtful that U.S. products can penetrate these markets as easily or profitably as the United States would like.

Therefore, the United States must rely on its own trade bloc in the Western Hemisphere. This, of course, does not mean total retrenchment, and no one advocates a new isolationism that would translate into bloc protectionism. For Washington, it means a completely new look at Latin America, that is, an unprecedented concentration on trade with the countries of the hemisphere. The Enterprise for the Americas Initiative and NAFTA must be seen in this light.

It is true that U.S. exports to Latin America did not represent more than 13 percent of total exports in 1991 (Hakim 1992: 96), but this was still more than U.S. sales to Japan (Pastor 1992: 108). Moreover, the rate of growth of U.S. exports in the hemisphere was, according to Robert Pastor, three times the rate for the rest of the world (Pastor 1992: 108). This means that "Latin America today offers the United States the key to enhancing its competitiveness and stimulating new growth" (Pastor 1992: 109). Consequently, Pastor believes, as do many other observers (Morici 1992; Baer 1991; Lowenthal 1990, 1993), that the Enterprise for the Americas Initiative served to boost the position of the United States vis-à-vis Europe and Japan in the Uruguay Round negotiations. It must be noted, however, that neither the Europeans nor the Japanese appeared to take notice of the initiative (Hakim 1992: 96).

There is no doubt that the United States can draw considerable advantage from NAFTA even if in the short term some labor-intensive jobs are transferred to Mexico. Production-sharing alliances (like those between Japan and some of its Asian partners) could be developed so as to allow the United States to concentrate on high-skilled jobs and to "create a more knowledge-intensive wealthy society" (Morici 1992: 103; Baer 1991: 40).

As for Mexico, if it wishes to enhance its economic productivity and continues to move toward a free market economy, it has very little choice but to turn to the United States. Opportunities elsewhere, in Europe notably, are very limited. The same applies to a few other Latin American countries, such as Chile.

No doubt the extension of free trade to the whole hemisphere is a long-term project, presenting enormous difficulties. Reluctance to enter into such a partnership with the United States is still strong in many countries. Old statist conceptions of the economy will be a stumbling block, and the United States has proven to be rigid on that score, although the Clinton administration has generated a slight twist in the direction of industrial policies. However, economic necessities may, in time, bring about some accommodation.

Few people see the advent of a three-bloc world system as either a desirable or foreseeable outcome of contemporary events. Indeed, there would be a high price to pay for the establishment of three economic fortresses. Everybody would lose in the process. There are also many factors—such as the military positions of Japan and Europe, technological requirements, and other considerations—that run contrary to such a rigid configuration. But it would be wrong to reject such a possibility too quickly. It may be worth remembering Thomas Hobbes's reasoning about the state of war. He considered it absolutely unsustainable among individuals, but he thought it could exist among large states, that is, masses impressive enough to deter one another. The balance-of-power system proved him right. Now that such a system is no longer possible because of the porosity of states, we may wonder if very large groupings, such as the big trade blocs, could not maintain, at least temporarily, a certain viable balance. That is not to say this viability would be positive, but it would not be inconceivable.

Transnational relations, though they occur mostly within the big blocs, may well prevent such a scenario from coming to pass.

The Transnational Level

Significant transactions across borders, independent of governmental structures, are a feature of our contemporary system. The fall of the Berlin Wall and the iron curtain has extended that reality to larger portions of the world. It is difficult, in this environment, to imagine an outright hardening of geographic entities. Our world is one in which Japanese and U.S. officials confront each other, sometimes dangerously, while Japanese businessmen invest in the United States, finance the U.S. government's debt, and own large portions of expensive land in the country. European farmers send hostile signals to Washington while U.S. businesses are flourishing in Europe.

But such transnational activities are limited compared with those that take place across borders. Even in the age of supersonic transportation and electronic communication, geographic proximity remains very important. A country like Canada experiences this cross-border activity frequently and intensely. In spite of all the links that bind Canadians to their former mother countries in Europe, the harsh reality is that their bed is made in North America. Crossing the U.S. border will always be easier—it is done almost unconsciously—than communicating with the rest of the world.

This is also true for the border between Mexico and the United States. Given the size of the population involved, the phenomenon is even more spectacular. Because of a large migration, the southern United States is, in cultural terms, almost becoming part of Mexico (Lowenthal 1990: 35). Half of the public schools in Los Angeles and in four southwestern states are now Hispanic. There are 20 million Hispanics living in the United States, and this population is growing more rapidly than that of the rest of the country.

Because of this growing population, "the line between domestic policy and Latin American policy" (Lowenthal 1990: 38) is harder and harder to draw. There may be a trend toward concentrating on domestic issues in the United States, but international issues are becoming more and more "intermestic," to borrow a recent catchword, so what is domestic is international and vice versa. This has made NAFTA an issue of immediate concern for the United States, a subject of heated internal debate wherein short-term disadvantages are weighed against long-term interests.

Moreover, while the United States is becoming somewhat more "Hispanicized," Latin Americans seem to draw closer to *their* northern neighbor. Most countries of the southern part of the hemisphere are now run by democratically elected governments. If ever new economic ventures bring with them more affluence among the population at large, chances are the cultural gap between U.S. citizens and Latin Americans, particularly Mexicans, will narrow.

Some U.S. analysts have already detected the signs announcing the rise of "a new North American political market of ideas" (Baer 1991: 148), thanks to "a universal science-based culture" (Baer 1991: 149). Throughout the hemisphere, people seem to express common aspirations. According to one author, there is "an awareness, even among ordinary people . . . of the possibility of a different future for oneself and especially one's children" (Langley 1989: 265). An "informal revolution is taking place" based on the U.S. model such that "the long-admired American experience of unshackling the individual so that society may benefit from his creativity . . . is an idea taking hold even among the lowliest street vendors in Latin America" (Langley 1989: 266). Have the ideals of Horatio Alger and Frank Capra spread south of the Rio Grande? Can we already talk of a common hemispheric culture? Such conclusions would certainly be premature for now, but there is no doubt that cultural transformations are occurring in parts of the very complex and diverse universe called Latin America. This may eventually lead to a certain cultural homogeneity. Meanwhile, a few caveats are in order.

First, the "universal science-based culture" is certainly and fortunately not about to materialize. There are too many indications that the peoples of the world, those of Latin America not the least, wish to benefit from more economic integration while keeping their roots, their identity, and their own culture.

Second, there are reasons to question the quaint U.S. tendency to see its own culture as not one among many but as *the* universal culture brought about by modernity. The "melting pot" experience and the successful exporting of U.S. mass culture have brought out the propensity of U.S. citizens to see their society as "the city shining upon the hill." Most people in the hemisphere would agree that the U.S. model should not prevail unless it is seriously amended. In other words, if there is eventually a common culture of the hemisphere, it should not be the U.S. culture writ large.

Third, what may well occur in Latin America, at least in Mexico, the Caribbean, and perhaps Central America, is a sort of "Canadianization" of the population, which suggests a greater cultural complicity with the United States. Canadians, even French-speaking Quebecois, have always accepted the United States' presence as a fact of life. They have found ways to confront the United States that do not sharply deny U.S. hegemony. "Hegemony can survive if it is accepted by those who are affected by it; it need not be imposed" (Poitras 1990: 30). Canadians may not realize it, but their standard of living is probably related to their acceptance (albeit reluctant) of U.S. hegemony. Chances are, we will witness a similar complicity among some of the peoples of Latin America in the years to come. That does not necessarily mean the loss of one's culture or complete Americanization; Quebec is a case in point. But it obviously means a definite recognition of a regional American system.

CONCLUSION

President Clinton scored a big victory when he won congressional approval of NAFTA in late 1993. He went out of his way to give this event political as well as economic significance. In the presidential discourse, NAFTA became a symbol of the United States' willingness to turn toward its neighbors and the rest of the world, to sympathize, share, and cooperate. The president made sure that NAFTA would not be seen as simply the aggrandizement of "Fortress America." He immediately carried the spirit of trade liberalization to the APEC conference, to Asia, and later to Europe, where the members of GATT finally concluded the Uruguay Round negotiations and agreed on the creation of a World Trade Organization.

This sequence of events fits in very well with the wishes of most of the liberal elites of the United States who refuse to see in NAFTA anything but a step toward global trade liberalization. Such optimism is well reflected in the following:

> By widening both the market and the range of available labor skills, NAFTA will enable North American firms and workers to compete more effectively against foreign producers. The resulting United States trade gains with Europe and Asia could, over time, outweigh the more immediate increase in regional trade. (Hufbauer and Schott 1993/1994: 109)

Some were more pessimistic and feared retaliation on the part of other trade bloc members:

> If the United States pushes FTAs only southward, it will certainly invite a defensive, if not retaliatory, bloc in Asia. Divisions will be sharpened and the world economy fragmented into 3 blocs. (Bhagwati 1993: 161)

Has this pessimism been proven wrong by U.S. goodwill and liberal words? Unfortunately, in spite of the fact that U.S. officials want to present their country "as the world's foremost free trade nation . . . protectionism is alive and well in the nation's capital, with more than 8000 tariffs and 3000 nontariff ledgers. . . . [T]here are also a plethora of options available to restrict international commerce in the future" (Fry, Taylor, and Wood 1994: 304).

With such protectionist behavior still common, in spite of President Clinton's noble declarations, it is hard not to acknowledge the possibility of reciprocity on the part of other trade blocs. U.S. citizens have not yet parted with the strong sense of exceptionalism that makes them expect from others a fairness they don't always practice themselves.

That is why it is difficult, for the moment, to conceive of a total reconciliation between regionalism and globalism unless a global U.S. hegemony is still thought possible. There are many indications to the contrary. We must, then, consider seriously the new orientation of the United States toward a regionalist policy in the Americas.

2

Mexico's Hemispheric Options in the Post–Cold War Era

◆

Guadalupe González & Jorge Chabat

During the past decade, Mexican foreign policy has entered a stage of profound transformation in its conceptual and instrumental dimensions. This transformation is not surprising, for despite the fact that government rhetoric has insisted on the historical continuity of Mexican foreign policy, it has changed in response to the internal and external developments of the 1980s, including the economic crisis of 1982. This change, which predates the fall of the Berlin Wall, has had a direct impact on internal politics and has implicitly redefined the terms of Mexican participation in world politics. In fact, Mexico's foreign policy has shifted from an ultradefensive, ideologically driven position to one of active pragmatism.

THE FACTORS OF CHANGE:
EXTERNAL PRESSURE AND ECONOMIC MODERNIZATION

The gradual transition from relative isolationism to participative realism has been provoked, in part, by changes in the international environment. The trend toward increasing globalization of production processes, the transnationalization of financial and technological flows, and the creation of regional trading blocs have increased the economic costs of tagging behind the trendsetters, especially for intermediate areas in the world economy, such as Mexico, or those frankly on the periphery, such as some Latin American countries. This new international environment has placed new demands on the foreign policies of these countries.[1] The economic challenge that was already self-evident in the 1980s has been accompanied by a global geopolitical transformation in the wake of the fall of the Berlin Wall.

39

However, for Latin America, the impact of the end of the Cold War has been mixed (Castañeda 1990). Although it has undoubtedly reduced global tensions and loosened the ideological constraints and alignment requirements for the region, the end of the Cold War also represents a decrease in Latin America's strategic importance and, probably, its exclusion from the new poles of economic power, especially for the more geographically distant countries.

In the particular case of Mexico, the aforementioned international developments have accelerated the redefinition of its external links, a process initiated during the 1980s as an urgent response to the crisis of the Mexican economic model. The changes to these two aspects of state policy have also affected its political system. However, the pace of systemic change has not been as rapid, despite the fact that one of the bastions of resistance to domestic political change gave way after internal and external pressures led Mexico to allow international observers to be present during the 1994 elections.

After the 1982 financial crash, the new president, Miguel de la Madrid (1982–1988), decided to make radical and profound changes in the economic development strategy. He deregulated the economy, lifted heavy trade barriers in order to gain Mexico's admittance into the General Agreement on Tariffs and Trade in 1986, and privatized hundreds of state-owned enterprises. However, he was not successful in either reducing inflation or attracting foreign investment. It was not until Carlos Salinas de Gortari (1988–1994) took power that these goals were fulfilled, thanks in large measure to the perspective of a free trade agreement between the United States and Mexico.

The new economic model, based on a strategy of promoting exports and attracting foreign investment, has affected the diplomatic arena substantially. Mexican diplomacy has adopted a supportive role in the effort to insert the country into the world economy, which has involved searches for new markets, the modification of Mexican laws to attract foreign capital, the renegotiation of external debt, and active participation in international and regional economic organizations. However, this openness to the outside has meant, in the short term, an acceleration of commercial integration with the United States.

The concentration of economic interaction with the United States, which follows a historical pattern, obviously derives from the geographical position of Mexico. In 1993, 78 percent of Mexican exports went to the United States and 68 percent of imports came from that country. In terms of volume, trade with the United States reached a total of $78.7 billion, almost four times the volume registered in 1987 ($21.5 billion) (International Monetary Fund 1994: 300). These figures indicate that Mexico has a greater concentration of two-way trade with the United States than does any other Latin American country, with the exception, but only for exports, of Guatemala (see Table 2.1). When these figures are compared with those for trade between Mexico and Latin America, which represents around 5 percent of total Mexican trade, the weight of the U.S. option is self-evident. Obviously, a radical modification of one country's trading pattern is almost impossible in the short term. The Mexican concentration on the U.S. market is the product of a historical integration developed over the past decades that cannot be abruptly altered.

Table 2.1   Latin American Trade with the United States (percentage of total country trade, 1993)

	Exports	Imports
Argentina	9.06	22.61
Bolivia	26.49	24.23
Brazil	20.69	23.61
Chile	17.33	22.56
Colombia	40.46	35.69
Costa Rica	56.27	53.80
El Salvador	50.37	42.92
Guatemala	87.89	45.38
Honduras	66.59	55.95
Mexico	78.42	68.24
Nicaragua	42.46	20.07
Panama	37.20	27.08
Paraguay	7.63	23.18
Peru	21.18	30.08
Uruguay	9.14	9.30
Venezuela	46.76	40.33

Source: IMF, *Direction of Trade Statistics Yearbook,* 1994.

The importance of the United States for Mexican foreign policy does not derive uniquely from this commercial dimension. The United States is also the main source of foreign capital for Mexico (around 60 percent). Moreover, the highly populated and porous 2,000-mile-long U.S.-Mexican border makes interaction a fact of life. Currently there are 300 million legal crossings every year (Lowenthal 1987: 49). The border is crossed every day by 6,600 tractor trailer trucks and 21,000 passenger vehicles (Testimony 1994). These numbers suggest that the border region, far from being a desert that keeps both countries separated and distant, is a dynamic zone that tends to draw both societies together through heavy traffic of goods, persons, and services.

Therefore, for Mexico, the negotiation of a free trade agreement with the United States represents the institutionalization of a de facto process set in motion decades ago that predates the formal diplomatic project. It does not necessarily mean that Mexico's options of participating in other economic blocs have disappeared in the long run but rather that these options are simply not viable in the short term, despite the government's rhetoric about the diversification of Mexico's foreign policy. In fact, the emphasis on diversification was one of the obsessions of dictator Porfirio Díaz at the end of the nineteenth century. At that time, Díaz wanted to counterbalance the influence of the United States by forging closer ties with Europe. Similar intentions have been clearly expressed by the Salinas administration, which coined the concept of "complementarity" in reference to regions other than the United States.[2] According to this concept, the European Union (EU), the Pacific Basin, and Latin America cannot be considered as *alternative* blocs to North America in the Mexican international economic strategy, but they are seen as *complementary* (Rico 1992). From this standpoint, Mexico is trying to find a balance in its relationship with the United States, avoid international isolation that might reduce its room to maneuver, and set the foundations for the long-term diversification of its external economic relations.

The emphasis on Mexico's links with Latin America, which does not fit with the cold logic of trade figures, has resulted in an increasing lack of coordination between the country's economic and political/diplomatic offices. Some argue that two foreign policies currently coexist in Mexico: one, pragmatic and economically oriented, looks to the North to help fulfill its goal of making Mexico a First World country; the other, traditional and ideologically driven, looks to Latin America and utilizes multilateral diplomacy as its main tool. From this perspective, the first orientation responds directly to the requirements of the economic model, and the second is rooted in political constraints related to the internal legitimacy of the Mexican regime (Chabat 1991). This argumentation suggests that the government's rhetoric about diversification basically plays an internal legitimizing role and is not necessarily related to a real effort toward balancing the United States' influence.

It is difficult to establish the real weight of internal and external factors in this discourse of complementarity. However, it is not possible to deny the legitimizing role of foreign policy in internal politics. The Mexican political system has undergone major transformations during the past decade. Traditional corporatism has been severely undermined as opposition parties grow in strength and as broad sectors of society make increasing demands for the democratization of

the regime. This process has weakened traditional forms of internal le-
gitimization linked to revolutionary nationalism and the idea of national unity vis-à-vis the concept of representative democracy (Loaeza
1988: 98). However, the Mexican government's reaction has been to
appeal to these old concepts, especially in the face of foreign criticism.

During the 1980s, internal pressures for democratization provoked political instability. Paradoxically, this led to increased criticisms from the outside, thus fueling a nationalistic response on the
part of the government that clashed with its economic reform
agenda. Indeed, tensions between the movement toward trade liberalization and the pace of internal democratization have been characteristic of the past two Mexican administrations. Although pressures from the U.S. government decreased notably by 1987–1988,
when a victory of the moderate left candidate Cuauhtémoc Cárdenas
appeared to be a real possibility, Mexican democracy has been under
scrutiny from several sectors of U.S. society. Even though the image
of Mexico—and particularly that of President Salinas—has improved
significantly since 1989, there have been serious attacks on the authoritarian nature of the Mexican political system, corruption, and
the lack of respect for human rights. These criticisms were particularly harsh in the United States during the ratification of the North
American Free Trade Agreement (NAFTA) in 1993. Both the guerrilla revolt in Chiapas at the beginning of 1994 and the subsequent
assassinations of the Revolutionary Institutional Party (PRI) presidential candidate, Luis Donaldo Colosio, and party secretary-general
Francisco Ruiz Massieu contributed to renewed deterioration of Mexico's image and paved the way for further external criticisms. Faced
with this negative climate of opinion in the United States, the Mexican government has dedicated significant resources to promoting
the image of the regime and some of its projects. Promotion of
NAFTA alone is thought to have cost at least $25 million ("Trading"
1993; Einsenstadt 1993).

Increased problems with traditional strategies of political legit-
imization in Mexico have also had an impact on the consensus built
around the country's foreign policy. In the past, one of the central
tenets of the policy was a conviction of the illegitimacy of seeking
outside help to advance internal political agendas. Until recently, attempts to find outside support—particularly from the United States
—were publicly denounced as something akin to high treason. However, in the 1990s it has become very common for parties and
groups, including the once ultranationalist left and the PRI itself, to
look for political allies and support on the outside (Dresser 1991).
Thus the panorama confronting Mexican foreign policy makers at
the end of the twentieth century is particularly complex. On the one

hand, increased economic openness has in fact deepened the linkage to the U.S. economy, making the strengthening of commercial ties with Latin America difficult in the short term. On the other hand, this rapprochement with the United States is nurturing the discourse of diversification and fueling diplomatic activism with the region. This ambivalent policy has provoked a mixed response from Latin America, which considers Mexico as both a bridge to the U.S. market and a competitor with no real interest in the processes of regional integration.

This lack of confidence in Mexico's Latin American identity has been provoked, as we will see in detail below, by a certain lack of Mexican enthusiasm regarding the integration of other countries to NAFTA. However, it does not mean that the Latin American option or, for that matter, the European and Asian options are canceled. Indeed, it is possible that the strengthening of links with the United States through NAFTA could paradoxically establish for the first time in Mexican history the foundations for a real diversification of Mexican foreign economic policy.

THE NATURE OF CHANGE:
FROM NATIONALISM TO UNIVERSALISM

The change in Mexican foreign policy has occurred at both the instrumental and conceptual levels. The instrumental dimension has undergone a profound modification in terms of interaction with the external world. During the 1980s the Mexican government had to face new and difficult challenges from the outside that involved the presence of nongovernmental actors, particularly the media, which proved to be a constant headache for the de la Madrid government.[3]

Initial responses to this new external reality were disjointed and torpid. However, the de la Madrid administration increasingly took to employing tools, such as lobbying, formerly perceived to be at variance with the traditional principle of nonintervention (according to which even the expression of opinions on the internal politics of other countries is proscribed). A propaganda campaign directed toward the U.S. media was one manifestation of changing government tactics, although it proved quite inefficient. Mexico also accorded extra attention to consulates in U.S. territory to defend the rights of Mexicans abroad. At the same time, the de la Madrid administration was actively involved in bilateral and multilateral economic negotiations on commercial and debt issues.

All of these tools were used intensively by the Salinas government as well. The Salinas administration launched another major lobby and propaganda effort in the United States—involving paid TV advertisements asking people to write to their congresspersons— that, in strict terms, was incompatible with the traditional concept of nonintervention. The anti-immigration policy of California governor Pete Wilson—which led to the approval of Proposition 187 in November 1994—also provoked strong protests by Salinas administration officials, protests that, ironically, were qualified as interventionist by the defenders of the proposition.

These changes at the instrumental level had a significant influence on traditional concepts of sovereignty not only in government rhetoric but in broad sectors of Mexican society as well. Mexico's traditional relationship with the outside has been, in general terms, traumatic. The outside was seen "in Mexico, for profound historical reasons, as a source of dangers, not of opportunities" (Zaid 1984: 7). As long as the closed economic model prevailed in Mexico, this concept of the external world was in fact quite functional. However, the governmental acknowledgment of the new foreign environment did not come until the Salinas administration, and the change in rhetoric was gradual.

In May 1989 the Mexican government modified regulations under its Foreign Investment Law to allow 100 percent of foreign capital into Mexico. Yet the law itself was not changed until December 1993. Furthermore, in mid-1989 President Salinas explicitly denied the possibility of commercial integration with the United States when he said that "Mexico does not belong and does not want to assimilate itself to any economic zone or political bloc" (*El Financiero* 1989). One year later, after news of impending free trade negotiations with the United States was leaked to a U.S. paper, the government tried to maintain an image of independence from Washington. The official discourse shifted to emphasize that the risks involved in the negotiation of the free trade agreement were minor. This line of argument was clearly laid out in the "recommendation" made by the Mexican senate to President Salinas in the wake of a national consultation on free trade and one week before the presidents of Mexico and the United States officially announced the beginning of the negotiating process of the agreement: "This agreement—contrary to a common market—would preserve the political and economic sovereignty of the country and would allow Mexico to establish its commercial policy with the rest of the world" ("México" 1990).

During the rest of his term, Salinas maintained an ambivalent position that stressed the risk of "being left out, marginalized from the new processes of world integration, the large flows of exchange" (Salinas de Gortari 1990) but also insisted that friendship with the United States would not come "at the expense of the values that determine our essence and constitute us as a nation" ("Assessment" 1989).

The Salinas administration was also very reluctant to accept any kind of supervision of the internal political process. Until the beginning of 1994, the government rejected emphatically the presence of international observers with such arguments as "The discussion on our democracy has no borders; it has only one definite judge: the Mexican people" (Salinas de Gortari 1990) or criticisms of an "ideological hegemony" that tries to universalize "a democracy for export in which the commercial manipulation replaces the autonomous political will of the voters"("Discurso" 1990; Lomas 1990). However, during the elections of August 1994, the Mexican government finally admitted "international visitors" to legitimize the electoral process. This decision notwithstanding, Mexico has consistently rejected mechanisms for supervising the implantation of democracy proposed by international organizations of which it is a member, a position that has in fact distanced it from the rest of Latin America (Bloomfield 1994).

The acceptance of the universal dimension of Mexico among society as a whole has also been gradual but in many ways surprising. A poll conducted immediately after information on free trade negotiations was leaked to the media in 1990 revealed that 59 percent of Mexicans were willing to see Mexico join the United States *if that would mean a better standard of living* ("Integración" 1991). Another poll, published in May 1992, showed a substantial change in Mexico's opinion of the United States between 1988, when only 37 percent of the participants had a "favorable" opinion of the "Colossus to the North," and 1991, when 52 percent expressed a favorable perception (Opinión 1992). This trend was also reflected in opinion polls on NAFTA, which was attracting around 60 percent of popular support in 1992 and 1993.[4] These polls suggest the existence of a radical change in Mexico's popular perception of the outside world and, especially, of the United States.

At the same time, the figures cited here should not be seen as suggesting that the Mexican government and public opinion have embraced the external world without resistance, for traces of nationalism do appear in Mexico from time to time. However, the change has been significant: from a perspective that stressed the advantages of diminishing international contact, the emphasis has finally shifted to the advantages of integration with the "ruling centers of world dynamism," as President Salinas himself asserted. How is this transformation of the traditional concept of sovereignty affecting Mexico's relations with areas other than the United States? Let us take a closer look at this question.

STRENGTH AND WEAKNESS OF THE DIVERSIFICATION POLICY: THE ROLE OF LATIN AMERICA

The emphasis on the diversification of Mexican foreign policy is as old as the foreign policy itself. President Salinas acknowledged that "our fundamental strategy has been the diversification of foreign relations" (Salinas de Gortari 1991). The Mexican secretary of foreign affairs Fernando Solana, who served under President Carlos Salinas de Gortari from 1988 to 1993, said it even more explicitly: the strengthening of links with Latin America and Europe is a way to "build spaces of equilibrium in the relationship with the United States and Canada" (Claps 1991: 1-A, 39-A). However, in commercial and investment terms, the links have been traditionally concentrated on the United States. President Salinas himself apparently attempted to diversify Mexico's economic relations during his period in office. Although the limited success of a visit to Europe early in 1990 seemingly convinced Salinas that there were no economic alternatives to the United States,[5] it appears that his administration felt the need to explore other options in an effort to counterbalance Washington's importance as economic integration with the United States progressed. However, approaches to the Pacific and European blocs were not immediately successful.

The Pacific Basin alternative, although attractive given the importance of Japan in the world economy, has important limitations. As Riordan Roett pointed out, one drawback is the potential for deterioration in U.S.-Japanese relations; in such a scenario, Washington could perceive a rapprochement between Mexico and Tokyo as a threat to its own interests (Roett 1991). On the other hand, whereas investment from Korea, Taiwan, and Singapore has shown a high degree of dynamism, Japan has maintained a prudent approach toward NAFTA.

Prospects for strengthening economic links with the European Union also face obstacles despite significant ties with Germany, Mexico's third-largest commercial partner and third-largest source of foreign capital, and Spain, which is important culturally as well as commercially. As a result of the economic crisis in the former socialist countries of Eastern Europe and the aggravation of the ethnic conflicts there, the EU has two immediate priorities: the consolidation of the process of economic integration in Western Europe and the political and economic stabilization of Eastern Europe. Therefore, its interest in Latin America in general, and Mexico in particular, is secondary.

In economic terms, Mexico's relationship with Latin America is even less important than its links with Europe or the Pacific Basin.

The region represents around 5 percent of Mexico's total trade and is totally irrelevant as a source of foreign capital. Nonetheless, a close relationship with the area has certain advantages since Latin America has never had any hegemonic pretensions with regard to Mexico. Furthermore, Mexico and Latin America are linked by a common cultural legacy, have endured interventions from the United States and other big powers, and share the challenge of solving serious economic problems. For these reasons, Latin America has been the main target of the Mexican diversification policy. President Salinas strengthened Mexico's participation in the Rio Group (formerly the Group of Eight), whose annual meetings bring together all the Latin American presidents. In addition, in July 1991, Salinas sponsored the First Iberoamerican Summit in Guadalajara. The countries represented were Argentina, Bolivia, Brazil, Chile, Colombia, Costa Rica, Cuba, the Dominican Republic, Ecuador, El Salvador, Guatemala, Honduras, Mexico, Nicaragua, Panama, Paraguay, Peru, Portugal, Spain, Uruguay, and Venezuela. Although the results of this summit and the following one in Madrid were inconclusive, its inception suggests the existence of Mexican leadership in the area.

The creation of the so-called Group of Three (G-3), formed by Mexico, Venezuela, and Colombia, is another manifestation of Mexico's interest in Latin America. Despite the fact that Venezuela and Colombia represent less than 0.4 percent of Mexico's total trade, they have a political importance, especially in the light of the potential for conflict in Central America and the Caribbean. Indeed, the G-3 countries were at the heart of the Contadora Group, created in 1983 to deal with the Central American crisis. More recently, in October 1991, the G-3 members invited Fidel Castro to a meeting in Cozumel, where they urged the Cuban leader to make reforms in his country. Consequently, the G-3 should be regarded more as a consultation mechanism for future crisis in the region rather than as a trading bloc.

At this point we should also mention the September 1991 signing of a free trade agreement between Mexico and Chile, two years before the approval of NAFTA by the U.S. Congress. This agreement was clearly intended to reduce the political impact of NAFTA negotiations, for at .04 percent of total volume, Mexico's trade with Chile is as insignificant as its commercial exchanges with Venezuela and Colombia. However, Chile's economic health has led to an invitation to enter NAFTA in the near future, which was announced during the Summit of the Americas in Miami in December 1994.

Despite Mexico's sponsorship of the aforementioned groups and the trade negotiations with certain other Latin American countries, Mexico has been seriously at odds with the rest of the region and with the Organization of American States (OAS) on topics such as democracy and human rights. In 1990, for example, the Mexican government was severely criticized by the Interamerican Commission on Human Rights for irregularities in the electoral processes of 1985 and 1986 (Chabat 1991). In December 1992 divergences with the rest of Latin America were very evident when Mexico was the *only country* to vote against a proposal making democratic government a requirement for membership in the OAS (there were twenty-seven votes in favor and two abstentions). However, even in the absence of drastic changes in its position, Mexico's decision to allow foreign observers to be present during the August 1994 elections gives a reason to expect greater discretion in its opposition to some forms of external surveillance of electoral processes. Such a change in attitude was apparent during the Summit of the Americas, and it should reduce the distance separating Mexico from the rest of Latin America on such issues.

From the perspective of commercial integration, it seems that since the approval of NAFTA Mexico has been very reluctant to allow new members into the agreement. According to a White House internal document leaked to the *New York Times* on March 1, 1994: "Mexico is not interested in allowing other countries in the region into an arrangement that offers considerable benefits, which were achieved because of its relationship to the United States" (Bradshe 1994).

The Mexican secretary of commerce, Jaime Serra Puche, denied this report the next day (Hall 1994). However, two months later, Serra Puche himself expressed Mexico's "rational and legitimate concerns" about the limits that the varying degrees of development of Latin American countries pose to NAFTA's expansion: "We can't have one rule that allows everyone to join. Some countries wouldn't fit," because of their state of development ("Mexico's" 1994). Nonetheless, it seems that Mexico has tempered its original reluctance to admit other countries into NAFTA out of fear that the United States would establish bilateral pacts with other Latin American countries that could affect its interest in a more negative way.[6] In any case, the Latin American free trade zone proposed for the year 2005 assumes the incorporation into an American Free Trade Agreement (AFTA) of most of the countries in the region, and Mexico has no power to stop this development.

From this standpoint, it seems evident that a relationship with Latin America will be important for Mexico as far as it affects Mexico's relationship with the United States through AFTA. At the same time, Mexico may become more attractive to other blocs in economic terms if its economy turns out to be more competitive and its internal market grows.[7] At the political level, Latin America is likely to take on greater importance in the eventuality of a concrete crisis (such as turmoil in Cuba or Central America). For this reason, Mexico cannot distance itself from the region and the defense of its immediate national security interests.

CONCLUSION

The change experienced in Mexican foreign policy during the past decade, although incomplete, is clearly visible now. From a defensive, ultranationalist position, Mexico has moved toward a more pragmatic approach in which Latin America plays a minor role in economic terms. Latin America's economic importance could increase, however, in light of AFTA. Although it would be better for Mexico in the short term to limit the expansion of NAFTA, it seems that this process is unavoidable. Nonetheless, Mexico will preserve a certain degree of bargaining power vis-à-vis the United States during the next several years because of the importance of commercial exchanges with its northern neighbor. Representing approximately 8 percent of total U.S. trade, Mexico is the United States' third most important commercial partner. If Mexican trade continues to expand at the pace of the past six years, it is reasonable to expect a broadening of the volume of trade with other regions as well. Although the percentages are unlikely to change drastically in the short term, this expansion would give Mexico a new continental dimension. Indeed, the rhetoric of Latin American unity maintained for some years by the Mexican government will probably finally become true, thanks to the United States.

NOTES

1. For an overview of the new demands of the international environment and how governments react to it, see Rosati et al. (1994).

2. During his visit to Argentina in October 1990, President Salinas stressed that the Latin American efforts of commercial integration and the integration to the United States were "complementary" ("Mexico" 1991).

3. For a description of the new tools Mexico began to use during the 1980s, see Chabat (1990).

4. According to a poll by the Mexican government's polling unit, in October 1992 64.3 percent favored NAFTA, while in September 1993 the percentage was 53.7. This fall in support can be explained by the problems NAFTA faced in 1993. However, a majority of the population still supported the free trade agreement (Golden 1993).

5. According to the *Wall Street Journal,* President Salinas declared after his trip to Europe that "the trip convinced me that we have to move faster toward commercial integration in North America" (Moffett 1990).

6. Apparently, the United Stated has threatened to sign bilateral agreements of its own with Latin American countries if Mexico and Canada oppose the broadening of NAFTA (Crane 1994).

7. President Salinas himself suggested the possibility that Mexico would become "more attractive" for Asian countries with the approval of NAFTA ("John" 1992).

3

Canada in the Americas: The Impact of Regionalism on a New Foreign Policy

◆

Gordon Mace & Jean-Philippe Thérien

This chapter analyzes Canada's foreign policy in the regional context of the Americas. The first part of the chapter focuses on the period 1960–1980, and the second part examines the period from 1980 onward. In both sections, a short review of the changes that have characterized the evolution of the international system is followed by an analysis of how Canada's response to these changes has affected its relationships with the rest of the hemisphere. We argue that Canada's behavior toward the region of the Americas has to be understood in the broader framework of Canadian foreign policy and that Canadian foreign policy itself has to be understood in the broader context of its international environment.

We begin with the post-1960 period because before 1960, except for the special case of the Caribbean, the Canadian government felt no need to develop a regional strategy extending beyond the Rio Grande. Many observers saw Canada as a regional power without a region (Holmes 1970: 34). Although Canada did begin in 1940 to broaden its diplomatic network to encompass certain Latin American countries, it did so unenthusiastically. Government missions to Latin America in 1946, 1953, and 1958 gave rise to constant endeavors at rediscovering the Latin American region (Ogelsby 1976: 164). Characterized by its low profile, Canada's presence in Latin America was ultimately based on the private initiatives of merchants, bankers, investors, and missionaries.

The Canadian government's passivity toward the hemisphere was notably illustrated by its long-standing refusal to join the Organization of American States (OAS). Canada's position can be explained in part by the lukewarm attitude of the United States, which feared intrusion by pro-British interests in hemispheric affairs. Also, given its strong involvement in the UN and the limited resources at its disposal, Canada did not want to disperse its efforts across too many international organizations. Finally, Canada was reluctant to join an institution that would have forced it to take sides either against the United States or against its Latin American partners. Considering this political atmosphere of prudence mixed with indifference, Canada's decision to maintain diplomatic relations with Fidel Castro's Cuba stands out as an atypical demonstration of leadership (Randall 1977: 209). That decision enabled the Canadian government to underscore its ability to act independently of the United States, but it was still far from expressing a long-term, structured policy toward the region.

1960–1980: THE POSTWAR ORDER IN QUESTION

A Changing International System

Profound transformations and numerous challenges characterized the international system between 1960 and 1980. Overall, the most striking change was the decline of strategic concerns and the rise of economic preoccupations. Contrary to the most pessimistic expectations, the balance of power between the superpowers held firm, the result being an era of prolonged détente. On the other hand, the commercial and financial systems established after World War II proved to be more fragile than expected. The subsequent economic instability and overall slowdown of growth became hallmarks of the new international order.

Although the United States held on to its status as the world's greatest power, the period from 1960 to 1980 brought about a gradual loss of U.S. hegemony. Whereas the United States accounted for nearly half of the world's gross national product in 1945, that proportion was reduced to 23 percent by 1974. As the devastated economies of Europe and Japan completed their reconstruction, the international system became more polycentric. The decline in U.S. competitiveness generated ever higher deficits in its balance of trade. Combined with a reckless U.S. budgetary policy, this situation led to a breakdown in the rules of the international economic order. In August 1971, U.S. president Richard Nixon took a series of unilateral measures that included scrapping the principle of the dollar's convertibility to gold and imposing a surtax on U.S. imports. These measures, whose effects were especially felt in Canada, paved the way for an overhaul of the Bretton Woods consensus. In 1976, the International Monetary Fund made official the transition from a system of fixed exchange rates to one of floating exchange rates.

The deficiencies of the world economy were further aggravated by the 1973 energy crisis. In Western countries, the Organization of Petroleum Exporting Countries (OPEC) served as an easy scapegoat for escalating inflation and general economic stagnation. It is nonetheless true that the repercussions of the initial oil price shock were considerable. The sudden rise in the price of energy prompted a noticeable deterioration in the trade balance of all oil-importing countries in both the North and the South. For the first time in history, Third World exporters of raw materials revealed how vulnerable the economies of developed countries could be to outside forces.

The oil crisis served as a springboard for demands in favor of a new international economic order. Throughout the 1970s, the developing countries used their automatic majority in the UN with the objective of profoundly transforming the structure of international economic relations. Catalyzed by OPEC's success, the new solidarity among developing countries also resulted from other factors: decolonization, the creation of the Group of 77 in 1964, the return of China to the international scene in 1971, and the first strides of the new industrial countries of Latin America and Asia. The South had poorly estimated, however, the North's resistance to change. After the election of U.S. president Ronald Reagan in 1980, the idea of global negotiations was quickly eliminated from the international agenda.

One prime vector for restructuring international power after 1960 was unquestionably the establishment on all continents of institutional mechanisms for regional integration (Lindberg and Scheingold 1970). Today hindsight allows us to affirm that, of all the regional international organizations created at that time, the European Economic Community (EEC) is the only one to have lived up to initial hopes. With its rapid growth in membership and the intensive development of its areas of cooperation, the EEC has remained a unique example. Yet, though the successes have been less dazzling, comparable undertakings on other continents have also helped underscore the notion that the nation-state is not a fully adequate instrument for dealing with the political and economic challenges of the international environment.

Canada's Third Option

The changes affecting world politics between 1960 and 1980 had a considerable impact on Canada's external relations. On the political front, the trend toward the diffusion of power relegated Canada to a role more in line with its capabilities and resources than the one it had acquired by default in 1945. On the economic front, Canada's interests encountered an international climate more menacing than ever. Exacerbated by numerous factors, including limits on access to the U.S. market, the end of Europe's reconstruction, Great Britain's entry into the EEC and that country's dropping of its system of preferential tariffs with Canada, the emergence of Japan and the new industrial countries in international trade, and the growing number of potentially protectionist regional groupings, this threatening situation ultimately explains why, in defining its foreign policy, the Canadian government moved to make international competitiveness an ever more central theme.

For the Canadian foreign policy elite, the evolution of the postwar order from 1960 on signaled the need for significant reorientations if Canada was to prosper and maintain its role in the international system. The eagerness of certain circles in the federal bureaucracy to introduce important changes in Canadian foreign policy coincided with the election in 1968 of a Liberal government. The new prime minister, Pierre Trudeau, almost immediately launched an extensive foreign policy review; the general guidelines for the review process were adopted by the cabinet in December 1969. The main points were that foreign policy should be an extension of internal policies and Canadian interests, that foreign policy should be seen in its totality, that Canada should remain active in international affairs but in more modest ways, and that continuous coordination would be necessary for optimum effectiveness (Granatstein and Bothwell 1990: 31). A White Paper on Canadian foreign policy was made public in 1970. The document contained six major orientations that were to guide Canada's foreign policy throughout the 1970s and early 1980s: to foster economic growth, to preserve sovereignty and independence, to contribute to peace and security, to promote social justice, to help develop the quality of life, and to maintain environmental harmony (Gouvernement du Canada 1970: 14). The White Paper contained six booklets, one of them devoted to Latin America, but none addressing the Canadian-U.S. relationship.

The 1971 "Nixon shock," more than anything else, made clear to the Canadian government that the world had changed and that the external environment had become a lot more threatening to Canada's position in the world system. That the Nixon measures were made public without any prior consultation with Canadian authorities only served to drive the point home. Now Canada was no longer even sure it could count on its neighbor and principal ally. The Canadian response to a changing overall environment was made public in 1972 through what were to be called the "Options Papers," published under the signature of the secretary of state for external affairs, Mitchell Sharp. The Third Option, the one adopted by the Canadian government, was an overall policy orientation that would guide domestic as well as external federal policies.

At its inception, the Third Option strategy had a larger domestic than external content. Internally, it implied more state intervention in the economy, the adoption of an industrial strategy, and the use of protectionist measures to keep strategic economic sectors out of the grasp of foreign enterprises (Pentland 1982). The concept of an industrial strategy never really materialized, but the federal government became more active in the Canadian economy through instruments such as the Canadian Development Corporation. The strategy also favored strong economic nationalism, as reflected in the establishment of the National Energy Program (NEP) and the creation of the Foreign Investment Review Agency (FIRA).[1]

In terms of foreign policy behavior, the Third Option strategy implied, essentially, an effort to diversify Canada's foreign partners. This was to be done at the political-diplomatic level by the federal government itself; in economic affairs it was to be achieved by way of government support for the Canadian business community with funds made available through the Canadian International Development Agency, the Export Development Corporation, the Canadian Commercial Corporation, and the Industry and Commerce Department's twin programs of Export Markets Development and Projects Promotion.

The Third Option strategy identified Japan and the EEC as the initial targets of the diversification effort. With regard to these targets, the strategy was not successful. Significantly, however, an extensive study of Canada's diplomatic behavior and disbursements made throughout the 1970s for programs related to the Third Option strategy has shown that very often the major target of such activities was, in fact, Latin America (Mace and Hervouet 1989).

This, of course, had little to do with what some see as today's emergent regionalism in the Americas. It was related, rather, to the fact that Latin America was then seen as a land of opportunity for Canadian business abroad, a view encouraged by the fact that Latin America at that time was the region where Canada's exports had the highest proportion of manufactured goods (Corbo and Havrylyshin 1980: 10). But more than that, it had to do with the upgrading of Canada's relations with Latin America subsequent to the important Canadian ministerial visit to the region in 1968.

This fact-finding mission to Latin America, the largest ever sent to that region, with five cabinet ministers and more than thirty civil servants, brought back significant data that, once fed into the policy review process, led to Canada's decision to "systematically reinforce" ties of all kinds with Latin America (Guy 1976: 377; Ogelsby 1976: 30–36, 182–183). The application of this decision took many forms throughout the 1970s. First of all, the Department of External Affairs established in 1971 a division for Latin America inside the Bureau for Hemispheric Affairs. The following year, Canada became an official member of the Inter-American Development Bank and obtained the status of permanent observer at the OAS, where it became involved in specialized agencies. The federal government also created, in agreement with its partners, joint consultative committees with Brazil, Mexico, Venezuela, and Argentina. Throughout the 1970s, Ottawa almost doubled its bilateral aid to Latin America[2] and encouraged trade and investment, with the result that at the end of the decade the region was importing more than 50 percent of Canadian manufactured goods sold to the Third World. It was also getting over 50 percent of Canada's direct foreign investment in the Third World, which accounted for a quarter of Canada's total foreign investment in 1976 (Mace 1989: 420–423; Ogelsby 1979; Canadian Investment 1981).

Hence, given the situation prior to 1968, it is not surprising that the 1970s were dubbed the "golden age" of Canada's relations with Latin America. But, again, this had little to do with regionalism. The nature of Canada's relations with Latin America during the 1970s stemmed much more from Ottawa's discovery of the region, from the economic opportunities associated with Latin American development at that time, and, more than anything else, from Canada's efforts to diversify its foreign relations.

As to the Third Option strategy, by the end of the 1970s it was widely deemed to have failed overall, a valid assessment if we consider the fate of Canada's relations with the initial targets of the Third Option, namely Japan and the EEC (Pentland, 1991: 129). But the validity of the assessment diminishes if we take into account the strength of the government's commitment to the initial policy objectives, which remained strong throughout the 1970s. In terms of general results, however, one has to recognize that the Third Option strategy was not a success: it was not able to modify in any significant manner the economic relationship between Canada and the United States.[3] The fate of the Third Option might have been different if the Canadian private sector had been more aggressive on foreign markets and if the launching of the strategy had not been immediately handicapped by the 1973–1974 oil crisis. All in all, it would be fair to say that the Third Option was a twenty-year strategy that was never really allowed to get under way. Canada's policy behavior during the 1970s can, ultimately, be summed up as economic nationalism on the domestic scene and an effort at diversification in the foreign policy field.

AFTER 1980: GLOBALIZATION VERSUS REGIONALISM

A Perspective on Systemic Trends

From 1980 to 1993, the postwar international order was shaken to its foundations with renewed intensity. The collapse of the Soviet Union and of its empire has had far-reaching repercussions. It has given unprecedented legitimacy to the market economy and has encouraged a process of democratization not only in Eastern Europe but also in Latin America, Africa, and Asia. From the standpoint of international institutions, the termination of the Cold War has given a new lease on life to the UN, which, for the first time, succeeded in applying the charter's collective security provisions in a credible manner (Rosenau 1992). Whereas in the late 1970s U.S. leadership was everywhere on the defensive, the United States looks now to be the only superpower. For Canada, continued U.S. power in the face of adversity has been a reassuring factor and has strongly influenced the government's international choices.

On the economic front, growth and international trade have remained very unsteady since the early 1980s. Weakened by a second energy crisis, which set off a tripling of oil prices in 1979, the world economy had to submit to the severe constraints imposed by a U.S. administration systematically opposed to inflation and in favor of free enterprise. Although a sustained recovery followed the severe recession of 1981–1982, it did not succeed in correcting the structural weaknesses of the world economy. In the mid-1990s, after the second recession in less than a decade, international economic activity remains marked by a profound lack of vigor (ONU 1992: 1–2).

The lackluster performance of the international economy since the early 1980s has been indissolubly linked to major disruptions in trade. With the crisis of trade multilateralism lingering, international commerce no longer acted as the engine of economic growth, as it had before. After avoiding the breakup of the General Agreement on Tariffs and Trade, the international community decided in 1986 to initiate the Uruguay Round, the most ambitious round of multilateral trade negotiations ever undertaken (Bhagwati 1991: 83). The negotiations finally came to a successful conclusion in December 1993. Yet for Canada the whole exercise and the world trade situation of the 1980s had revealed the necessity for significant modifications in economic and foreign policy orientations.

The unpredictability of the international trading system has also coincided with a series of disturbances in the international financial system. Over the past decade, the par values of the main currencies have fluctuated widely. In spite of various efforts to contain this source of disruption, the recent evolution of the exchange rates of some currencies shows that the international monetary order remains highly fragile (Rossant 1992). Third World debt—which rose to $1,500 billion in 1992—is another major source of tension that has affected the functioning of the international financial system since 1980 (World Bank 1992: 160). After the collapse of the Baker Plan (1985), the Brady Plan (1989) finally confirmed that the debt could never be entirely paid off. Worst-case scenarios have been avoided, but debt still represents the main external obstacle to speedier Third World development.

Uncertainties abound, and the evolution of the international environment proceeds within the ambit of two opposing trends. On the one hand, the interdependence and globalization of markets have become fundamental characteristics of the world order. On the other hand, the rise of three regional blocs in Europe, the Americas, and Asia indicates a trend toward the fragmentation of the international system. The European Union (EU) makes Europe the regional bloc whose degree of integration is the most advanced. Despite all the difficulties in forging a coherent European identity, the implementation of the Single European Act in 1993 demonstrates the dynamism of European cooperation and suggests that the EU will continue to be a powerful pole of attraction for other states. In the Americas, the 1988 Canadian-U.S. Free Trade Agreement (FTA) and the 1994 North American Free Trade Agreement (NAFTA) have made possible the emergence of an unprecedented continental regionalism, which, according to former U.S. president George Bush, could eventually stretch from Alaska to Tierra del Fuego. Finally, in Asia, the process of regionalization is different because it is developing with a minimum of institutions and bureaucratic mechanisms. Centered on Japanese monetary and industrial power and increasingly independent of the U.S. market, this zone of cooperation encompasses South Korea, Taiwan, Hong Kong, and the countries of the Association of Southeast Asian Nations. It is impossible for the time being to say which of these two forces—globalization or regionalism—will in the end prove more decisive, but it is clear that the disappearance of the common enemy, the USSR, may impede the preservation of unity that has characterized relations between the United States, Europe, and Japan over the past forty years.

The Americas:
A Growing Concern in Canadian Foreign Policy

Canada's attitude toward the sweeping transformations that have shaken the international system in the past decade or so has been mixed. Some of these changes were received favorably by the Canadian foreign policy elite. This is the case with regard to the dismemberment of the Soviet empire and the introduction of democratic rules and market-oriented strategies in the countries of the former Communist bloc. From a Canadian perspective, the end of the Cold War era, although not without its problems, should alleviate the danger of nuclear war and create opportunities for the establishment of a peaceful international system. For middle powers like Canada, it should also allow for greater flexibility in foreign policy behavior.

But, at the same time, other changes were not so favorably perceived in Ottawa. The increasing economic domination of Japan, the position of large European countries both in world markets and in their own geographical regions, the progress toward a single market in Western Europe, the difficulty of forging an agreement in the Uruguay Round and the ensuing threat for the multilateral trading system, and, finally, the increasingly protectionist attitude of the U.S. government as a result of trade problems, particularly with Japan, all of these contributed to creating an environment considered threatening to Canada's position in the international system. Moreover, the anxiety was heightened by the reputed weakness of Canada's basis for action, given the country's increasing public and private debt, the internal threat to its unity, its dismal record of investment in research and development, and its weak competitive position at the international level (Paquet 1991). Some observers have summarized Canada's difficult situation by referring to the "Argentinization" of the country.

New policy orientations were urgently needed to enable Canada to adapt to the new environment, and these were made possible with the election of a new Conservative government in 1984. Soon after the elections, the new government sent out a clear message: it wanted to break with the economic nationalism so prevalent in the 1970s. The most visible way to do this was to tackle that emblem of economic nationalism, FIRA. From then on, instead of screening foreign investment, FIRA would become an agency charged with enticing foreign investment into Canada. An effort was also made to reduce the growth of public spending and to trim the state apparatus through measures such as cuts in the federal bureaucracy, the introduction of a tax on goods and services, a reduction in transfer payments to provincial and local governments, and the privatization of crown corporations. In perfect step with the economic philosophy that was spreading throughout the Western world, the Conservative government managed successfully to demonstrate that Canada was now open for business; the private sector, both domestic and foreign, would find less state intervention in Canada and a more market-oriented economy.

New orientations were also adopted in matters of foreign policy. These were first made public in the mid-1980s, with the introduction of a Green Paper on Canadian foreign policy (Clark 1985). The Green Paper maintained traditional objectives associated with Canada's international role, but something new was added. Though trade had always been an important aspect of Canadian foreign policy, it was now emphasized that more had to be done to maintain and upgrade a Canadian presence in world markets. Canadian business abroad had to become more competitive, and to this end, the government had to provide support. The other important element was the announcement that Canada would have to reflect on the nature of its future relations with the United States. The "Options" method was retrieved in order to launch a process of consultation at the end of which the federal government would have to come to a decision concerning Canadian-U.S. relations (Clark 1985: 31–33). The Green Paper's title—*Competitiveness and Security*—eloquently summarized where the emphasis would be placed in Canada's future external relations.

Without a doubt, the most important foreign policy endeavor of the Canadian government in the second part of the 1980s was the decision to sign a free trade agreement with the United States. The last time an overall trade arrangement with the United States had been submitted for public approval in Canada, in 1911, it resulted in electoral defeat for Sir Wilfrid Laurier. Then, for more than seventy-five years, the subject was not raised again for extensive discussion. True, there was the Auto Pact of 1965 and the signing in 1982 of sectoral trade agreements between Ottawa and Washington, but at that time the options were left open. Not so in 1988–1989. After a fierce public debate, the Conservative Party was re-elected in 1988 on a platform built essentially around free trade with the United States. Some months later, the FTA was put into effect. Its enactment represents the most important shift in Canada's foreign policy behavior in the twentieth century.

The FTA did put an end to an old debate between proponents of continental free trade and advocates of a modern version of John A. Macdonald's 1879 National Policy of tariff protection (Gherson 1992: 155) and autonomous industrial development. The agreement basically meant that Canada was prepared to hitch its fate to that of the United States, confident that it could keep its autonomy in international affairs but at the same time unsure of the impact that this decision would have on the fabric of Canadian society.

Among Canada's top foreign policy elite, there are many who believe that the world is now reorganizing itself in "hub and spoke" arrangements (Hampson and Maule 1991: 13). The three most important such arrangements—the triad—are in Europe, with the German-French hub; in Asia, with Japan as the hub; and in the Americas, with the United States as the hub. In such a world, Canada has very little place to go, because the domestic threats to its unity and the problems it faces in terms of productivity and competitiveness impede its capacity to act on the world scene, particularly in Asia and Europe, where its influence is declining (Carre 1992; Ouellette, Henderson, and Livermore 1992). It was therefore considered vital that Canada secure a relationship with the United States and become a full partner in the regional system of the Americas (Hart 1991: 96). This was confirmed when the minister of foreign affairs, Joe Clark, addressed the meeting of the General Assembly of the OAS in November 1989: "Canada's joining of the OAS represents . . . a decision to become a partner in this hemisphere. For too long, Canadians have seen this hemisphere as our house; it is now time to make it our home" (Clark 1989: 1). This did not mean that Canada would withdraw from the rest of the world or disregard the UN and other multilateral organizations such as the Commonwealth or La Francophonie. Rather, it meant that henceforward the Americas could become as important as Europe for Canadian foreign policy; eventually, the Americas might even occupy a crucial position in Canada's foreign policy.

This is the rationale behind Canada's latest foreign policy moves. It is the basis of Ottawa's decision to sign and implement the FTA, and it explains the decision to participate in the negotiations leading to the signing of NAFTA. But Canada's increasing involvement in the region has by no means been limited to North America. The same rationale explains Canada's active intervention in Central America since 1986 and Ottawa's efforts at mediation in the case of Haiti. It is also closely connected to Ottawa's announcement in the fall of 1989 of a new Latin American strategy and to Canada's decision to become a full member of the OAS in January 1990. Such developments may indicate that counterweights to U.S. influence may soon have to be sought in the Americas rather than in Europe or even Asia, as was traditionally the case.

Ottawa's Latin American strategy was not given the prominence it might have received; furthermore, it was more a set of broad objectives than a concrete policy framework (Dosman 1992: 552). Yet it was nevertheless followed by concrete steps that demonstrated Canada's new commitment to the hemisphere, a commitment and an involvement that went far beyond NAFTA. Canadian diplomats became very active in OAS activities and took the lead in promoting solutions to problems that sometimes were not unrelated to Canada's own interests, such as disarmament and high-seas fishing, but also to problems that were in the interest of the whole American community (Dosman 1992: 546–547). This was the case, for example, when Canada sponsored the creation in the OAS of the Unit for the Promotion of Democracy. Ottawa was also involved in the promotion of more efficient and effective decisionmaking mechanisms in the OAS. Outside the OAS, Canada has been involved in the Central American peace process, having participated concretely in the United Nations Observer Group in Central America (ONUCA) and having played a security role in El Salvador, Haiti, and the Commonwealth Caribbean.

But as Dosman has pointed out, the Latin America constituency in Canada remains weak, and Ottawa still seems to lack a comprehensive framework for Canada's involvement in the region (Dosman 1992: 550–553). Inside the Department of Foreign Affairs and International Trade, diplomats responsible for Latin American affairs are often at a disadvantage when competing for attention from decisionmakers at the cabinet level. Funds are also lacking to support scientific and cultural exchanges that would be useful to better understand the evolving dynamics of the region. Steps have been taken, but more will have to be done to consolidate the relationship between Canada and Latin America. What, then, can we expect concerning Canada's future involvement in the hemisphere? How will Canada fit in the emerging architecture of the Americas?

CONCLUSION:
CANADA'S PLACE IN THE NEW REGIONALISM OF THE AMERICAS

Today things are moving rapidly in the Americas. Major progress has been made in terms of democratic development and respect for human rights. Governments, most notably in Mexico, Chile, and Argentina but elsewhere as well, have initiated significant economic reforms. From a commercial and economic point of view, the hemisphere itself is being reorganized, with the introduction of the FTA, NAFTA, the Southern Cone Common Market, and the Group of Three and the changes made to the Caribbean Community and Common Market (CARICOM), the Central American Common Market, and the Andean Group. All of these developments point clearly to a remodeling of the hemisphere, perhaps in the direction of a new regional system.

Canada's insertion in this new architecture of the Americas will likely be twofold. The most visible involvement at the start will naturally be in North America, where developments will affect Canada more than events anywhere else in the world. Here the name of the game will be NAFTA. Ottawa will be heavily involved in the implementation and functioning of NAFTA; it will strive at the same time to obtain for Canadian business the environment needed to reap all possible benefits from the arrangement. Progress has been made in the area of deregulation, but much more must be done in terms of education, training, and investment in research and development. In the near future, Ottawa, Washington, and Mexico will also have to deal with the expansion of NAFTA. Chile is now negotiating for full membership, and other Latin American countries are waiting on the doorstep. Studies have also shown that over the past twenty years many small countries of Central America and the Caribbean have been slowly drifting toward North America in matters of trade (Mace, Bélanger, and Thérien 1993). Decisions on these issues will not be easy to make.

Besides NAFTA, Ottawa will be closely monitoring the very real phenomenon of transborder regionalism, which might also become a concern for Mexico City and Washington. There is already a high level of more localized exchange across the Canadian-U.S. border (particularly in the east, in the far west, and in the Great Lakes region), and the same is true of the U.S.-Mexican border. Companies and local governments are involved; some, such as Quebec, the Maritimes, New York, and the New England states, have already established an institutional framework. This phenomenon probably poses no real or immediate threat to sovereignty, although Ottawa has expressed some concern (Ouellette, Henderson, and Livermore 1992: 5, 9); however, there will surely be management problems. In the long run, one can foresee the growth of transborder regionalism, and no one can exclude its possible impact on the remapping of North America, at least in the fields of economic and cultural affairs.

Leaving aside North America, it seems that Canada will have no other choice but to become more involved in the emerging regional system of the hemisphere. Canada will be increasingly pushed back into the Americas by the nature of the changes occurring in the world system (specifically, the hub-and-spoke arrangements) and by its own diminishing international influence, as can be seen particularly in the relative decline of its role in Europe. As a "new" country of the Americas, Canada can be expected to be a full-time participant and a devoted architect in the building of a regional system. To fulfill this expectation, Canada will naturally want to increase its overall interactions with its neighbors of the Americas other than the United States, particularly by supporting NAFTA's extension to other countries of the hemisphere. In addition to diplomatic and economic exchanges, this will imply encouraging more contacts between academics and public opinion leaders of Canada and Latin American countries. Canada will also be expected to offer financial support and technical expertise to subregional integration schemes and other multilateral institutions, as it did in relation to the Andean Pact in the 1970s and as it is still doing in relation to CARICOM.

We can also expect that Ottawa will want to apply to the Americas what has characterized Canada's traditional role in international affairs, namely the promotion of the principle of functionalism and the practice of an honest broker. In the first instance, this will mean strong support in favor of multilateral organizations, particularly the OAS, as the primary forums for settling disputes and managing problems. Concretely, this should take three forms: (1) promotion of organizational reforms within the OAS with the aim of more efficient functioning and decisionmaking; (2) support for a greater involvement of the OAS in the management of regional problems; and (3) promotion of values basic to Canadian foreign policy, such as those articulated by former secretary of state for external affairs, Barbara McDougall. These values are the promotion and protection of fundamental human rights; the development of democratic values and institutions; the establishment of "good government," meaning responsible decisionmaking with support from an attentive public administration; and the elimination of obstacles to international trade (*This Week* 1992: 1).

As to the role of honest broker, Canada has already played this part in Central America and Haiti. And there is little doubt that Canada will want to assume in the Americas the mediation role that has been so successful in the past and that is a widely respected feature of traditional Canadian foreign policy. As an extension of this concept, one can also speculate that in the more distant future Canada will look favorably on the formation of a "concert" of middle powers, one of whose functions would be to counterbalance the overwhelming presence of the United States in the region. Under no circumstances would this be a gesture of a confrontational nature, but, should it ever be established, this kind of structure would have to be considered one instrument among several endeavoring to facilitate mediation and problem solving in the region.

It seems that developments in the world system have imposed upon Canada a new role in the building of regionalism in the Americas. Steps have already been made in that direction, but only the future will reveal what the nature and scope of Canada's commitment to the regional system of the Americas will be. From the present vantage point, however, it seems that Canada will have no other alternative but to become more and more active in the community of the Americas.

NOTES

We would like to thank our colleagues Andrew Axline, Jonathan Lemco, Peter McKenna, and David Pollock, whose comments were extremely useful in revising this chapter. We would also like to acknowledge the generous financial support of the Fonds FCAR and the Social Sciences and Humanities Research Council of Canada.

1. The NEP was designed to protect the Canadian oil industry from total domination by foreign firms. The establishment of the crown corporation Petro-Canada was also a step in that direction. However, the program was strongly criticized by the governments of the western provinces, notably Alberta, while FIRA was criticized by a majority of the Canadian business community.

2. The level of aid rose from 7.5 percent in 1970 to 14.8 percent of total Canadian bilateral disbursements in 1979. This was done mainly at the expense of Canada's bilateral aid to Asia. But it must be kept in mind that, compared with Asia and Africa, Latin America was never a major recipient of Canada's aid

3. Canada's exports to the United States ranged between 60 and 70 percent of Canada's overall exports throughout the 1970s and amounted to 75 percent by the mid-1980s (Weintraub 1986).

4

Jamaica:
The End of the Postcolonial Era

———————◆———————

Anthony Payne

Throughout the first quarter of a century of its independence, the foreign policy of Jamaica was relatively straightforward. It reflected the basic contours of the international relations of the Caribbean as a whole, which were a classic form of what can be called North-South-East-West politics, shaped equally by the problems of development and underdevelopment (the North-South dimension) and the constraints of the Cold War (the East-West dimension) (Payne 1984). This matrix was extended a stage further because the Caribbean, uniquely in the developing world, belonged to both the great North-South systems to have grown up in the twentieth century: the American hemispheric system with the United States as core and Latin America and the Caribbean as periphery; and the European imperial system with Britain, France, the Netherlands, and, most recently, the European Union (EU) as core and Africa, the Caribbean, and the Pacific as periphery. Gaining independence in such a constricting geopolitical and geoeconomic environment, nearly all of the new states of the region pursued foreign policies that were judicious mixtures of adjustment and accommodation to more powerful states and forces (Braveboy-Wagner 1989). Their only real option was to seek to diversify their dependence by assembling a range of alternative patronage and protection networks on which they could draw.

Like most of their counterparts in at least the Commonwealth Caribbean, successive Jamaican governments handled this agenda well enough, for the most part picking their way carefully through the limitations imposed by the external environment they had inherited at independence. They took part in the various organizations that make up the UN system, joined the Commonwealth and for a while the Non-Aligned Movement, participated fully alongside other former European colonies in the negotiations with the European Community that inaugurated and sustained the Lomé process, and generally sought to use diplomacy to advantage whenever and wherever opportunity arose. They really ran into difficulties on only two fronts. One concerned relations with Cuba, which were developed on too intimate a basis in the 1970s by the first Manley government, thereby making Jamaica a focus of the Cold War and an object of U.S. hostility. The other, a perennial problem for Jamaica before as well as after the independence era, concerned relations with the rest of the Commonwealth Caribbean and the case for and against the regional integration of the English-speaking states. On this issue, even to this day, Jamaica has not resolved satisfactorily the balance that is appropriate between national and subregional policy frameworks. Nevertheless, aside from these awkward matters, Jamaica can be said to have established for itself a reasonably safe niche within the world order of the period from the end of World War II until the "great changes" initiated by the events of 1989 in Europe.

Jamaica's present foreign policy dilemma, like that of every other state in the developed or developing world, is, of course, that that order has now come to an end while the shape of its replacement is far from clear. This chapter begins, therefore, by identifying those aspects of the changing external environment that most directly bear on Jamaica, proceeds to chart the reorientation of foreign policy that has been undertaken in the country over the past few years, and then turns to consider at length the challenge presented to Jamaica by the "new regionalism" that has sprung up across the Caribbean in response to the recent U.S. embrace of an Americanist framework within which to deal with its immediate southern neighbors. This Americanist project unquestionably poses the most important set of external questions to confront Jamaica in the present period and perhaps in the whole of its postindependence history. The way these questions are resolved will affect not only Jamaica's position in the emerging world order of the 1990s but also its very identity as a nation-state.

THE CHANGING EXTERNAL ENVIRONMENT

Although the point is often missed in both journalistic and academic accounts of the post-1989 changes, the new order that is coming into being is characterized by something much deeper than just the end of the Cold War. Its essence consists of an interplay between a new but still unequal diffusion of power between the core states or blocs of the world (the United States, the EU, and Japan) and a new concentration of power in the hands of international capital. The core states cooperate up to a point to preserve and manage the system in a way that is broadly consistent with the interests of international capital, yet they simultaneously use many of the political, economic, and military means at their disposal to compete for national and/or regional advantage. They are, in other words, allies and rivals at the same time. Stripped of its rhetoric, that is the paradox at the root of the new world order. On its good days, it will no doubt look like a *pax consortis*, controlled efficiently by the Group of Seven countries via the UN, the International Montary Fund (IMF), and the World Bank on essentially the same liberal-capitalist ideological terrain. This conceptualization of the world order also precisely explains the roots of the two most important developments on the international scene that presently bear upon the prospects of Jamaica and the rest of the Caribbean. These are the implementation of the Single European Market (SEM) on January 1, 1993, and the completion on January 1, 1994, of the North American Free Trade Agreement (NAFTA).

The background to these initiatives is well known (Lodge 1993; Baer 1991). President François Mitterrand of France initiated the European project in a speech in 1984 in which he expressed the fear that Western Europe was being bypassed in the new technologies of the microchip, robotics, and lasers and argued that European firms needed to be able to operate freely across national boundaries if they were to compete globally in the future. These ideas were refined by the European Commission and subsequently published as the 1992 program. The program embraced a range of initiatives, including ambitious schemes to achieve economic and monetary union, develop the social dimension of Community policies, promote joint technological research, and help create the SEM. U.S. president George Bush launched the Enterprise for the Americas Initiative (EAI) somewhat later, in June 1990, initially only advancing relatively modest proposals for debt relief, investment promotion, and free trade within the Americas. This agenda also subsequently moved in a fast and exciting way to include the negotiation of NAFTA between the United States, Canada, and Mexico by August 1992 and the prospect, in the medium term, of a free trade area encompassing the entire Western Hemisphere. In other words, both initiatives originated as competitive responses on the part of core states or state groupings to strong political pressures to revitalize their own positions within the new global economy and thereby offset perceptions of relative decline. The United States and the EU were simply acting in their own best interests, as they understood them, in an increasingly integrated global market economy.

The joint threat that the SEM and NAFTA represented to Jamaica and the Caribbean has understandably been much less frequently noted in discussions, but it is nonetheless very real. For its part, the SEM has already generated both short-term opportunities and problems regarding Caribbean access to the EU market. The balance between the two has probably been roughly even. In the longer term, though, the Caribbean worry is that the completion of the single market and the pursuit of the other aspects of the 1992 program will strengthen those political forces in the EU preoccupied with redefining its identity within the wider post–Cold War Europe. The challenges involved in reshaping the meaning of European cooperation are obvious enough and may not leave much political energy for settling upon a new European relationship with the rest of the world, especially the poorer world. Moreover, it is the case that Lomé IV, the latest expression of the trade, aid, and cooperation agreements that have bound the EU to its former colonial possessions, runs out in the year 2000 and has already come under midterm review. Other EU agreements with other parts of the world are also due for renegotiation in this same period, leading to increasingly widespread surmise, much reinforced by some of the recent statements emanating from the Commission, that the EU will steadily restructure its relations with the rest of the developing world on a regional basis (Sutton 1993). In this scenario the privileges of all the Lomé countries would disappear, with Jamaica and the Caribbean being accorded a much lower priority by the EU.

NAFTA, for its part, poses a more immediate and considerable threat to the preferential access to the U.S. market that virtually all Caribbean Basin countries, including those in Central America, have enjoyed since the early 1980s under the terms of the Caribbean Basin Initiative (CBI). The fear is, obviously, that exports to and investment from the United States will be diverted toward Mexico to the CBI countries' disadvantage. This would lead to plant closures, increased unemployment, and widening balance-of-payments deficits, with all the attendant social and political consequences (Latin American Economic System 1993). The longer-term worry that follows from this is that the Caribbean Basin will become marginal to U.S. interests even within the Americas as public and private sector policymakers become more and more preoccupied with the bigger countries and more lucrative markets that exist in mainland South America.

The message of Jamaica and the other parts of the Caribbean is thus the same in both the European and American arenas of policy. They are in serious danger of being diminished as areas of concern on the part of their two most important modern patrons. They cannot any longer play their old Cold War cards in Washington and they cannot for much longer go on appealing to historical ties and the sentimentality of long-standing connections in Europe. Beyond a certain point, however, these two problems are not commensurate. At present the Caribbean remains poised between Europe and North America in the world order. But, as a colleague and I have previously argued, the two relationships "are working themselves out in different timeframes: Europe represents the legacy of the past, North America holds the prospect of the future" (Payne and Sutton 1992: 71–72). Needless to say, it would be pointless for Jamaica or any other Caribbean state to throw away past links with Europe before it has properly come to terms with its future ties to North America. The transition can, and should, be finessed. Nevertheless, the key political insight into the changing external environment in which Jamaica now has to operate remains the realization that all parts of the Caribbean are inexorably coming to be located, geopolitically and geoeconomically, within the Americas.

More generally, but just as importantly, Jamaica and the Caribbean cannot escape the realities of the new global political economy forged during the 1980s and early 1990s. This economy is characterized by a new concentration of power in the hands of international capital and a consequent intense competition for that capital and the markets it opens up between all states (Gill and Law 1988). A maxim has thereby been imposed on all developing states that in effect says, "The only thing worse than being exploited is not being exploited." In these circumstances, Caribbean countries, like all others, have inevitably already experienced enormous pressures to increase their economic competitiveness to the point where they can participate effectively in the global economy. This requires, at a minimum, both new outside investment in manufacturing and services as well as access to the markets of the developed world. To a considerable extent, therefore, foreign policy and diplomacy in the new world order have had to be brought into the service of development planning. Historically, Jamaican and Caribbean diplomacy has emphasized preserving the status quo; the dominant mood has been an awareness of constraint and vulnerability. The ideology of the world order of the 1990s is precisely the opposite of this: it stresses opportunities and both the risks and the rewards of embracing change. It undoubtedly expects a lot of small states with only limited resources and a relatively brief history of foreign policymaking, but they have had no choice but to adapt and try to cope.

FOREIGN POLICY ENVIRONMENT

Early Jamaican leaders were initially hesitant and uncertain in their dealings with the United States. This was partly due to their perception that the United States was significantly more powerful than their own country and partly due to their inherited colonial predisposition to look first to Europe for succor and support. To be sure, Jamaica's first postindependence government (1962–1972) left no doubt that it identified fully with Western economic and political interests. For example, whereas it had remained silent on U.S. intervention in the Dominican Republic in 1965, it condemned the Soviet invasion of Czechoslovakia in 1968. In the late 1960s, the Jamaican government also demonstrated a more lively interest in issues relating to apartheid and decolonization in southern Africa and even entered the Non-Aligned Movement as an observer. However, these shifts of policy, although not insignificant, were tentative so as not to damage Jamaica's overall standing as a loyal friend of the West, especially in relation to the "fight" against communism. Certainly, Jamaica had done nothing to bring itself to Washington's attention.

This changed dramatically in the mid-1970s. Michael Manley came to office in Jamaica in 1972 proclaiming the need for social and economic reform at home and an active "Third Worldist" policy abroad. His government thus set about renegotiating long-standing tax agreements signed with U.S.- and Canadian-owned bauxite and alumina companies operating in Jamaica, took an active stance in favor of international economic reform, and even dared to establish diplomatic relations with Cuba. In the early days the government was cautious enough to confirm with the United States that it could resume limited trade with Cuba without incurring penalties under U.S. laws and regulations. From these beginnings, however, the government became progressively more radical: in 1974 it declared itself a devotee of democratic socialism, and in 1976 it won re-election on a platform of anti-imperialism. During this period Manley flirted with the adoption of a full-fledged socialist strategy. In the end, his government backed away from this prospect but maintained what it could of its radicalism by means of symbolic foreign policy gestures. In this vein, Manley traveled to Cuba, where he heaped fulsome praise on Fidel Castro, played a leading part in Non-Aligned politics, and generally sought to promote Third World solidarity in opposition to Western interests.

Extraordinarily, the Jamaican government did not seem to realize, at least until it was far too late, that the United States would oppose and ultimately seek to undermine its foreign policy. A revealing example of this miscalculation is a meeting Manley had with U.S. secretary of state Henry Kissinger in late 1975. Manley later described that meeting: "Suddenly he raised the question of Angola and said he would appreciate it if Jamaica would at least remain neutral on the subject of the Cuban army presence in Angola. I told him that I could make no promises but would pay the utmost attention to his request." Kissinger then apparently brought up the separate matter of Jamaica's request for a U.S. $100 million trade credit. "He said they were looking at it, and let the comment hang in the room for a moment. I had the feeling he was sending me a message" (Manley 1982: 116). Although Kissinger's message was clear to Manley, five days later he nevertheless publicly announced Jamaica's support for Cuban involvement in Angola. The result was that U.S. economic aid to Jamaica was embargoed until the end of the Ford administration.

Whether or not one subscribes to the view that the United States actively sought to "destabilize" the Jamaican administration in the mid-1970s (Payne 1988), its hostility to Manley's ambitions and its capacity to harm them, especially in such matters as Jamaica's negotiations with the International Monetary Fund (IMF), undoubtedly did enormous damage. But Jamaica did not use the resources of foreign policy to ameliorate its relationship with the United States. Thus, during this period, Jamaica had come to the attention of Washington but had still not given sufficient priority to the vital matter of establishing a viable working relationship with the United States.

This pattern was broken by Edward Seaga when he became prime minister in 1980, and the change was epitomized by his success in securing an invitation to be the first foreign leader to visit newly elected president Ronald Reagan in the White House in early 1981. Seaga cleverly used this visit to proclaim his commitment to the capitalist path of development and to call upon the new U.S. administration to pay more attention to the problems of the Caribbean. Although the closeness of this early contact did not flourish as fully as Seaga had initially hoped—in fact, considerable tensions developed at times in his dealings with the State Department and other U.S. government agencies—as prime minister, he never deviated from his early awareness that relations with Washington were the most important dimension of Jamaican foreign policy. Indeed, they were critical to every aspect of the development strategy that the Seaga government espoused. Attracting more foreign investors; securing market access for Jamaica's new nontraditional exports, such as apparel; reviving and expanding the tourist industry; ameliorating the deflationary demands of the IMF—all depended on the support of the U.S. administration. Seaga, accordingly, was more than prepared to cut all of Jamaica's diplomatic and other ties with Cuba and to frustrate the efforts of the Caribbean Community and Common Market (CARICOM) to bargain collectively with the Reagan White House over the terms of its re-engagement with Caribbean affairs.

What is more, it became apparent during the 1980s that a returning Michael Manley government would maintain much of the new priority attached to relations with the United States. This shift was all the more significant precisely because the reformist thrust of the first Manley governments of the 1970s had been broken on the back of U.S. antagonism. Yet, by the middle of the decade, while still in opposition, Manley had signaled his change of approach. He traveled regularly to Washington, seeking meetings with Reagan administration officials, representatives of the IMF and the other multilateral agencies, and members of the influential "black caucus" in the U.S. Congress. The message was always the same: Jamaica under a future Manley government wanted to work with, not against, U.S. prescriptions for the Caribbean. Initially, this was received skeptically, but it proved to be true. On resuming office in February 1989, Manley inherited the structural adjustment program started under IMF supervision in the early 1980s and set about working with the IMF in a mood of resigned acceptance.

The "new Manley" also focused Jamaican foreign policy on Washington, just as he had promised in opposition. Significantly, the key post of ambassador to the United States was not given to a career diplomat but to a young but very able economist, albeit with a radical background, Richard Bernal. Bernal was also given a good deal of freedom by David Coore, Manley's minister of foreign affairs. As an economist, he was well equipped to handle discussions with the IMF and the World Bank, and he was particularly well placed in the Caribbean and Latin American diplomatic corps in Washington to take advantage of the opening offered by President George Bush's Enterprise for the Americas Initiative (EAI) in 1990. As a result, Jamaica has been able to position itself at the forefront of the debate about how the Caribbean should react to the EAI and all that it set in motion and over time has assumed the role of the leader of the Commonwealth Caribbean countries in all of their dealings with Washington in relation to this new agenda.

Jamaica was certainly better poised than any other part of the Caribbean to respond to the specific proposals contained within the EAI. The debt relief and investment promotion components required that beneficiary countries meet certain eligibility criteria. These consisted essentially of the possession of a stable macroeconomic environment and the pursuit of market-oriented policies as certified by the IMF, the World Bank, and the Inter-American Development Bank (IADB), which was given the primary role in the implementation of the EAI. As we have seen, Jamaica had been pursuing such policies since the beginning of the Seaga government. Under the stimulus of the EAI and in the face of renewed conflicts with the IMF over the failure to meet certain targets under the terms of the January 1990 agreement with the IMF, Manley's new government moved to emphasize the extent of its commitment to the philosophy of deregulation.

In September 1990 it floated the Jamaican dollar and a year later it lifted foreign exchange controls altogether (Payne 1992). In effect, Manley had decided that there was no alternative to private sector leadership of the economy, no other mechanism of production than the free market, and no other location for Jamaica than the U.S. sphere of influence with its associated promise of access to the U.S. market. As for the EAI eligibility criteria, Jamaica accordingly became the first Caribbean country and only the second country in the hemisphere to qualify fully. Its PL480 debt to the U.S. government was thus reduced by 80 percent in 1991 and it has subsequently received some financial support from the IADB Multilateral Investment Fund set up to promote private enterprise development.

Access to the other component of the EAI, the U.S. offer to sign trade liberalization agreements with groups of hemispheric countries, obviously required the involvement and support of the other CARICOM countries. The preliminary stage was the signature of a so-called framework agreement with the United States asserting support for a variety of liberal trading principles that reflected the economic philosophy of the Bush administration. Jamaica's diplomatic problem was that it was much further down the road of trade liberalization than any other Commonwealth Caribbean government. As it happened, the CARICOM heads of government were due to meet for their annual conference in August 1990, shortly after the EAI had been announced. At that meeting, the organization's secretary-general was mandated to convene a technical group to consider the U.S. initiative and make recommendations. The group concluded that, in light of the enthusiastic response of other central Latin American governments, many of which had moved quickly to sign framework agreements, and "the global trend towards the creation of regional blocs," the CARICOM countries needed to "indicate and maintain an active interest in the process." Moreover, its report noted that "the preservation of the integrity of the Caribbean Common Market would require that at least those CARICOM Member States which are members of the Common Market act jointly." As a consequence, its principal recommendation was that CARICOM should seek to negotiate a framework agreement with the United States as a group, albeit with the proviso that the agreement should include "explicit recognition of, and commensurate action for, their relatively lower level of, and constraints to, development" (CARICOM 1991).

This qualification reflected the hesitancy of the less developed smaller islands of the eastern Caribbean and in particular their concern about the impact of reciprocal free trade with the United States upon their tiny economies; the overall embrace of the idea of negotiating a framework agreement reflected Jamaica's advocacy of that position. The Jamaican government was asked to initiate discussions with the Office of the U.S. Trade Representative in Washington on behalf of all the members of CARICOM. A draft agreement was reached without too much difficulty and approved by the CARICOM heads of government, and a U.S.-CARICOM framework agreement was signed on July 22, 1991. The text was broadly the same as all the other framework agreements that had been negotiated with the United States. The effort of the Commonwealth Caribbean to obtain significant recognition of its lower level of development received relatively little response. In the end, the preamble to the agreement noted only that the economies of the subregion were "small and undiversified" and that "measures to improve the operation of the CBI [Caribbean Basin Initiative]" would be considered. Otherwise, it focused the attention of the new U.S.-CARICOM council on trade and investment on the following familiar issues: "investment liberalization including entry requirements . . . ; the review of investment aspects of tax treaties; market access barriers affecting both agricultural and industrial products; liberalization of trade and investment with other regional markets; [and] trade in services" (US-TR 1991).

Regional spokesmen took solace in the fact that, as in all the framework agreements, any topic relating to trade or investment could be raised at any time by either party on the council. By contrast, U.S. participants in the talks drew the conclusion that the preoccupation of the Commonwealth Caribbean with its special status only pointed out the continued lack of realism in the region, Jamaican attitudes notwithstanding, regarding the need to become more competitive and trade its way out of underdevelopment.

Nevertheless, Jamaica and the other CARICOM states had taken a decisive step toward the wider embrace of hemispheric free trade; they had signaled their intentions. However, as was made clear by U.S. officials, concluding a framework agreement did not in itself guarantee that the United States would go on to engage in talks on free trade or sign an actual agreement. In any case, from February 1991 onward, the United States was preoccupied with the negotiation of NAFTA with Canada and Mexico. The message transmitted to all other aspirants in the hemisphere was that the United States would turn to them only when this was satisfactorily achieved. Even so, the existence of ongoing NAFTA talks could not but shift the debate about the future of free trade in the Americas toward, first, the impact of a NAFTA deal on the rest of the hemisphere if it was not extended and, second, the best available mechanism for gaining access to NAFTA if the consequences of exclusion looked dire. The problem was particularly intense for all the beneficiary countries of the CBI because NAFTA threatened to make the preferential access to the U.S. market (which they had won back in the days of Cold War politics) relatively less advantageous for some of their products.

Most CBI countries responded by expressing their desire to come to terms with NAFTA. Jamaica was particularly articulate in its adoption of this position, under the leadership of both Michael Manley and his successor (Manley retired because of ill health in March 1992), P. J. Patterson. Its specific proposal was for parity with NAFTA as a transitional arrangement—in other words, granting CBI countries the same conditions of market access to the United States provided to Mexico under NAFTA—followed by a phased entry into NAFTA on a reciprocal basis over a suitable adjustment period (Bernal 1992). The implication of this proposal was that the Jamaican government was prepared to give greater priority to its future trading relations with the United States than to its existing (and future) trading relations with the EU under the Lomé Conventions. Although this offer was not spelled out, it is reasonable to assume that Jamaica believed, as did most analysts, that the negotiation of reciprocal free trade with the United States might well require it to forsake the non-reciprocal aspect of its previous trading agreement with the EU and replace it with the standard "most favored nation" formula. The bottom line for Jamaica was, and is, to maintain for its apparel industry, which had grown considerably during the 1980s and early 1990s, access to the U.S. market equal to that of Mexico and to become a key foreign exchange earner. However, Jamaica's stance unavoidably brings into question the degree to which it genuinely speaks for all other CARICOM states, many of which have not yet thought through their position vis-à-vis NAFTA. Early reactions suggested that the smaller eastern Caribbean states in particular may decide that they have more to lose from the abandonment of Lomé than from the exclusion from NAFTA. At some stage, therefore, they may choose negotiating priorities that differ from Jamaica's.

The question of how best to react to NAFTA, which is the point highlighted by the potential Jamaican–eastern Caribbean division within CARICOM, has developed into the key issue for all states within the Caribbean Basin. It has spurred a complex rethinking of the meaning of regionalism in the Basin that must be examined in detail in order to assess whether it opens up new foreign policy options for Jamaica.

THE NEW REGIONALISM OF THE CARIBBEAN

The best starting point to discuss this new regionalism is still CARICOM. From its inception in 1973, CARICOM faced a dichotomy within the regional integration movement that came to be known as "deepening" versus "widening." The former group wanted to intensify cooperation among the core Commonwealth Caribbean members of CARICOM on a range of issues; the latter advocated a minimalist program based on free trade and functional linkages that included the wider Caribbean. Neither objective was really achieved. CARICOM survived longer than many regional integration movements but at the price of stagnation. Its failures were increasingly recognized, and in 1989 a major inquiry into its functioning was launched by the West Indian Commission, a group of distinguished regional figures led by Shridath Ramphal, the former Commonwealth secretary-general. The commission sought to resolve the organization's problems by proposing a simultaneous deepening and widening of CARICOM (West Indian Commission 1992). Its key proposal in the first regard—the establishment of a permanent body made up of three former political leaders that would drive the internal integration process forward—was rejected by the heads of government. Thus the "deepening" issue remains unresolved.

However, the commission's solution to the "widening" dilemma has aroused interest and appears likely to come to fruition. It proposed the creation of a new body, the Association of Caribbean States (ACS), anchored on CARICOM but open to the wider Basin region. As the commission argued in its report:

> Put simply, the peoples of CARICOM and their Governments must no longer think in narrow terms merely of "the Commonwealth Caribbean", but in wider terms of a "Caribbean Commonwealth"—and must work to fulfil this larger ambition. The ambition itself must encompass, besides the 13 CARICOM countries, all the countries of the Caribbean Basin. It must reach out, therefore, to all the independent island states of the Caribbean Sea and the Latin American countries of Central and South America whose shores are washed by it. And it must be open as well to the Commonwealth of Puerto Rico, the island communities of the French West Indies, the Dutch islands of Aruba and the Netherland Antilles, the US Virgin Islands and the remaining British dependencies. (WIC 1992: 449)

The ACS was envisaged as "being functionally active in an integration sense" (WIC 1992: 446) and a wide set of possible areas of cooperation was listed, including the negotiation of special trading terms, the widening of communication links, cooperation in tourism and health matters, the management of the resources of the Caribbean Sea, and the curbing of drug trafficking. Nevertheless, the aim was not to be too specific at too early a stage—for it was recognized that formidable constitutional and cultural difficulties lay in the way of the project—but rather to give voice to the idea and subsequently propose it to the governments of other Caribbean Basin countries.

Much of the detailed planning remains to be done. Nevertheless, political support for the ACS concept has grown. Michael Manley was asked out of retirement, as it were, to conduct what was called a "probe" of non-CARICOM views of the proposal. As a result of his mission, a group of technical staff was gathered together and charged with preparing a paper on an organizational structure for the ACS in time for a document that was signed in Barbados in July 1994 at the time of the annual CARICOM heads of government meeting. There was, for a time, a danger that the whole project would be seen in Central America and the other non-English-speaking parts of the region as too much of an extension of CARICOM. The CARICOM states are, after all, only a small part of the wider Basin region, yet the tenor of the discussion of the proposed ACS seemed to presume that the Commonwealth Caribbean countries would unquestionably be at the core of such a wider grouping. It seems, though, that CARICOM's leaders have since softened their stance; the governments of Colombia, Venezuela, Mexico, and Suriname have all expressed their desire to join the ACS.

Indeed, in October 1993 the leaders of these four countries met with CARICOM leaders in Port of Spain in Trinidad and signed an action plan on economic cooperation. CARICOM leaders welcomed the decision of Colombia, Mexico, and Venezuela (the so-called Group of Three [G-3] to establish a free trade arrangement among themselves to coincide with the inauguration of NAFTA on January 1, 1994. Venezuela had concluded a one-way free trade deal with CARICOM a year earlier, and one outcome of the Trinidad meeting was the likelihood of a similar agreement being signed between CARICOM and Colombia by the end of 1994. For his part, Mexican president Carlos Salinas de Gortari formally welcomed the possibility of free trade with CARICOM, and it was announced that such discussions would also be initiated with Mexico. Although all the leaders decided to proceed on a bilateral basis, the idea of joint free trade involving CARICOM, Suriname, and the G-3 was clearly at the forefront of the October 1993 discussion. Mexico's position is the critical one, since its involvement would serve, in effect, to attach the whole group to NAFTA.

The varying positions of other important Caribbean states further complicate prospects for the development of new forms of Caribbean regionalism. The Dominican Republic, for example, conventionally attempts to straddle the Caribbean and Latin America, participating in Lomé, seeking membership in CARICOM, and yet, in other respects, working more closely with its Hispanic rather than its West Indian neighbors. Its foreign minister, Roberto Raina, conducted an extensive tour of Venezuela and no less than seven CARICOM countries in November 1993, talking the language of economic and cultural cooperation. Earlier in the year CARICOM's leaders had agreed to promote ties with Cuba by establishing a CARICOM-Cuba Mixed Commission similar to existing joint bodies with Mexico and Colombia. Some leaders also expressed their support for Cuba's admission into the ACS as a founding member. However, the idea of the Mixed Commission was not well received in Washington and is clearly something of a risky initiative on CARICOM's part in light of past U.S. prejudices. At the same time, the obduracy of the U.S. position cannot but act as a brake on Caribbean organizations that are re-embracing Cuba.

The response of the Central American states to the new regionalism is perhaps the most critical to the Caribbean states. For the fact is that the restructuring of international relations has placed the Caribbean, for virtually the first time in its history, in an economic and political predicament similar to Central America's; so near in one sense and yet so far in others. After all, all the states of the Basin, island, enclave, and isthmus are small; they are all pursuing a judicious mixture of development and security on broadly the same terrain; they are all affected by the EAI and NAFTA; and in the future they may be embraced within a single regional relationship with the EU that supersedes both Lomé and the San Jose process, which has linked Central American countries to the EU since the mid-1980s. From an optimistic viewpoint, this holds out the possibility that the concept of the Caribbean Basin may become internalized by political, business, and intellectual leaders in both "halves" of the Basin and, as such, come to shape foreign policy responses to external threats.

For the moment, the signs are, admittedly, more mixed, with integrative and disintegrative tendencies pushing in opposite directions. Ties between Central America and the Caribbean undoubtedly became closer when these two regions began to form groups in response to the EAI and NAFTA initiatives. Led by the Washington-based business pressure group Caribbean/Latin American Action (C/LAA), the regional private sector began to argue the case for greater Basin-wide cooperation (C/LAA 1990/1991). The government of Governor Rafael Hernandez Colon in Puerto Rico also sought to promote closer links between Central American and Caribbean political leaders, inviting both Honduran president Rafael Callejas and Michael Manley to the Caribbean Basin business conference in San Juan in August 1991 and setting up the Caribbean Basin Technical Advisory Group (CBTAG) to facilitate joint policy-making between the two parts of the Basin. Callejas and Manley got on well together, met again in December of that year at the C/LAA conference in Miami, and initiated the first ever joint meeting of Central American and Caribbean foreign ministers, which took place in San Pedro Sula, Honduras, in January 1992 (CBTAG 1992). CBTAG constituted, in embryo, a workable institutional framework for closer Caribbean Basin cooperation and was capable not only of organizing relations with the EAI and NAFTA but also of promoting regional economic integration within the Basin itself. It was a highly creative innovation by the Puerto Rican government and a genuinely novel moment in the affairs of the countries of the Caribbean and Central America.

However, from this high point, there is no denying that the process of Basin-wide dialogue has subsequently run into difficulties. The Hernandez Colon administration was defeated in elections in November 1992 and was replaced by a regime committed to negotiating statehood for Puerto Rico within the United States. As a result, CBTAG has been effectively disbanded and Puerto Rico has substantially withdrawn from the regional diplomatic scene. Within the Commonwealth Caribbean, Manley's retirement had removed the person most supportive of Basin linkages. Patterson, who succeeded Manley, was not as interested in the effort, and no other CARICOM head of government has come forward to take the initiative. The early discussions of the ACS also appeared to be too closely aligned with CARICOM from a Central American perspective. Most important, reflecting and exacerbating these problems, a major row over bananas developed during 1992. The EU was trying to reconcile its promise under Lomé to provide a protected market in bananas for producers of its former colonies with its commitment to establish the SEM. The dilemma for the EU was more acute still because the case against continuing protection was also strongly being made by the United States and Latin America within the Uruguay Round of the General Agreement on Tariffs and Trade. The dispute pitted the smaller Caribbean banana-producing states, mainly in the eastern region but also including Jamaica, directly against the more competitive "dollar-banana" states of Central America. The eventual, highly complicated compromise, based on tariffication rather than quotas, was struck in mid-December 1992 after much lobbying and political conflict. For the Caribbean, it was not as good a deal as Lomé, but it was still too protectionist from the point of view of Central American producers.

All this, to state the obvious, scarcely helped engender friendly relations on other important regional issues in the emerging Caribbean–Central American dialogue. It seemed for a while as if the political discord arising from the banana dispute would also linger, with the Central American leadership apparently backing various European efforts to challenge the new regime established in the December 1992 compromise. However, a second joint meeting of foreign ministers took place in Kingston, Jamaica, in May 1993, and Manley's subsequent probe of key Central American countries in connection with the ACS helped reduce tensions. Talks have also taken place between officials of the secretariats of CARICOM and the Central American Common Market, and a cooperation agreement has been signed. The intention of both sides appears to be to set the banana issue aside as much as possible in order to facilitate collaboration on other matters. Evidently, though, Central American leaders have not deferred to Caribbean leadership on the ACS. Some were attracted by the potential of the work of CBTAG and still see the case for wider Basin cooperation in negotiation with the United States and the EU; nevertheless, their dominant view has been that the Caribbean is the weaker half of the Basin and needs, as it were, to come to them, rather than the reverse. These leaders will certainly not tolerate CARICOM's attempt to control the agenda of the ACS, and it is not yet apparent that they will even join. Indeed, in the absence of an appropriately supplicant approach by the CARICOM states, the inclination of many Central American countries may be to reorganize their relations with the United States either bilaterally or, at best, on a common Central American basis.

NAFTA is thus central to both the Caribbean and Central America. For the moment, these regions' governments have joined to back the bills tabled in the U.S. Congress by representatives from the state of Florida. This putative "Caribbean Basin Free Trade Agreements Act" would give the CBI countries parity with Mexico in terms of tariffs, rules of origin, and quota elimination for a three-year transitional period, during which time they would be expected to pursue programs of liberalization and adjustment. At the end of the transition, they would seek some form of access to NAFTA on the basis of trade reciprocity. As yet, the Clinton administration has not expressed a firm view on these bills, indicating only its willingness to have them submitted to the Office of the Trade Representative for study. Beyond that, the political signals have been mixed. During the 1992 presidential election, Clinton and other campaign spokesmen spoke out firmly against using U.S. taxpayers' money on initiatives, such as the CBI, that could be construed as subsidizing the export of U.S. jobs. Future vice president Albert Gore was particularly condemnatory, declaring that he had voted against the CBI when he was a congressman. More recently, though, Clinton was persuaded to meet with the leaders of the four largest CARICOM states, Jamaica, Trinidad and Tobago, Barbados, and Guyana, in August 1993, and at the end of these discussions he promised to instruct his trade representative,

Micky Kantor, to undertake a study of the impact of NAFTA on the smaller Caribbean economies. At present, therefore, the U.S. administration's mind is not made up on the issue of parity legislation, and it is impossible to know what the U.S. Congress will make of the two bills before it.

From the perspective of the CBI countries, the concepts of parity and transition are a formula around which everyone has been able to gather for the moment. If passed, the Caribbean Basin trade act would obviously give all parts of the region breathing space. But it does not, and cannot, avoid the deeper questions posed by the whole EAI and NAFTA process. Some of the tactical issues are necessarily outside the region's control. The United States will decide whether to open NAFTA to the rest of the hemisphere, and if so, how. There may be a queue; there may be a threshold system in which aspirant countries are, in effect, told to ready themselves for reciprocity in advance of detailed talks; there may be a preference for bargaining with groups of countries organized regionally rather than with single states. All of this remains to be clarified, which is what makes the notion of a transitional period of parity useful from the Caribbean Basin perspective.

At the end of the transition, however, the fundamental issue will still have to be decided, and hard choices will have to be made by all parts of the Basin. The widest available negotiating unit would be the ACS, but precisely because it might involve all the states of the Caribbean Basin, including Mexico, it is the least likely. A joint Central American–Caribbean group is also thinkable, although this would require immediate and urgent work on the part of the various component states. The most likely possibility is that CARICOM and Central America will negotiate as separate subregional units, although there is the possibility that the regional mechanisms will not hold together in the face of difficult negotiating choices. In short, the unfolding of what we have called the new Caribbean regionalism is still at too early a stage for analysts to make predictions. What is apparent is that these new organizations and linkages will form the framework within which individual Caribbean and Central American states have to shape their particular foreign policies.

It is time, then, to return to the specific case of Jamaica and consider the options that this new agenda offers its leaders. The Jamaican government has expressed its firm support for the Caribbean Basin free trade legislation, and its ambassador in Washington, Bernal, has spoken effectively in favor of CBI parity before congressional committees. He also plays an active role within the CBI group of ambassadors in Washington. Therefore, for the moment, there is no reason to think that the Jamaican government has any intention of diverging from a regional approach, either of a wider Basin or a narrower CARICOM nature. Its active engagement with the NAFTA agenda does, however, give it the option of breaking ranks and acting either unilaterally or jointly—perhaps with Costa Rica, which is the Central American state most similar to Jamaica—to initiate negotiations with the United States in advance of the remaining states of the Basin. This could still be presented positively, from a regionalist perspective, as the action of a key state pioneering a path toward reciprocal free trade with the United States, a path that could be trodden by the other members of the group in due course. It is difficult in the present circumstances to assess the likelihood of this sort of development: it depends more on the policies adopted by the other states than those pursued by either Jamaica or Costa Rica. However, given the pathbreaking shift in economic liberalization made by successive Jamaican administrations over the past decade or so, it is hard to imagine the Patterson regime not seeking to take the final step of entry into a U.S.-led free trade zone. If that necessitated a split within CARICOM, the price might well be one that was worth paying.

CONCLUSION

The seismic changes being wrought in the international system by the SEM and NAFTA signal, in effect, the end of the postcolonial era for Jamaica. To put it another way, the period in which the legacies of a European colonial history could provide a measure of protection from destabilizing external forces has come to a conclusion. Jamaica now has to find its way by its own means in what is a new world. The argument of this chapter is that, to all intents and purposes, Jamaica has already made the key choice, which is to align itself firmly with all that is going on economically and politically in the Americas. This road of development will have far-reaching implications for the economy, society, and polity of Jamaica. Some implications have been considered in this chapter; others cannot yet even be conceived. It is important, however, to note that the choice that has been made also has major cultural implications. Jamaica's unique national identity will be threatened, and certainly changed, by all the attendant consequences of deepening Americanization. This does not have to mean that cricket will be replaced by baseball in the affections of Jamaicans, but it will call into question the particularity of things Jamaican that has been such an appealing feature of this island society in the past thirty years or so of its independence from Britain.

5

Venezuela, *el Gran Viraje*, and Regionalism in the Caribbean Basin

◆

Andrés Serbin

In this chapter the impact of external events and a domestic economic crisis will be analyzed in relationship to the reformulation of Venezuela's economic and foreign policy during the second presidency of Carlos Andrés Pérez (1989–1993). During this period, the government introduced its so-called *gran viraje*, or a radical turn in policy direction. Specifically, the chapter will analyze in detail how the articulation of a new economic policy relates, first, to the reformulation of Venezuela's foreign policy and, second, to a prioritization of subregional issues. These developments have occurred within the context of a strong push toward regionalization as a response to pressures from the international system as well as domestic demands for reform. The chapter concludes with a positive assessment of Venezuela's attempt to create linkages between its new economic and foreign policy objectives as they relate to regionalization.

GLOBAL AND HEMISPHERIC CHANGES AND THE PROCESS OF REGIONALIZATION IN THE CARIBBEAN

Over the past decade, a series of international events has raised concern among Latin American and Caribbean countries that they might find themselves marginalized from the international system. This perception is due to three factors: first, the loss of strategic importance of the region as a whole as a result of the end of the Cold War; second, the paralyzing effects of the debt crisis and the lost decade, in terms of economic development and growth, of the 1980s; and, third, the consequences of the debt crisis for Latin America's entry into a resurgent international economic system.

Latin America's fear of economic marginalization, with its concomitant reduction of foreign investment and commercial trade, was reflected in the willingness of the region's countries to abandon the inward economic development model that had characterized the decades prior to 1980. At the same time, these countries recognized the renewed economic importance of the United States for the region, which generated an enthusiasm for the possibilities associated with integration (Hurrell 1992: 124–128). This change in economic orientation occurred after the implementation of structural adjustment programs and the economic restructuring that had accompanied the process of democratization in Latin America.

As the international system is becoming increasingly divided into economic and trading blocs, Latin America has responded by stressing the need for hemispheric regional integration. Compared with previous attempts at regional integration, the present reaction on the part of Latin American and Caribbean countries is decidedly different, in part because of the effects of structural adjustment unleashed by the debt crisis of the 1980s.

There is an obvious congruence of economic policy orientation at the hemispheric level, as countries of the region respond to the new climate of integration. More specifically, there is a growing consensus regarding the need to deepen the processes of trade liberalization through the implementation of various free trade agreements and the acceleration of plans for subregional economic integration. Some of these plans are of recent origin, whereas others have been in the planning stages for many years. At the same time, there is a consensus that market mechanisms need to be deepened and the region needs to push forward with economic adjustment programs, even though these call into question the long-favored indigenous development strategies associated with import substitution industrialization (CEPAL 1991b). The emphasis on liberalizing trade and attaining economic growth through the increase of exports is part of a strategy that intends, first, to expand the space for regional economic activity in the name of competitive advantage and larger markets and, second, to guarantee Latin America a more favorable position in the international system.

In sum, faced with the globalization of the world economy and the emergence of three economically important trading blocs that have growing interregional trading relations, countries in Latin America and the Caribbean have opted to create regional nuclei "through the assistance of agreements that reinforce the privileged ties between states that share the same geography, history, culture and economy" (CEPAL 1991b: 4).

The Caribbean Basin has been especially sensitive to the process of regionalization because, immediately after the end of the Cold War, when the developed West headed into an economic recession, the region's strategic importance declined significantly, and the extraregional countries that had traditionally been involved in its affairs gradually withdrew.

From a strategic and geopolitical perspective, the consequence of this important change has been a shift in the priorities that make up the security agenda of the Caribbean. The Cuban-Soviet threat of the Cold War period has given way to the problems of drug trafficking, south-north migration, and environmental concerns, all of which are considered important issues from the perspective of extraregional actors such as the United States and those European countries with former colonies in the Caribbean (Serbin 1991a, 1992a; Griffith 1991). By contrast, for the countries of the region, the major security issues increasingly revolve around questions of economic vulnerability and political stability; the need to devise a development strategy that responds to new global pressures; the consequences of occupying a position of disadvantage in the international economy; and the impact of various preferential and nonreciprocal trade agreements, such as the Caribbean Basin Initiative (CBI), the Lomé Convention, the North American Free Trade Agreement (NAFTA), and the European Union (Serbin 1991a).

Given this new context, regional integration initiatives modeled on the Central American Common Market or the Caribbean Community and Common Market (CARICOM) have moved to the forefront. At the same time, the Caribbean Basin's loss of strategic significance has led regional middle powers to attempt to fill a void by creating a free trade agreement between Colombia, Mexico, and Venezuela, or the Group of Three (G-3), an initiative that strongly emphasizes cooperation with Central America and the island nations of the Caribbean. This agreement has been received very favorably by the smaller nations in the Caribbean Basin, both because it promotes closer ties between Central America and the Caribbean and because it broadens the geographic conception of the region to the whole of the Caribbean Basin, including important middle powers. This now-enlarged understanding of the Caribbean Basin has been formalized through the creation of the Association of Caribbean States (ACS), which came into existence in July 1994 (WIC 1992; Serbin 1992b, 1993a).

This development, which represents an important change in interregional relations, is due to two related factors: the need to establish closer alliances at the regional level in order to strengthen the position of the Caribbean in multilateral forums and the need to deepen cooperative and integrative processes at the subregional level in order to expand existing economic opportunities and to make possible a more effective and more competitive integration of the region into the international economic system.

The benefits of this new regional dynamic are evident in other spheres. First, there has been a noticeable increase in subregional diplomatic activities and initiatives. The countries of Central America and of CARICOM have participated in the Rio Group and have become more active within the Organization of American States (OAS). There has also been extensive cooperation between English- and Spanish-speaking countries in the search for a solution to the Haitian crisis. Second, interregional relations will doubtless become even more intensified through a dual process of deepening already existing integration arrangements and negotiating new free trade agreements between principal regional actors. CARICOM, the Central American System of Economic Integration, the G-3, the ACS, and the free trade agreements between the G-3, CARICOM, and Central America are all examples of this new interest for regional cooperation.

Within this general framework of developments, the Venezuelan case provides an interesting example of a country that has had to respond to global, hemispheric, and domestic pressures. The resulting policy reforms, known as the gran viraje, are as much a result of events external to Venezuela as they are a consequence of domestic and regional developments. Together, these propelled the country to significantly change its foreign policy, and it is to this we now turn.

EXTERNAL PRESSURES AND DOMESTIC CRISIS: THE GRAN VIRAJE AND VENEZUELAN FOREIGN POLICY

At the global, hemispheric, and subregional levels, Venezuela's international reputation is due both to its consolidated democracy, established over thirty years ago, and to its oil wealth, which is the key component of a foreign policy whose goals extend beyond those of countries of a similar size. During the 1980s, however, Venezuela's relatively stable position suffered several significant transformations. The combined effects of the decline in oil prices on the international market and the impact of the external debt provoked an unprecedented economic crisis that called into question the very stability of Venezuela's democracy (Tulchin et al. 1993). In the late 1980s, deficits in the external account, fiscal and monetary problems, and the unwillingness of the international banks to grant loans worsened economic conditions. Furthermore, the presidential elections of 1988 effectively guaranteed that the government would maintain an expansive fiscal policy, which caused a sharp drop in foreign reserves (Ortiz Ramirez 1992: 40–41).

In 1989, Carlos Andrés Pérez assumed the office of the president, marking the beginning of a major policy reorientation in Venezuela. The government's new position was known as the gran viraje, and it was grounded in the need both to reorient the country's economic policy to counteract the effects of the economic crisis and to reorganize the political system to adjust to this economic imperative.

The country's new economic strategy was marked by a series of radical initiatives that were intended to introduce some dramatic restructuring. Elements of this strategy included a reduction in public spending, the elimination of direct and indirect state subsidies, an increase in the price of gasoline and services, deregulation, privatization, industrial retraining, and the reduction of customs duties. Together these elements were designed to help reduce the fiscal deficit, liberalize exchange and interest rates, control prices, and open the economy to trade and international competition. This radical program was accompanied by a new development strategy that increasingly relied on outward-oriented growth and trade liberalization. The development strategy marked a fundamental shift in the country's traditional economic and political orientation and provoked serious political and social consequences (Toro Hardy 1992; FUNDAFUTURO 1992; Romero 1994; Naim 1993).

These changes, and their concomitant social and political costs, generated a strong reaction from various sectors of the population. The subsequent caracazo of February 1989, shortly after Pérez assumed power, as well as the aborted coups of February 4, 1992 (Sonntag and Mangón 1992; Serbin 1992c), and November 27, 1992, led to a rearticulation of Venezuela's foreign policy objectives. Henceforth, the country would pursue a more active trade policy with an emphasis on increasing exports and creating ties with nearby trading nations through free trade agreements and subregional integration (Rojas 1992).

The Eighth National Plan outlined the development strategy by which Venezuela would seek to improve its position in the international system. There were five major objectives: (1) The government would adopt an aggressive stance on international issues. (2) Venezuela's foreign policy would assist the country's economic objectives through the defense of free trade, Latin American economic integration, and the strengthening of international democratic solidarity. (3) There would be a new focus on regional integration, the strengthening of institutions of cooperation and integration, the development of trade agreements, the coordination of macroeconomic policy, and the forging of strategic alliances in various fields (technology, culture, and politics). (4) The government would conduct an aggressive trade diplomacy, on both the bilateral and multilateral fronts, in order to expand the markets for Venezuelan exports. (5) Venezuela would join the General Agreement on Tariffs and Trade (GATT) and establish channels of communication between the government and international institutions of cooperation and integration (CORDIPLÁN 1990; cited in Cardozo de Da Silva 1992a: 5).

In accordance with these five objectives, the government outlined a commercial policy based on three pillars: (1) There would be a gradual liberalization of the Venezuelan economy with the intention of promoting increased efficiency and competitiveness in the industrial and agriculture sectors. (2) There would be an active strategy of commercial integration and negotiation with the objective of expanding markets, trade, and investment opportunities for local agents. (3) There would be a policy for the promotion of exports with a special emphasis on nontraditional exports (Rodríguez Mendoza 1993a). The goals of these three pillars were in turn expressed by three interrelated components—tariff policies, association and integration, and the promotion of exports—that formed the basis of Decree no. 239, promulgated on May 24, 1989. This decree laid the foundation for the New Commercial Policy (NPC), which served as the blueprint for the government's new policy orientation (Ortiz Ramirez 1992: 15).

During the first four years of Pérez's presidency, the government made the greatest progress in the objectives of the first pillar: a radical program designed to reduce tariffs was introduced and was later accelerated in 1992. As for the second pillar, Venezuela made astonishing progress toward achieving its economic integration objectives. First, it developed closer economic ties with Colombia, to the point that Venezuelan-Colombian trade was the largest bilateral exchange within both the Andean Pact and the trade agreement of the G-3. As such, the integrative process inherent in the Andean Pact moved forward despite the temporary self-exclusion of Peru and Bolivia's increasingly important trading ties with the countries of the Southern Cone Common Market (MERCOSUR). Second, Venezuela entered into free trade negotiations with Chile and began discussing the possibility of nonreciprocal trade agreements with Central America and CARICOM. Third, Venezuela gained observer status in CARICOM in 1991. And fourth, in August 1990, Venezuela joined GATT. With respect to the third pillar, the government introduced a series of reforms, including the elimination of export subsidies, a partial simplification of the procedure to begin exporting merchandise, an attempt to introduce custom drawbacks, the privatization of ports, and the creation of a Bank of Foreign Trade. Together these measures significantly increased nontraditional exports.

For the most part, Venezuela's nontraditional exports were developed to take advantage of the opportunities for trade offered by the various free trade and integration agreements at the subregional level. For example, let us consider Venezuela's commercial exchange within the Andean Pact, the country's most active trading arrangement: more than 45 percent of nontraditional exports went to Latin America in 1992, the year the pact was introduced, compared with 35 percent in 1989 (Acosta 1993: 19). Despite the fact that the expansion of nontraditional exports faced many difficulties and obstacles, it is obvious from these figures that Venezuela's private sector has become an important support base for the new policies of increased trade and subregional integration, as well as the policy to promote foreign trade (Rodríguez Mendoza 1993a).

The Venezuelan government has deliberately sought to buttress its new commercial strategy and regional position on the diplomatic and political front through a series of subregional, regional, and hemispheric alliances that draw on its extensive prior experience in the region. The government adopted a two-pronged strategy, namely, to deepen already existing ties with countries in the region and to actively participate in new regional initiatives. Therefore, in an attempt to reinforce the country's capacity to negotiate and to fill an expanding leadership gap in the Caribbean Basin, Venezuela renewed its ties with various Latin American countries through organizations such as CARICOM, the Andean Pact, and the Latin American Integration Association and with the countries of Central America directly. In addition, it joined new political organizations, such as the Rio Group, and along with Mexico and Colombia, Venezuela formed the G-3, in an attempt to promote political and economic consensus (Cobo 1992; Serbin 1992b, 1993b).

In conclusion, it could be argued that the gran viraje was a development strategy designed to promote Venezuela's traditional and nontraditional exports. The Pérez government, starting with a diagnosis of the dangers and pressures facing the country's traditional and chief export—oil and its derivatives—unveiled a development strategy that outlined the steps required to maximize the competitive advantage of oil. This strategy also proposed a series of steps that would liberalize trade and commerce and would promote integration and the expansion of economic activity so that the country's nontraditional exports might be diversified and increased. Within the context of this new development strategy, regionalization became an essential component of Venezuela's new foreign policy, and it sought to maximize the country's previous successes in economic cooperation, political concertation, and geostrategic alliances.

VENEZUELA'S FOREIGN POLICY
AND THE PROCESS OF REGIONALIZATION

Although Venezuela's foreign policy objectives in the period of the gran viraje clearly marked a departure in a new direction, they were nevertheless conditioned by a series of consequences from previous foreign policy experiences as well as by a collection of adverse external circumstances. For example, when the gran viraje was introduced, the government persisted with a somewhat overambitious foreign policy that included participating in international programs and forums whose purposes were quite distinct from Venezuela's immediate policy objectives. These included the Comisión del Sur and presidential participation in hemispheric and international organizations. However, the events of February 4 and November 27, 1992, forced the government to re-evaluate its foreign policy and to scale down its international activities. Moreover, the government's overambitious policy objectives had been seriously questioned by various domestic sectors and, especially, by the press (Romero 1987).

As a result of this reassessment, there was a gradual refocusing of Venezuela's foreign policy to correspond to its position in the Caribbean Basin. There were two principal reasons for this refocusing: first, geographical location dictated that these countries provided the most accessible and fluid markets for Venezuelan exports; and second, there was the historical experience of prior relations and alliances within the Caribbean Basin.

There were, however, two exceptions to this subregional trend. First, there was Venezuela's commitment to continued participation in the Organization of Petroleum Exporting Countries (OPEC). Venezuela was a founding member of OPEC and preferred to continue benefiting from setting international prices for hydrocarbons and responding to pressures on the cartel's activities from industrialized nations, even if these opportunities were sometimes restricted because of frequent disagreements and breaches of promises within the cartel. Moreover, Venezuela preferred this option despite the vicissitudes of the international petroleum market and the frequent political and economic challenges faced by members of the cartel.

Second, Venezuela continued to search for potential foreign investors in Europe and Asia to further develop its mining and energy sectors, because existing foreign investment from North America was insufficient. The search for foreign capital has been linked to two economic imperatives: the development of megaprojects in the petrochemical, aluminum, gas exploration, bauxite, and carbon industries and the expansion of the petroleum sector to render it more international. In fact, Venezuelan Petroleum (PDVSA) has initiated an active international campaign designed to penetrate the markets of industrialized countries in order to guarantee the distribution of Venezuelan hydrocarbons. In order to facilitate this objective, PDVSA has obtained the assistance and cooperation of transnational corporations in the United States and Europe. Despite these efforts, foreign capital investment and joint ventures with transnational corporations in the national petroleum sector continue to be severely restricted by the legislation that nationalized the petroleum industry in 1975. Finally, it should be noted that at the beginning of 1992 the international expansion of PDVSA was limited by a presidential decree, ostensibly because of the government's budgetary restrictions (*LAWR* 1992: 1).

These international activities aside, Venezuela's foreign policy has revolved around the following five issues: (1) relations with the United States in general and, more specifically, oil exports, NAFTA, and the Enterprise for the Americas Initiative; (2) the process of economic integration with Colombia; (3) the reactivation of the Andean Pact and the determination to avoid the difficulties that plagued the original agreement in the 1970s by promoting a new focus; (4) the establishment of the G-3 and the difficulties of enacting a free trade agreement with Mexico; and (5) the continuation of traditional relations with Central America and the Caribbean. The process of regionalization has provided Venezuela the opportunity to maximize the benefits associated with creating stronger links between the countries of the Caribbean Basin, largely by broadening the concept of the Caribbean Basin to include both the United States and the countries of the Andean region (Serbin 1990). Let us now consider each of these objectives in turn.

In general terms, it can be said that regionalization emerged as an initial response to changes in the international system and new pressures and demands exerted by both the new international order and Venezuela's domestic crisis. As such, it is difficult to determine whether there is an explicit regionalization strategy for the long term. However, what is possible to discern is that regionalization, as a response to the withdrawal of international actors from the Caribbean Basin, is based on much more than simply economic and commercial considerations—although these are clearly at the base of the Venezuelan government's NPC and gran viraje. Still, regionalization is more appropriately understood as a combination of economic, geostrategic, and political considerations as well as historical and cultural coincidences.

Relations with the United States

The United States is Venezuela's principal market for its oil exports and chief source of its imports. Moreover, the United States is regarded as Venezuela's traditional ally from the Cold War period. Since the beginning of the gran viraje, the importance of this traditional alliance has been reaffirmed by Venezuela, especially during the political turmoil of 1992, when many feared that a military government might take over in Caracas. It was widely hoped that the United States would extend to Venezuela the support that it has accorded other Latin American countries in the recent wave of redemocratization and consolidation.

In 1991 more than half of Venezuela's exports and nearly 70 percent of direct exports of petroleum and its derivatives went to the United States. The United States was the source of more than 40 percent of Venezuela's imports and approximately half of all its foreign investment. Venezuela's foreign debt, meanwhile, is almost entirely owed to U.S. banks. On the political front, relations between the two countries historically have been important because of common interests that have corresponded to Venezuela's foreign policy priorities, especially at the subregional level: democratic political stability, drug trafficking, the environment, regional conflicts, and human rights.

By comparison, Venezuela has maintained a somewhat limited—although relatively stable—importance in the hierarchy of U.S. interests. In commercial terms, Venezuela was the United States' second largest Latin American trading partner in 1991, after Mexico. Venezuelan investment in U.S. oil companies such as Citgo, Champlain, and Unoven has remained significant, and Venezuela is considered to be a reliable and well-situated provider of oil, despite its flirtation with OPEC politics. In fact, following the Gulf War, Venezuela became the United States' second most important supplier of oil. Historically, Venezuela has always fulfilled its contractual petroleum obligations to the United States despite its active participation in OPEC. However, it is worth noting that Venezuela's goal of becoming, through a preferential agreement, the United States' strategic ally by virtue of the fact that it is a reliable supplier of oil has never materialized.

Venezuela hoped that a commercial and investment agreement signed between it and the United States in April 1991 would lead to a free trade agreement similar to NAFTA. However, U.S. trade representatives have repeatedly stressed that Chile will be the next country to be considered for membership. Venezuela's slow economic restructuring and stabilization and precarious political situation have been to blame.

Finally, Venezuela has attempted to increase the amount of its nontraditional exports to the United States in the hope of fixing its trade imbalance; however, this attempt has been hindered by nontariff protectionist barriers in the steel, cement, and aluminum sectors. This is especially frustrating for Venezuela since, despite its membership in GATT, which favors the export of nontraditional products to the North American market, oil continues to dominate Venezuela's export structure, making up nearly 90 percent of its exports to the United States (Cardozo de Da Silva 1992a).

Relations with Colombia

Trade integration has proceeded apace between Venezuela and Colombia, primarily because of the complementarity between their economies, the similarities between their adjustment programs, and the geographical proximity of the two nations. However, the acceleration of the integration process has been threatened by internal political problems in both countries, as well as by some border tensions, which have caused a resurgence of nationalism on both sides of the border. Nevertheless, the accomplishments tend to outweigh the difficulties, and the Venezuelan-Colombian trade axis has guaranteed the success of the Andean Pact, certainly when one compares the pact to its predecessor, the Acuerdo de Cartagena (CEPAL 1991a).

Within the framework of accelerating the process of subregional integration, the Andean Pact stands out as the pre-existing structure that has most readily accommodated the objective of establishing a free market and customs union. And within the Andean Pact, Venezuela and Colombia have had an established free trade zone and policy of open skies since January 1992. In just one year after the pact was instituted, trade between these two countries had surpassed U.S. $965 million, a 53 percent increase over 1991, and Colombian exports to Venezuela had doubled. Venezuela is now Colombia's second most important source of imports, after the United States, and trade between the two countries represents the greatest bilateral commercial relationship in the region (*Economía Hoy* 1993a: 9).

The Andean Pact

The Colombian-Venezuelan success story has not been matched by similar advances among the other member states of the Andean Pact for the period 1992–1993 primarily because of the difficulties in establishing a common external tariff and a free trade zone. But trade within the Andean Pact increased significantly in 1992 and 1993 despite the conduct of Peru and Bolivia. Following a diplomatic impasse with Venezuela after Peruvian president Alberto Fujimori's *autogolpe* in 1992, Peru has essentially excluded itself from the affairs of the Andean Pact, preferring instead to conduct bilateral trade agreements. Bolivia, meanwhile, is becoming increasingly integrated into MERCOSUR, and it is possible that it will become formally integrated into this organization. Should this happen, Bolivia would have to withdraw its membership from other subregional trading groups, as regulations forbid dual membership. On the horizon, Ecuador has advanced in its free trade negotiations with Colombia and Venezuela and is positioning itself for eventual membership in the G-3 (Ochoa Antich 1993).

In 1992 trade between the member countries of the Andean Pact reached a historic record of U.S. $2,120 million, representing a 17.9 percent increase from the previous year (*Economía Hoy* 1993b: 18). Venezuela's subregional exports are the second most voluminous among members of the Andean Pact but display the fastest rate of increase in the region (Rodríguez Mendoza 1993b). However, despite the fact that 83 percent of inter-Andean trade is made up of manufactured goods, in accordance with the Junta del Acuerdo de Cartagena (JUNAC), Venezuela's exports within the Andean Pact continue to be dominated by petroleum and petroleum derivatives (Rodríguez Mendoza 1993b; Carmona Estanga 1993: 2–3).

The establishment of a free trade zone in the Andean region—even if Peru were excluded—would introduce an "open integration model" that, in principle, should not be restricted by a common external tariff. In fact, during Pérez's presidency the president of the Institute of Foreign Trade proposed that the member countries of the Andean Pact should begin negotiating closer commercial relations with MERCOSUR (Rodríguez Mendoza 1993b).

The G-3 and Relations with Mexico

Since 1989 Venezuela has also been actively involved in the G-3. The G-3's original objective was to act as a regional body for consultation and evaluation, and it was created to consider the possibility of establishing a free trade zone, with a special emphasis on commercial and energy issues, and to encourage cooperation with the countries of Central America and the Caribbean (Grupo de los Tres 1991).

Despite the obvious asymmetries in the size and potential of the economies of each of these countries, especially as they relate to trade relations with the United States, there are several reasons that Mexico, Colombia, and Venezuela have been actively working toward a free trade agreement. From the Venezuelan and Colombian perspective, the G-3 offers the possibility of strategically positioning themselves for eventual membership in NAFTA. From the Mexican perspective, the G-3 is a relatively inexpensive way of counterbalancing the political effects of closer integration with Canada and the United States. The practicability of the Venezuelan and Colombian objective can be questioned, but it clearly was a motivating factor when the G-3 was formed. The expansion of the regional market remains a long-term goal of both Venezuela and Colombia, and they maintain that Mexico will provide the most accessible avenue for closer trade relations with the United States. The Mexican government's long-term objective for the G-3 is probably to facilitate its Central American foreign policy; this objective "is based on pushing through the Darien jungle as opposed to keeping Latin America divided into two" (Zapata 1992).

There is some reason to doubt the compatibility of these proposals and their resilience to external events. In a study published in 1991, the Economic Commission for Latin America maintained that

> one possible development path is the eventual consolidation of the G-3 and the creation, in the medium term, of a free trade area between Mexico, Colombia and Venezuela. While the possibility of a convergence of interests is high, the different national goals that exist relative to the common protectionist structure toward third nations and the question of the increasing integration of the Mexican economy with that of the United States through NAFTA, makes it highly improbable that the G-3 will manage to set up a customs union. (SELA 1991b)

These issues were very much in evidence during the trilateral negotiations that took place on February 11 and 12, 1993, in Caracas. The differences between the three countries, as well as the difficulty of ensuring that elements of the G-3 agreement were in harmony with those governing Mexico's eventual membership in NAFTA, were recognized by all participants. In fact, the G-3 free trade agreement was signed in 1994.

The Caribbean and Central America: The Concerns of the G-3 and the Role of Venezuela

Beyond these immediate economic intentions, the countries of the G-3 share extensive experience in political matters, as is evidenced by the Contadora Group, the San José Agreement, and the increased attention being paid to the subregional situation since the end of the Cold War produced a geopolitical vacuum in the Caribbean Basin. All three members of the G-3 have been equally concerned about the political stability of Central America and the island nations of the Caribbean and about an eventual political transition in Cuba and its impact on the region as a whole (Serbin 1992b, 1993b).

The G-3 is especially interested in establishing cooperative links with the countries of Central America and the Caribbean. G-3 members have accomplished this by signing a series of nonreciprocal trade agreements with the countries of Central America and CARICOM. In addition, Mexico, Colombia, and Venezuela have observer status in CARICOM and are founding members of the ACS.

Venezuela's trade links with the Caribbean are modest: in 1991, Caribbean trade represented only 2.3 percent of total Venezuelan exports (Molina Duarte 1992). Still, Venezuela's interest in the non-Spanish Caribbean extends beyond issues of trade. Because this region is the main passage through which Venezuela receives the majority of its imports and, more important, through which it sends its petroleum exports, the area is of strategic interest, too. In other words, even a hint of political instability in the Caribbean represents a threat to Venezuela's economic interests and political stability.

A similar situation exists vis-à-vis Central America, a region in which Venezuela has become increasingly involved politically since the 1970s. Despite the limitations of the Central American market, Venezuela has developed a trade surplus in its commercial relations with the region, with a notable increase in its nontraditional exports. In a move designed to further develop this trend, in July 1991 Venezuela signed a working paper for a commercial and investment agreement with Costa Rica, El Salvador, Honduras, Guatemala, and Nicaragua. On February 3, 1993, this working paper was countersigned, although under nonreciprocal conditions, by the other members of the G-3. This agreement has been opposed by certain elements of Venezuela's private sector, especially the Association of Venezuelan Exporters; these same elements opposed a similar agreement with CARICOM.

CONCLUSION

Venezuela's recent foreign policy experience since the initiation of the gran viraje has been marked by the acceleration of processes of regionalization in the Caribbean Basin. Both domestic and external pressures have come to bear on Venezuela's decision to tighten up its economic and political relations with its neighbors at the subregional level. On balance, the results of this policy change have been very positive for Venezuela in terms of its trade, political, and diplomatic objectives. This conclusion is true despite several limitations, such as the domestic consequences of this policy shift, the limitations of the extent of export diversification and commercial opening, the degree of involvement of the private sector, and changes within the public sector.

From the perspective of Venezuela's foreign policy objectives, the results of the policy changes are equally positive. Venezuela has been successful at meeting its new economic priorities as they relate to the imperatives of adjustment and restructuring. At the same time, the country has accomplished its geopolitical objectives as these relate to the promotion and consolidation of subregional alliances and cooperation. These successes have come despite the fact that Venezuela has had to scale down its role as an international actor and refocus its attention on a smaller field of action.

However, the gran viraje has not been without its critics. Some have pointed out the lack of continuity in the objectives of Venezuela's foreign policy; the absence of a clear and coherent strategy toward the industrialized nations, especially the United States; and the possible divisions within the actions and initiatives of this foreign policy. In response to these criticisms, it should be noted that since 1990 the gran viraje has outlined a foreign policy along regional lines with clear and realistic objectives. Moreover, these objectives are more in line with Venezuela's economic and geopolitical reality and can better assist in the promotion of the country's interests and objectives within the Caribbean Basin.

Venezuela's retreat on the foreign policy front at the international level and concentration on regional issues are a reflection not only of an accelerated process of regionalization in the Caribbean Basin but also of an unconscious diversification of economic and political ties at the global level. This process, in turn, is due to the increasing fragmentation of the international system into three main economic blocs and the increased protectionism of the industrialized nations. Regionalization is also a result of domestic political and social instability following two attempted coups, social and political tensions, and the removal from office of President Pérez in May 1994 following accusations that he misappropriated party funds. Given these events, it is not surprising that the process of regionalization upon which Venezuela has embarked, especially for the years 1989–1993, is beginning to be perceived as "parochial" in some national sectors (Weill 1993). These sectors have criticized the limitations of this process in terms of providing Venezuela with a more advantageous position in the international scene.

6

Colombia's Assertive Regionalism in Latin America

◆

Juan Gabriel Tokatlian & Arlene B. Tickner

The central objective of this chapter is to describe and evaluate the role of regionalism in Colombia's foreign policy in the 1990s. In order to achieve this goal, we will attempt to identify the most significant characteristics of the post–Cold War international system and their implications for the nation's status on a global level. Additionally, we will review the preponderant tendencies of Colombian foreign policy, in particular during the presidency of César Gaviria Trujillo (1990–1994). We will also analyze the place and scope of the *concertación*, integration, and cooperation policies in the country's approach to Latin American and hemispheric issues. Following this discussion, we will evaluate the concrete practices of the Rio Group and the Group of Three (G-3) and the achievements and shortcomings of the Colombian-Venezuelan integration process. As a result, we hope to extract a series of conclusions in regard to the scope, opportunities, and restrictions that Colombia faces on an internal and external level with respect to the formulation of a strategic policy in favor of an assertive regionalism.

THE GLOBAL CONTEXT: TRANSITION AND CHANGE

In order to examine the potential, extent, and limitations of Colombia's international insertion and the place of regionalism in Colombian foreign policy orientations, it seems essential to introduce a brief summary of the state of international relations in the 1990s as related to the country's position in the world system. In this regard, it is possible to identify at least three lines of development. First, events such as the dissolution of the Soviet Union, the collapse of "real socialism" in Eastern Europe, and the unification of Germany have led analysts and observers to affirm that the Cold War has ended and that a new world order, conceived in the West and orchestrated from Washington, has replaced the pre-existing order. Although there is unanimity on the assertion that the ideological conflict between East and West has ended, a clear consensus does not exist regarding the truly novel character of the order described. Nevertheless, the conclusion of this conflict has not been (and may not necessarily be) balanced and stable: disorder and chaos will most likely increase, in both the center and the periphery, in the passage toward more lasting, mature, and intricate forms of order. In short, the so-called new world order seems to constitute more an ideal goal than a consummated reality.

Second, in an attempt to identify a "scheme of leadership," global attention has centered almost exclusively on the United States. For some experts, notwithstanding the collapse of the USSR, we are currently witnessing a relative though notorious decline in U.S. power because of the erosion (economic, in particular) of that country's directive capacity in global issues (Calleo 1987; Kennedy 1987). For others, the material vitality and political will of the United States continue to exist, leading them to conclude that this nation may be able to expand its leadership condition more easily in the new global context (Strange 1988; Huntington 1988/1989; Nye 1990). The optimism of some specialists leads them to insist that the United States is the exclusive architect of a unipolar world (Krauthammer 1991). This assertion disregards the consolidation of multipolar arrangements in the economic and technological spheres during the 1980s, the still viable Russian nuclear arsenal, the slow but ascending military capacity of Japan and China, and Washington's severe educational, financial, and commercial ills. In evaluating the issue of international leadership, one must avoid confusing determination with capability, associating willingness with opportunity, and equating desire with potential. The distance between what the United States would like to accomplish and what that country can realistically hope to achieve should serve to moderate what has been exalted as the unsurpassable U.S. monopoly of the world stage.

Third, in an assessment of the evolution of "global systems," emphasis has been placed upon the prolonged cycles of international history; the goal has been to explain hegemonic modifications from a less mechanical, deterministic viewpoint by combining the material and ideological, the internal and external, and the persuasive and coercive aspects of hegemony. Thus, for authors such as Cafruny, the world is currently experiencing a phase of minimal U.S. hegemony, which has followed periods of integral (1944–1960) and declining

(1960–1971) hegemony (Cafruny 1990: 111–114). In the most recent period, which was initiated by President Richard Nixon's decision to eliminate the gold exchange standard in 1971 and is marked by a shift in the global balance of economic power, U.S. hegemony is characterized by the following traits: (1) neoliberalism constitutes the hegemonic ideology; (2) market forces provide the basic organizing principle of the system; (3) more than a practice of consensual or negotiated leadership, a tendency toward unilateral authority is evident; (4) an increasingly contested, unequal distribution of costs and benefits is observable, in which the United States transfers increasingly greater burdens abroad, encumbering even its closest and most reliable allies; and (5) the basis of elite unity (on an international level) resides in the cooptation of national leadership groups that enjoy a relatively narrow, increasingly wavering base of social support. In summary, minimal hegemony rests upon a precarious type of regime in the medium and long terms that lacks a substantial challenge or resistance to the established order but is marked by multiple contradictions. The absence of an antihegemonic bloc contributes to the maintenance of an elemental consensus. Nevertheless, the lack of an organized, effective opposition does not imply that concrete, permanent options have been established to conciliate the different interests in conflict and thus transcend the political-economic discontinuities present in the system.

In light of the profound transformations that have occurred, and those that are currently in progress, it is imperative to situate international relations within a renewed center-periphery framework, incorporating some additional components into this fertile approach. Although it is true that the distances and discrepancies between North and South are tending to increase, the peripheral status of a specific nation need not be eternal as a result. The major weakness of the dependency perspective in Latin America is its implicit resignation (the unsurpassable structural impediment) and its single option for escape (total, revolutionary transformation). From a structuralist perspective, it is not unrealistic to consider forms, mechanisms, and strategies that would allow a country such as Colombia to avoid complete international marginalization (a sort of "periphery of the periphery") and to diversify its global insertion with relative imagination and persistence.

Having made the foregoing reflections, we will highlight several tendencies that are characteristic of the present decade. To begin with, during this period the so-called new international market relations have become as important as traditional political-military relations when defining power equations on a global level. In addition, the final portion of the century will continue to witness unresolved tensions between globalization and regionalization. Although globalist attempts at financial and market liberalization with a strong multilateral accent are clear, simultaneous efforts to create commercial blocs on a regional level have become generalized (Rosales 1990). Simultaneously, during the 1990s the regional homogeneity of developing countries has become gradually but noticeably weakened. All-encompassing terms such as the "Arab world," the "African world," or the "Latin American world" have appeared to lose force. In the case of Latin America, what Rico described as the existence of "two Latin Americas" (Rico 1986) has become apparent: while northern Latin America (Mexico, Central America, and the Caribbean) is economically assimilated into the strategic hold of the United States, South America is still somewhat marginal vis-à-vis Washington. Toward the end of this century, the "new" issues of the global agenda will gain importance—the environment, illicit drugs, migrations, human rights, and widespread criminality,[1] among others—whereas topics such as foreign debt, technological transfer, and inequality will be displaced. Finally, during the remainder of the present decade, the reformulation of two central concepts in international relations may seriously affect Latin America. Although a movement in favor of the notion of limited and diffuse sovereignty is striving to replace the principle of unlimited, absolute state sovereignty, the transformation of the principle of nonintervention into the criterion of "qualified" intervention under certain conditions has become clear.

Within this context, the considerations expressed above mitigate the somewhat excessive euphoria of a large number of U.S. (and Colombian) analysts who affirm that the United States is, and without a doubt will continue to be, the indisputable hegemon well into the next century. Although the United States' zeal for leadership clearly persists, it will be difficult to restore its status as a sole power in world affairs. The Pax Americana is less an alternative for a bright future than part of a supposedly great past.

However, in order for a country such as Colombia to formulate a strategic approach to its foreign policy, and to regionalism in particular, it must avoid conceptual confusions. In this regard, one must separate the global and regional dimensions of hegemony. Although on an international level, a progressive "dehegemonization" favoring a relative increase in the margins of autonomy of some emerging powers in the Third World (in Asia, for example) is observable, in the Latin American context, a U.S. "rehegemonization" (which occurred particularly during the 1980s) is apparent. This latter process has become even more noticeable during the 1990s, with a dissolved Soviet Union, a Japan relatively uninterested in the region (except for specific cases), and a European Union marginally inclined to associate itself commercially, technologically, and financially with Latin America as a whole.

An additional observation regarding hegemony and its impact upon Latin America is required at this point: in order to ensure its leadership in the hemisphere, the United States will probably employ "positive" instruments of persuasion and approximation in its treatment of the most important Latin American countries.[2] Nevertheless, when Washington perceives one of the region's nations as a "problem country" for reasons considered threatening to U.S. national security—drug trafficking, the degradation of the environment, massive migration, and rampant corruption, among others, are issues that exacerbate this condition—the use of "negative" coercive mechanisms to guarantee U.S. domination in the continent will not be discarded (Cardona and Tokatlian 1991: 16–21). With varied emphasis and diverse combinations, the "carrot" and "stick" will continue to be distinct but complementary means—depending upon the case in question—in U.S. policy toward Latin America. Thus, although U.S. hegemony has somewhat deteriorated on a global scale, Washington has experienced an accelerated, penetrating regional hegemony.

The preceding observations have several implications for Colombian foreign policy. First, they suggest the need for serious strategic reflection concerning a desirable orientation and possible behavior on both a continental and global level. Second, they establish limits and opportunities with respect to the nation's desire to formulate an assertive external conduct that will increase its international negotiating power. Third, they lead to a cautious reflection concerning the conceptualization and practice of autonomy in the global affairs of peripheral nations.[3] Fourth, they suggest the need to concentrate upon domestic issues: rather than external phenomena, it will clearly be internal elements—political, social, economic, cultural, scientific, and military, among others—that will help achieve a vigorous, dynamic, and consistent global insertion.

COLOMBIAN FOREIGN POLICY: HORIZONS AND DILEMMAS

For Colombia, the beginning of the 1990s coincided with the inauguration of a new administration, that of Liberal president César Gaviria Trujillo (1990–1994). Within the framework discussed above, it is pertinent to identify the most noteworthy characteristics of this government in terms of its general macroeconomic and foreign policies.

Upon assuming office, President Gaviria encountered a changing and contradictory international reality and a complicated domestic scene. In both cases, plausible policy options were relatively scarce, while margins for maneuverability were extremely limited. According to official perceptions, the major task to be undertaken was a more effective insertion into global markets in the shortest time possible, given that a country such as Colombia could not continue to passively await favorable changes in the international climate. It appeared that the predominant view of the executive power was that short-term alternatives were extremely limited and, as a result, should be taken advantage of to the maximum. Thus, after Gaviria's inauguration, the Modernization Plan for the Colombian Economy (or the *apertura*), launched by President Virgilio Barco (1986–1990) in February 1990, was accelerated, resulting in substantial changes in the country's customs and tariff policies,[4] foreign exchange and banking regimes, labor legislation, treatment of foreign capital, and the intervention of the state in the economy. Additionally, domestic issues were a priority at this time, temporarily displacing possibilities for strategic formulations in the field of foreign policy: from the National Constitutional Assembly (1990) and the new constitution (1991) to dialogues with guerrilla organizations (1991–1992) and the "plea bargaining" system (*política de sometimiento*), introduced specifically for Medellín cartel drug traffickers (1990–1992), governmental efforts and resources were concentrated internally.

There was a relatively high degree of coherence between the Gaviria and Barco administrations: several officials served under both presidents, and their foreign policies were similar in terms of discourse and general orientation. The Gaviria administration maintained emphasis on certain objectives introduced by the previous administration, such as the search for an active economic diplomacy (in particular, those aspects related to commercial and financial apertura), the modernization of the country's foreign policy apparatus, the preservation of a relative degree of autonomy, the improvement of national negotiating power, and the diversification of Colombia's political ties on an international level. Simultaneously, the Gaviria administration emphasized basic concepts and criteria, including the advocacy of a "nonideological" approach to foreign policy, the "denarcotization" of the agenda with Washington, and the opening of the country in different dimensions of its internal and external affairs (Gaviria Trujillo 1992).

Nevertheless, these orientations were gradually modified for practical reasons rather than conceptual motives. The ideological dimension of diplomacy lost importance in a world context characterized by the disappearance of the Soviet Union, the crisis of ideological paradigms, and the growing significance of pragmatism. The attenuation of the drug issue vis-à-vis the United States became more difficult with Pablo Escobar's escape from prison in 1992, the alarming growth of the heroin business in the country, and, more recently, the Colombian government's continuance of the plea-bargaining system, extended recently to include members of the Cali cartel (Tokatlian 1994: 77–117). The apertura policy confronted a recessive global environment and the exacerbation of protectionism in the United States and Europe.

On another level, multilateral policies gained significant impulse in the Gaviria administration. This impulse resulted from a set of basic canons that had guided the country's international conduct particularly since the presidency of Belisario Betancur (1982–1986): the preservation of a relative degree of autonomy in the international sphere through the improvement of national negotiating power strengthened through group initiatives; the promotion of associative and common actions with the goal of reducing eventual external tension and vulnerability (political, economic, and military) that might have affected Colombia; the growth of the nation's international visibility, designed to avoid isolation and eliminate the possibility of negatively internationalizing local conflicts; and the assurance of an elemental level of regional support for central positions that were defended and sustained by the country in continental and global arenas. In this sense, one might highlight the consistent backing Gaviria gave to, among others, the G-3, the commitment adopted in favor of strengthening the Andean Group, the active support offered to the Rio Group, the dynamic participation in the Group of Friends to the General Secretary of the UN in consolidating a peace agreement between the government of El Salvador and the Frente Farabundo Martí de Liberación National (FMLN), and the permanent efforts devoted to the Cairns Group in the Uruguay Round negotiations of the General Agreement on Tariffs and Trade. Simultaneously, an important profile in the UN and the Organization of American States (OAS) confirms the significance of multinational arrangements for Colombian foreign policy.[5] In consequence, and keeping in mind the internal and external restraints identified above, this area of Colombia's international policy will probably be reinforced in the future (Ministerio de Relaciones Exteriores 1994).

While a strategy aimed at diversifying the country's economic ties on a global level has been promoted, the reality is that commercial, financial, and technological relations with the United States and the European Union continue to predominate in Colombia's foreign policy. This situation has become even more evident following the approval of a series of commercial preferences from both counterparts (the Andean Trade Preference Act, approved by the U.S. Congress for ten years, and the Special Cooperation Program, originally approved by the Europeans for a period of four years and renegotiated for an additional ten) in recognition of the Andean nations' (Colombia, Peru, Bolivia, Ecuador) fight against drugs. Other than the case of Venezuela, a country with which Colombia consolidated a highly significant exchange, the goal of noticeably increasing new and diverse commercial associations did not materialize from 1990 to 1994. With the 1993 approval of the North American Free Trade Agreement (NAFTA) by the U.S. Congress, Colombia, as with other Latin American nations whose trade is concentrated in the U.S. market, will probably be less inclined to persist with efforts at diversification, in order to gain eventual access into NAFTA.[6]

On an institutional level, the Gaviria administration sought to accelerate national attempts at modernizing the country's foreign policy apparatus (Jaramillo 1991b). The Supplementing Law 33 of March 16, 1990, which sought an administrative *aggiornamento* in the management of international affairs, Law 11 of January 21, 1991, providing for the reorganization of the Ministry of Foreign Relations, and Decree 10 of January 3, 1992, which introduced an organic statute for the country's foreign service, constitute important renovating instruments that give the ministry the tools necessary to design and execute a more consistent, aggressive international policy. Nevertheless, toward the end of the Gaviria government, the Ministry of Foreign Relations had yet to be sufficiently strengthened. In fact, this institution is increasingly being converted into an inoperative entity that obstructs rather than guarantees the country's internationalization process.

On another front, and notwithstanding the difficulties present in the Ministry of Foreign Relations, the Presidential Advisory for International Affairs was created in 1990 to overcome the traditional fragmentation and refine the level of coordination of Colombian foreign policy. Parallel to this, the Ministry of Foreign Trade was created in 1992 in order to expand and promote the country's commercial relations in a more dynamic, institutionalized fashion. Since its creation, the country has assumed a more energetic role in advancing multilateral trade arrangements. Bilateral agreements have been signed with numerous countries and a series of commercial missions have been conducted in order to improve Colombia's commercial image abroad. Finally, in February 1994, the Ministry of the Environment was created, reflecting the importance of environmental issues for the country's internal affairs and the potential of this topic in incrementing Colombia's negotiating status on regional and global levels.

THE REGIONALIST COMPONENT OF
COLOMBIAN FOREIGN POLICY: OPTION OR UTOPIA?

To what extent have symbolic expressions of adherence to regionalism (as evidenced by the constitution and official declarations) been met by a consistent policy of prioritized strategies for addressing the subcontinent? Drawing from Andrew Hurrell's definition, one might understand regionalism as "a set of policies by one or more states designed to promote the emergence of a cohesive regional unit, which dominates the pattern of relations between the states of that region" (Hurrell 1992: 123). More specifically, there are three terms that are regularly employed interchangeably, without much distinction or clarity, that might characterize this set of policies described by Hurrell: concertación, cooperation, and integration. Rather than representing a minor question of semantics, the absence of precision and transparency in the definition of these concepts has had highly negative consequences for both Latin American foreign policy in general and integration policies in particular. As a result, it seems appropriate to introduce a more solid terminological base that will permit us to approach regionalism in a better, creative fashion. The three terms might be envisioned as different means of gaining bargaining power, resources, and mutual support in order to eventually negotiate access into the broad, hemispheric bloc proposed by the Enterprise for the Americas Initiative and inaugurated with NAFTA. They can be defined as follows:

- *concertación:* a mechanism through which two or more governments act together in the state domain, in general on a diplomatic level, with political objectives regarding other individual or collective actors.
- *cooperation:* a process by which the state, with the active collaboration of some segments of civil society (especially the private sector), produces selective, timely, and feasible projects and agreements that are largely of an economic and commercial nature but have a political background between two or more parties and eventually between nearby countries and other counterparts.
- *integration:* a more extensive, intensive, complex, and profound process between two or more nations that implies a social, political, economic, cultural, scientific, diplomatic, and even military linkage and an interdependence of enormous proportions, stimulated by the governments but with a highly dynamic, protagonistic participation of varied agents of the societies involved.

In this sense, the Rio Group (which includes thirteen Latin American countries that have established permanent consultation mechanisms) is an example of concertación; the G-3 (Mexico, Venezuela, and Colombia) is an instrument of cooperation; and the structure generated between Colombia and Venezuela in recent years tends to be an archetype of integration.

The conceptual precision of these explanations has serious political and institutional implications. In particular, our identification facilitates the design of strategic foreign policy proposals with respect to regionalism. It also helps to determine the requirements of an efficient bureaucratic coordination needed to manage different issues, distinct objectives, diverse periods of maturation, and multiple actors operating domestically and abroad. At the same time, this clarification alters the realm of perception; the regionalist schemes listed are not similar to one another—each is different in terms of its function, value, and significance—and it is not necessary for a country such as Colombia to be present in all of them. In conclusion, a series of differing perspectives regarding regionalism must be revived; if it is not, all attempts at dynamic internationalization and autonomous global insertion will inevitably falter.

The attention given to regionalism in the 1991 constitution is highlighted in the following (Vargas de Losada 1991):

- Preamble: "The people of Colombia, in exercise of their sovereign power, . . . and committed to promoting the *integration of the Latin American community* [emphasis added], decree, sanction and promulgate the following Political Constitution of Colombia."
- Article 9: "The foreign relations of the State are founded upon national sovereignty, respect for the self-determination of different peoples and the recognition of the principles of international law accepted by Colombia. Simultaneously, *Colombia's foreign policy will be oriented towards Latin American and Caribbean integration* [emphasis added]."
- Article 227: "*The State will promote economic, social and political integration with other nations, in particular with the countries of Latin America and the Caribbean* [emphasis added], through the celebration of treaties that create supranational organisms, *including the conformation of a Latin American Community of Nations* [emphasis added] on the bases of fairness, equality and reciprocity."

Such examples permeate the entire constitution, and they represent a significant transformation in the country's perception of its place in the subcontinent and in the world in general. From the role of archipelago, sustained by the constitution of 1886, the country shifted toward a more associative position, bolstered by the 1991 constitution, in which the people, the government, and the state, as diverse actors on a national and regional level, share a clear commitment to regionalism in the terrain of ideals.

This commitment notwithstanding, in practice Colombia's regional conduct has yet to demonstrate that Latin America is an important part of the country's foreign policy. In fact, one might affirm that, with respect to the subcontinent, a reactive foreign policy has dominated over a proposal-oriented one. Thus Colombia's Latin American policy seems to be guided more by transient determinism than by strategic planning.

One explanation for this conduct is clearly the effect of more important temporal issues (among others, drug trafficking, human rights, commercial and financial negotiations with the United States and the European Union, and activities related to the process of apertura and internationalization), which occupy and at times saturate the attention of the executive office and its different decision-making entities linked to Colombian foreign policy. In addition to this, a permanent concern for domestic issues, in particular those relating to public order (guerrilla groups, paramilitarism, and drug-related violence) and those that affect the population as a whole (for example, the 1992 energy crisis, the need for a comprehensive social policy, urban and rural insecurity, and the state of internal commotion) contribute to the excessive concentration of the present administration upon national affairs.

To a certain extent, the strategic preferences granted to the various processes of subregional affiliation in the economic and political spheres (the Andean Group, the G-3, Colombia-Venezuela, the Rio Group) reflected the reactive nature of the Gaviria administration's Latin American policy. Upon assuming office, Gaviria identified the importance of Latin American regionalist processes in his foreign policy in the following order: the Rio Group, the Andean Group, the Latin American Integration Association, the G-3, Venezuela, Ecuador, and the OAS (Jaramillo 1991a); only one year later, the priority became Venezuela and then the G-3 and the Andean Group simultaneously (*El Tiempo* 1992).[7]

At the beginning of the Gaviria administration, the Rio Group was accorded a high degree of importance in Colombia's Latin American policy agenda, reflecting the country's desire to establish itself as a protagonist in regional affairs and to strengthen Latin America's negotiating power on a global level. For Colombia, the major worth of this group resided in its political significance and its potential for cohesive dialogue with the United States and Europe in particular. The centrality of issues such as human rights, narcotics, multilateral organizations, and commercial cooperation in the Rio Group's agenda coincided with the priority that these topics received in Colombia's foreign policy. In addition, it was crucial for Colombia to politicize this agenda, allowing for a potentially less technical, more realist treatment of the issues mentioned.

Nevertheless, only a year later (1991) a series of problems that emerged within the Rio Group caused the government to lower the organization on its list of priorities. In brief, these difficulties were related to the agenda, to the mechanisms for consensus, and to the issues of foreign policy in the respective member countries.

The problems in the Rio Group's agenda have been and continue to be multiple in nature. The numeric increase in member countries, combined with an excessive expansion in the topics supposedly covering the interests of the group's governments, has led to a lack of order in its priorities.[8] In addition, an absolute vagueness in the intraregional and external treatment of these same topics has reduced the credibility of the group. Moreover, a highly reactive, less proposal-oriented tone in the elaboration of these issues has reduced the leverage of the Rio Group as a cohesive, energetic association vis-à-vis other individual or collective counterparts.

The difficulty inherent in reaching a "strong consensus" within the Rio Group has also become truly alarming. There are a large number of external motives that certainly impede the achievement of basic, substantive agreements. Nevertheless, the Rio Group must carry out a more serious regional and national analysis in order to understand and thus overcome its greatest obstacles.[9] It is easy to achieve a "weak consensus" (all against the universal "plague" of narcotics, all in favor of the "massive" transfer of technology, all in favor of "really" strengthening multilateral mechanisms for dialogue and discussion, etc.). However, the consolidation of a majority that might convert rhetoric into practice, theory into praxis, and a defensive posture into an offensive position has been virtually impossible in recent years. The case of the Rio Group seems to demonstrate that the creative alliance of individual national interests is incompatible with a powerful regional interest.

At present, practically all of the countries in Latin America define their respective foreign policies as pragmatic. This generalized self-description is rooted in the fact that existing global restrictions seem to impose a sort of individual transactional logic, in particular with regard to Washington, which is shared by the majority of Latin American nations. The predominant rationale is that an "excessive" unity with regional partners reduces the possibility of obtaining individual benefits from stronger counterparts in the international system. On a rhetorical level, Latin America constitutes the epicenter of the respective foreign policies of the region's countries; nonetheless, national discourses fail to coincide with actual practice. At the beginning of his administration, President Gaviria proposed the creation of a Latin American Forum, with the goal of surpassing the isolated treatment of international issues and promoting greater regional dialogue and cooperation (Gaviria Trujillo 1992: 37). The Colombian president did not persist with this proposal, but his idea highlights the urgent need to reach a realistic balance of the state of political concertación in the region, particularly with regard to the Rio Group.

The G-3, created in 1989 during the Barco administration (Ministerio de Relaciones Exteriores 1993b), followed a productive experience with concertación between Colombia, Venezuela, and Mexico (and Panama) in the Contadora Group and expressed the three countries' interest in promoting an economic, cultural, and political harmonization that might strengthen their influence on a regional level (Cardona 1992). For President Gaviria, the initial priority in this process was the consolidation of the country's integration with Venezuela, from which negotiation with Mexico could then proceed (*El Tiempo* 1992). The Ministry of Foreign Trade believed that a commitment to free trade with Mexico and Venezuela would grant Colombia the possibility to be part of a large North, Central, and South American network (*El Espectador* 1992).[10] For the Ministry of Foreign Affairs, the G-3 was one of the fundamental "pillars" of Colombian foreign policy, although its management of the pro tempore secretariat of this organization was excessively discreet (Arias 1991).

The G-3 was originally conceived as a political-diplomatic organization with subregional goals (to reinforce Colombia's projection in the Caribbean Basin, of high geopolitical significance for the country) and global objectives (to better coordinate the three countries' positions in different multilateral forums). The group's slow transformation—which by no means represents the disappearance of its political foundations and diplomatic qualities—is a reflection of the wishes of the member countries' governments to encourage a more dynamic regional economic activity. Additionally, it has become clear that a growing economic linkage between the three nations has contributed to the strengthening of political ties that were established since the Contadora and Rio groups.

While the commitments achieved in the G-3 have been largely of an economic nature, the group has also exercised considerable political influence on a subregional level, especially in Central America and the Caribbean.[11] However, internal and external difficulties continue to condition and limit the transformation of this interesting cooperation process into a fundamental integration scheme. On a procedural level, a fragmented, even dysfunctional treatment of the issues included in the negotiations has been evident. While various Colombian ministries share responsibility for the management of different high level groups, the lack of a centralized coordination and planning order has increased segmentation and reduced the government's bargaining capacity.

In this respect, it is important to note that the Ministry of Foreign Relations has become increasingly displaced in the management of the G-3 negotiations, whereas the Ministry of Foreign Trade has assumed a central role in the orientation of trilateral relations. This is a result of several factors, including President Gaviria's interest in intensifying the economic component of linkages between the three countries, the greater dexterity of the foreign trade ministry (over that of foreign relations) in advancing the country's international economic relations, and the new reality generated by NAFTA and the importance of consolidating commercial commitments that may facilitate economic agreements with the United States in the future.

Additional impediments include the asymmetries of the Colombian, Venezuelan, and Mexican economies, distinct expectations in the three nations regarding the group,[12] and differences regarding the pace of adjustment processes, harmonization of macroeconomic policies, and political reform. With regard to this last point, the private sectors of the three countries have begun to insist that they be consulted for the negotiation of this type of agreement more so than in the past and that such arrangements be reduced in speed in order to allow respective national producers to adapt to the challenges generated. Finally, events such as the failed coup attempt in Venezuela in February 1992, the forced resignation of President Carlos Andrés Pérez in 1993, the inauguration of Rafael Caldera's presidency in Caracas in the midst of severe social and institutional problems, Colombia's political and economic difficulties on a domestic level, the armed uprising of January 1, 1994, in Chiapas, Mexico, and the assassination of the Revolutionary Institutional Party's presidential candidate, Luis Donaldo Colosio, will clearly continue to modify the velocity with which the agreements advance.

The Colombian-Venezuelan integration process was initiated in February 1989, when the two countries signed an accord in which several committees (the Permanent Commission of Conciliation, the High Commission, and the National Commissions of Frontier Issues) were created in order to elaborate recommendations in the areas of transportation and border commerce, customs, agriculture and industry, oceanic delimitation, international rivers, drug trafficking, recuperation of stolen vehicles, labor and migration, the environment, energy and minerals, communications, culture and education, and binational ethnic groups (Ministerio de Relaciones Exteriores 1993a). When efforts to revive the Andean Group failed in late 1991, following Peru's and Ecuador's refusal to adopt the common external tariff, Colombia and Venezuela decided to advance bilaterally with the free trade agreement originally established by that group.

A combination of historical elements, geographical realities, political motivations, social linkages, cultural foundations, and diplomatic needs have led Colombia (and Venezuela) to comprehend the enormous importance of motivating and intensifying the binational integration process. In the 1990s it has become crucial for Bogotá and Caracas jointly to confront requirements for internal development and aspirations for external autonomy. As a result, during the Gaviria administration Venezuela became a vital reference point for Colombia's international relations and its sustained effort to vigorously reinforce bilateral interdependence.

Since the beginning of this process, the nature of Colombian-Venezuelan relations has been altered substantially: a relationship marked by antagonism[13] has been gradually converted into one characterized by collaboration and compromise, with the goal of maximizing mutual advantages and capabilities. Perhaps the most significant progress has been made in the commercial area, where bilateral trade increased approximately 300 percent between 1989 and 1993[14] and substantial reciprocal investments have been made. Despite the improved relations in commercial and other areas (Pardo García-Peña 1993), the countries have disagreed on a number of issues and have not implemented many of the commissions' recommendations (Cardona et al. 1992). Simultaneously, the domestic problems identified earlier as obstacles to the G-3 negotiations have impeded the progress of the bilateral integration process. Although the advances made since 1989 will clearly be impossible to erase, it is difficult to predict the effects that the elections of Rafael Caldera in Venezuela and Ernesto Samper in Colombia will have upon Colombian-Venezuelan relations. Nevertheless, notwithstanding the difficulties presently faced by both nations, an authentic political determination to advance with the integration process seems to predominate.

CONCLUSION

Although Colombia has attempted to respond to a new, largely different continental and global reality in recent years with creative and effective foreign policy measures, a series of external and domestic factors continue to inhibit the creation of a truly successful, strategic formulation of the country's international relations with respect to regionalism. Thus the nation faces a series of challenges, specifically on the internal front, that hinder the consolidation of an assertive regional policy. The Gaviria administration made relevant efforts to improve and increase Colombia's Latin American profile, and future Colombian governments will be able to expand the hemispheric insertion of the country based on these efforts. The internationalization process has become irreversible for a country such as Colombia and requires a more dynamic, participatory, and consistent foreign policy. The new constitution of 1991 offers a point of reference rich in premises and ideals that in the future should materialize in a more Latin Americanist, continental orientation on the part of the country's leadership. At present, Colombia is a relevant actor in the regional sphere, and because of its resources, capacities, and will, it should occupy an important place in the concert of the Americas in the future.

The country is also redefining its profile in the regional and global spheres. Under the Betancur (1982–1986), Barco (1986–1990), and Gaviria (1990–1994) administrations Colombia advanced a restructuring of its international behavior. The country has been characterized by a type of triple association. First, it has identified itself with the West in cultural terms, sharing values such as the defense of democracy, pluralism, and dissent, as well as in an economic sense, immersing itself in the capitalist system. Second, the country is part of the periphery of world politics and, as such, has needs, demands, and aspirations of well-being, security, and independence similar to those of its Third World counterparts. Third, in the Latin American sphere, Colombia occupies an intermediary status as a result of its diverse sources of demographic, natural, material, and strategic power, leading it to assume proposal-oriented and distinctive positions. Additionally, and from a geopolitical perspective, Colombia holds "a quadruple inscription in the Latin American scheme: it is an Andean country, it forms part of the Caribbean Basin and the Pacific, and at the same time is an Amazonian nation" (Cardona and Tokatlian 1993: 142). This multiple identification constitutes an extremely valuable asset for the praxis of a singular, assertive foreign policy.

In conclusion, these elements form a set of essential factors that must be taken into consideration to understand the design and implementation of Colombia's regional policy. This policy reflects the country's intention and determination to create an autonomous capacity for itself in a moderate but firm manner and to seek a greater bargaining power while exercising a more active role in hemispheric affairs. Certainly, this type of conduct will most likely continue to characterize Colombian foreign policy in the 1990s.

NOTES

1. This topic has been discussed very little in the existing literature on the new global agenda, but its importance will probably grow during the 1990s. According to Arlacchi, the definition of criminality on a large scale includes four manifestations with international implications: organized crime, economic and financial crimes, political and administrative corruption, and illegal lobbying (Arlacchi 1988).

2. The Enterprise for the Americas Initiative, announced by President George Bush in June 1990, is an important example in this respect.

3. In essence, during the 1970s and 1980s in Latin America, the exercise of autonomy in foreign policy was believed to rest on political variables, the distancing from or challenges to the regional hegemonic power, and a type of economic autocracy. In the 1990s new criteria have emerged affirming, for example, that autonomy is sustained by commercial, financial, and technological factors. These criteria place a greater accent on the pragmatic collaboration with the continental hegemon and redefine the standards of economic and political sovereignty. Instead of pursuing the diversification of dependence as an objective of foreign policy as before, a country now has to ensure a hierarchic link with the most powerful actor on a hemispheric level, in other words with the United States, in the least amount of time and to the greatest extent possible (Gómez, Drekonja, Tokatlian, and Carvajal 1993).

4. In September 1991 President Gaviria announced an accelerated tariff reduction, originally programmed for 1994 by the previous administration.

5. In this regard, it is important to highlight the recent nomination of former president Gaviria as general-secretary of the OAS.

6. Countries that stay out of NAFTA will face the double jeopardy of competitive disadvantage in the U.S. market vis-à-vis Mexico and other eventual members and similar disadvantages in member countries vis-à-vis the United States (Erzan and Yeats 1992).

7. See interview with President Gaviria regarding Colombian foreign policy in *El Tiempo* (1992).

8. An eloquent example of this can be found in the "Declaración del Grupo de Río en Santiago de Chile," approved by the heads of state during the Seventh Presidential Summit of the Rio Group in October 1993. The extensive declaration (30 points) makes reference to almost all topics and dimensions of international politics, without an elemental sense of priority. For example, it seems as important to reaffirm the regional commitment to "promote sustainable development" (point 8) as it does to underline "the need to progressively improve the quality of education in our countries" (point 15), reiterate the "determination to promote and protect human rights" (point 18), and support "the candidacy of Rafael Moreno to the General Direction of the United Nations Food and Agriculture Organization [FAO]" (point 28). It is interesting to note that the Rio Group's candidate for the FAO was not elected; Jacques Diouf from Senegal won the number of votes necessary to occupy this post. In this respect, see Oviedo (1993).

9. The Rio Group's approach to the debt crisis is probably the clearest example in this respect. All of the governments of the region sought to moderate the actions of the rest, to the point where moderation brought with it immobilization and an absence of originality. As a result of the obvious differences between the Latin American countries, a minimum common denominator for negotiating with other state and nongovernmental actors was never reached. At present, this topic has disappeared for all practical purposes from the Latin American agenda, placing the Rio Group in a fragile and almost erratic position with regard to other, more powerful counterparts for whom the issue of the debt has ceased to represent a problem.

10. See interview with Juan Manuel Santos, minister of foreign trade, in *El Espectador* (1992).

11. The group's attempts to serve as a discreet bridge, not a mediator, between Cuba and the United States and to encourage peaceful democratic change in the island are noteworthy in this respect. From the Colombian perspective, additional support for these initiatives from countries such as Canada and Spain is highly positive.

12. Although for Mexico the G-3 constitutes a mechanism through which that country can counterbalance its association with NAFTA, allowing it to maintain a certain degree of political influence in the region, Colombia and Venezuela may hope to accelerate their acceptance into NAFTA through this process, as well as strengthen commercial ties with Mexico, Central America, and the Caribbean (Serbin 1993a: 120–129).

13. Historically, bilateral relations have been dominated by a dispute over the delimitation of a region located in the Gulf of Venezuela. For an extensive discussion of this issue, among others, see Eastman and Cabra (1987); Obregón and Nasi (1990); Vázquez Carrizosa (1983).

14. According to sources at the Colombo-Venezuelan Chamber of Commerce and Integration, in 1989 trade between the two countries amounted to U.S. $391 million, and in 1993 bilateral commerce reached approximately U.S. $1.2 billion.

7

Peru:
Atypical External Behavior

◆

Ronald Bruce St John

Regionalism, in particular enhanced regional economic integration, is an idea that has clearly taken hold today in the Western Hemisphere. The negotiation of the North American Free Trade Agreement, the revitalization of the Central American Common Market, and the creation of the Southern Cone Common Market are only a few of the steps taken in recent years to set in place the first building blocks of a hemispheric free trade system and possibly a regional economic community. Much of the current progress on economic- and trade-related issues in Latin America is linked to the Enterprise for the Americas Initiative announced by former president George Bush in June 1990. Most Latin American governments greeted this proposal for a free trade system with enthusiasm. It fueled expectations that economic integration had become a feasible goal that would boost regional growth prospects. The end of the Cold War and the concomitant decline in U.S. hegemony contributed to the current positive atmosphere for sustained cooperation among the nations of the hemisphere.

Regional cooperation on either the political or economic fronts is hardly a new theme in inter-American relations. The nations of the Western Hemisphere have a long history of political and economic integration efforts—at both the regional and subregional levels. This is particularly true for Peru, where a strong sense of solidarity with its American neighbors characterized its foreign policy from the outset of the independence era. The Peruvian government was actively involved in a series of hemispheric gatherings, and it later played a leadership role in the promotion of continental solidarity and development. Peruvian diplomacy subsequently expanded in scope and direction to champion, first, inter-American cooperation and, more

recently, international solidarity. Unfortunately, few of these diplomatic efforts produced the desired political or economic gains, and
none resulted in a strong record of sustained performance. Many of
the Latin American countries today, in particular Peru, remain
plagued by the severe social, economic, and political problems that
hampered earlier integration efforts.

This chapter first briefly examines the central role the related
movements of continental solidarity and regionalism have played in
the historical experience of Peru. The focus then turns to the post-
1980 international political and economic environment and the impact recent changes there, such as the Third World debt crisis, U.S.
policy orientations during and after the Reagan administration, and
difficulties encountered by the Andean Pact, have had on the external policy of Peru. Significant domestic forces and events, including
the rise of terrorist movements in Peru and the increase in coca production, are also examined because they have had a surprisingly important impact on contemporary Peruvian foreign policy. The chapter concludes with an evaluation of the policies implemented by the
current Peruvian government to address the multitude of internal
and external forces affecting its foreign policy in general and its approach to regionalism in particular.

TRADITIONAL APPROACHES

The governments of Gran Colombia and Peru first called in mid-
1822 for the congress of American states, which finally opened in
Panama four years later. The principal objective of the Panama Conference was to form a continental federation to reduce discord
among member states, defend the independence of Latin America,
and counteract the influence of the Holy Alliance. Delegates to the
conference concluded four conventions, the most important being
a treaty of perpetual union, league, and confederation. Since the
government of Colombia was the only signatory to ratify any of these
conventions, the Panama Conference failed to meet its formal objectives. It remains notable, nevertheless, because it marked the formal beginning of the movement for enhanced continental solidarity
(Barrenechea y Raygada 1942).

Peruvian diplomacy throughout the Panama Conference displayed a bifurcation of interests and concerns that long marked the
Peruvian stance on the question of continental solidarity. On the one
hand, a feeling of kindred spirit and solidarity, if not interest in formal union, typified Peruvian diplomacy toward its South American
neighbors. On the other, increasingly bitter rivalries with adjacent

states over territorial claims and boundaries worked against any movement toward unity. These two opposing forces characterized Peruvian foreign policy into the early twentieth century (St John 1992b: 1).

General Andres Santa Cruz announced in 1836 the formation of the ill-fated Peru-Bolivia Confederation, the only serious effort at South American regional integration from the collapse of Gran Colombia to the contemporary period. In theory, the newly formed federal republic, consisting of North Peru, South Peru, and Bolivia, was made up of sovereign states. In reality, it was subordinate to a powerful central government headed by Santa Cruz as supreme protector. The Peru-Bolivia Confederation in form bore a remarkable similarity to the Federation of the Andes proclaimed by Simón Bolívar in 1826. Like its precursor, the confederation generated considerable internal and external opposition. Defeated at the bloody battle of Yungay, Santa Cruz resigned his authority as supreme protector and dissolved the confederation (Ortiz de Zevallos Paz Soldán 1972: 67–71).

The 1845 election of Ramón Castilla to the presidency of Peru was a milestone in the development of Peruvian foreign policy as well as in the promotion of continental solidarity. During two terms in office, Castilla actively pursued closer ties with Bolivia and Ecuador as part of a broader scheme to promote wider hemispheric cooperation. The Castilla administration also attempted to continue the work begun at the 1826 Panama Conference through a new international conference that opened in Lima in late 1847. The Lima Conference produced four treaties, the most important of which was a treaty of union and confederation (Barrenechea y Raygada 1947: 27–28).

The Castilla administration, responding in part to threats of intervention from outside the hemisphere, later proposed a treaty of defensive and offensive alliance with the aim of uniting the Latin American nations for their common defense. The resulting 1856 Continental Treaty, signed by representatives of Chile, Ecuador, and Peru, incorporated principles long advocated by the Peruvian government, including nonintervention and respect for the territorial integrity of member states. While the pact also created a congress of plenipotentiaries to act as a consultative body, there was nothing in the agreement that either constituted or laid the groundwork for a union of the signatories. The Castilla administration pursued wider support for the Continental Treaty; however, none of the signatories ever ratified the agreement (Ulloa Sotomayor 1938: xciii–xcvi).

The decade of the 1860s offered the Peruvian government a unique opportunity for enhanced regional status and wider continental leadership. The legacy of the Castilla years included a coherent, comprehensive foreign policy grounded in the principles of nonintervention, national integrity, and continental solidarity. In addition, improvements to the structure and organization of the diplomatic corps developed the machinery necessary for a more effective foreign policy. Faced with exciting new prospects, successive Peruvian presidents in the two decades before the War of the Pacific (1879–1883) pursued related foreign policy objectives but with little success.

In the four decades following the War of the Pacific, Peruvian diplomacy concentrated on the recovery of the two Peruvian provinces, Tacna and Arica, that remained in Chilean hands at the end of the war. At the same time, the Peruvian government made progress in resolving its complicated, often interrelated boundary disputes with Bolivia, Brazil, Colombia, and Ecuador. In both issue areas, but particularly in its dispute with Chile, Peru looked to the U.S. government for support in obtaining a favorable outcome. In part for this reason, the most important influence on Peruvian foreign relations throughout this period was the growing ascendancy of the U.S. government, together with private interests from the United States, in the political and economic affairs of Latin America.

Cautious optimism tempered by pragmatism characterized the Peruvian approach to the 1945 discussions that eventually led to the founding of the UN. Deeply concerned that any new international body would fully recognize regional jurisdiction in matters of peace and security, the Peruvian delegation to the San Francisco peace conference was a strong and articulate voice for the primacy of regional structures. Later, as an active participant in the new international body, Peru remained a strong supporter of regional organizations, especially when questions of regional peace or security were concerned. Consistent with this approach, the Peruvian delegation joined other American states at the Rio Conference in 1947 and the Ninth Inter-American Conference in Bogotá in 1948 to develop institutions and procedures to maintain peace among themselves (Wagner de Reyna 1964: 295–298).

Reflecting this preference for enhanced regional cooperation, the Peruvian government in 1954 joined its Pacific neighbors in announcing that none would unilaterally diminish its claim to exercise sovereignty and jurisdiction over the continental shelf and insular sea to a distance of 200 nautical miles without prior consultation and agreement. At the same time, Peru, Chile, and Ecuador declared their intention to enforce their claims to sovereignty by all necessary means, including force. Before the end of the year, the first foreign fishing fleet had been captured and fined, an event that became commonplace throughout the decade. To many observers, the growing involvement of the Peruvian government in the more controversial aspects of the law of the sea seemed a natural extension of its long-time commitment to territorial questions (Ferrero Costa 1979: 43–89).

The two decades after World War II presented exciting new challenges and opportunities for Peruvian fore ign policy. With the apparent resolution in 1942 of its remaining territorial dispute, the Peruvian government began to resume the leadership role in continental affairs it had forsaken in the aftermath of the War of the Pacific. Peru demonstrated a growing interest in Latin American economic cooperation and development, and it participated in multilateral conferences and declarations on maritime fishing and mineral resources. It also joined the Latin American Free Trade Association when that body was created with much enthusiasm in early 1960.

In early October 1968, the armed forces of Peru ousted the civilian government of Fernando Belaúnde Terry and initiated a twelve-year period of military government commonly referred to as the *docenio*. In addition to measures to assert heightened Peruvian sovereignty, the revolutionary government of the armed forces demanded a radical reorientation of the inter-American economic and political system. In fact, its early policies in this regard constituted a systematic questioning of the principal institutions of the entire system, including the Organization of American States (OAS), the Inter-American Treaty of Reciprocal Assistance, and the Inter-American Development Bank. The military government called for an end to the OAS embargo of Cuba and pushed for creation of an economic front directed at the United States. It cosponsored resolutions to relocate the seat of the OAS from Washington, D.C., to a site in Latin America and to modify the OAS charter to include recognition of the right to ideological pluralism in the Western Hemisphere. Finally, the revolutionary government called for the reorganization of the Inter-American Development Bank to eradicate paternalism, a concept that it defined largely in terms of alleged U.S. control (St John and Gorman 1982: 179–183).

The formal movement toward enhanced subregional cooperation had begun during the first Belaúnde administration with the 1966 Declaration of Bogotá, which committed the signatories to negotiate an agreement for economic integration. The Cartagena Agreement, which established the Andean Common Market or Andean Group, followed three years later. The Andean Group subsequently pursued a number of collective policies consistent with the objectives of the Peruvian government. These included a code for the common treatment of foreign capital, industrial programming among member countries, and the establishment of a common external tariff.

The Peruvian economy clearly reaped important trade advantages from its early participation in the Andean Common Market. Unfortunately, prolonged debate over the implementation of many of its more controversial policies later retarded progress toward meaningful economic integration (Vargas-Hidalgo 1979).

CHANGING POLICY ENVIRONMENT

The 1980s proved to be a challenging decade for the Peruvian government. A wide variety of regional and extraregional forces combined to create a dramatically new policy environment for decisionmakers in Lima. A period of declining tension between the superpowers was followed by the implosion of the Soviet Union and the end of the Cold War. The Third World debt crisis proved especially difficult for Peru, and the Andean Pact encountered new obstacles to integration. Finally, the burgeoning trade in narcotics transformed a serious domestic insurgency into a major foreign policy issue.

The second Belaúnde administration, installed in 1980, reaffirmed the Peruvian commitment to regional cooperation; but its choice of a development model dependent on both the U.S. government and the international financial community slowed progress toward Andean integration. Hamstrung by $9 billion in foreign debt, an International Monetary Fund (IMF) standby agreement, high levels of unemployment, and an acute dependency on the vagaries of commodity export prices, the Peruvian government elected to pursue economic growth under a more open economic system based on tariff reductions and a more liberal policy toward foreign capital. This new economic model called for modifications in the foreign investment code and a suspension or liberalization of sectoral industrial programs. The Peruvian government also lowered tariffs on industrial products, which made progress toward a common industrial tariff, already years behind schedule, virtually impossible. To promote foreign investment, Peru later joined Colombia in liberalizing the regulations governing profit remittances by foreign companies. Finally, the Peruvian government firmly opposed the earlier tendency of the Andean Group to take political stands on nonpact issues (St John 1992b: 207–208).

As Peru struggled to reorder its economic policies, it searched for a more positive relationship with the United States. Unfortunately, the growing ambiguity that characterized U.S.-Peruvian relations, an uncertainty that stemmed from the conflicting demands of Peruvian nationalism and the need for U.S. cooperation to achieve both domestic and foreign policy goals, left little room for sustained improvement. On the economic front, the Belaúnde administration clashed with Washington over levels of economic assistance and U.S. enforcement of countervailing duties on Peruvian textiles. Repeated crises also developed over a dispute with Eastern Airlines concerning carrier routes and landing rights (St John 1984: 305–306).

In addition, the Reagan administration rejected Peruvian support for the Contadora Group, which sought a negotiated solution to the crisis in Central America. In turn, the Peruvian government labeled U.S. policy toward the war in the Falkland Islands as blind and anachronistic and lambasted Washington for its support of Great Britain (Rudolph 1992: 85–86). At one point, President Belaúnde even suggested ousting the United States from the OAS. When the United States invaded Grenada, the Peruvian government deplored the action, condemning interference in the internal affairs of another country.

In the end, the economic problems of Peru, made worse by natural disasters, growing insurgency problems, a burgeoning traffic in narcotics, and bickering within the ruling party, proved more than the Belaúnde administration could manage. With a substantial debt load in place, the effect of the increase in international interest rates in 1981–1982, combined with a sizable drop in the purchasing power of commodity exports, was especially painful for Peru. Higher interest payments and lower export earnings, termed the "scissors effect," caused severe economic problems for the Peruvian government and people. By the time Belaúnde left office in 1985, the rate of inflation approached 200 percent, the highest recorded in Peru to that time, real wages had plunged some 40 percent since 1980, and per capita income was down to the level of the mid-1960s. The external debt approached $14 billion, with full service on the debt requiring all of Peru's 1985 export earnings and an estimated 133 percent of 1986 earnings. In a period of prolonged crisis, the one issue most Peruvians agreed upon was that the new president, Alán García Pérez, was inheriting the worst economic crisis of the century and quite possibly the worst in Peruvian history.

The García administration (1985–1990) quickly concluded that full service on the external debt was unthinkable. In consequence, the Peruvian government soon declared that it would limit interest payments on its debt to 10 percent of export earnings. At the same time, it rejected the IMF as the formal mediator between Peru and its consortium of private lenders. Instead, it promoted collective action by all Latin American states to develop a common approach to the issue of Third World indebtedness. Complementary measures announced by the Peruvian government included a halt to payments on medium- and long-term private foreign debt and a prohibition for two years on the remission abroad of foreign currency derived from profits and royalties. Peru later experienced difficulty in negotiating a common approach to the debt question when most Third World states rejected the 10 percent policy as unworkable (Ferrero Costa 1987: 58–60).

In a conciliatory gesture, the IMF initially stretched its rules and accepted partial payments on the Peruvian debt; however, when the Peruvian government refused to correct its arrears, the IMF declared it ineligible for future loans. The IMF decision spotlighted the existing impasse, and it also formalized Peruvian isolation from foreign government lenders and commercial banks. The IMF cutoff also hampered Peruvian attempts to obtain new loans from the World Bank, one of its few remaining potential sources of outside credit. Matters worsened in 1986 when the World Bank, followed by the Inter-American Development Bank, suspended loan disbursements because Peru was overdue in repaying outstanding debts (Crabtree 1992: 25–68).

Throughout the García presidency, a wide variety of international movements and organizations increasingly consumed the limited resources of the Peruvian government. Consequently, Peruvian foreign affairs assumed an extracontinental dimension that deviated from its traditional focus on regional and subregional issues. After breaking diplomatic relations with the South African government and participating actively in antiapartheid conferences, for example, the foreign minister of Peru was elected president of the UN World Conference on Sanctions Against South Africa in mid-1986. In part to publicize its debt policy, the Peruvian government also took a more active role in the Non-Aligned Movement. For a time, there was even speculation that García might be the next president of the movement, a prospect he did not rule out until late 1988. At the same time, the García administration maintained an independent, if uncritical, posture toward socialist countries. In line with this policy, Peru pursued a closer association with the social democratic groups of Western Europe and hosted the Seventeenth Congress of the Socialist International (Berrios 1986).

In the second half of the decade, the Peruvian government also took a more activist approach to a variety of more traditional international organizations. Viewing the Latin American Economic System (SELA) as an important forum in which to generate support for its economic policies, it hosted the Twelfth SELA Meeting of Foreign Ministers in Lima, where the group provided measured support for the Peruvian position on foreign debt. Peru was also a founding member of the Andean Reserve Fund and promoted the creation of

a Latin American monetary fund to include regional economic powers such as Argentina and Brazil. In the OAS, the Peruvian government proposed the creation of the International Organization for
Latin America and the Caribbean to serve as a permanent mechanism for regional political consultation. However, Lima denounced
the Inter-American Reciprocal Assistance Treaty in 1989 to protest
the U.S. invasion of Panama. Elsewhere, informal political discussion
and networking continued in a number of international forums, including the Contadora Group, the Contadora Support Group, and
the Group of Eight (Ferrero Costa 1987: 73–74).

The activist foreign policy of the García administration, resulting
from both domestic pressures and new international openings, did
little to improve bilateral relations with the United States. Unresolved issues related to the external debt, a civil aviation accord, increased bilateral aid, and protectionist sentiment toward Peruvian
imports had carried over from the previous administration. In addition, new initiatives, such as Peruvian condemnation of U.S. policy in
Central America and the 10 percent repayment policy, put Lima on
a collision course with Washington. Although less than 20 percent of
Peruvian obligations were owed to North American banks, the U.S.
government feared that other debtor nations, where North American
liabilities were considerably larger, might be tempted to adopt the
Peruvian solution. Finally, the García administration frequently employed strong language and a confrontational style in dealing with
the White House. Although much of this rhetoric was probably intended for domestic Peruvian consumption, it exacerbated Peruvian
relations with the United States.

The Maoist Sendero Luminoso, or Shining Path, movement,
which launched a "people's war" in mid-1980, was followed four years
later by the appearance of a second armed organization, the Movi-
miento Revolucionario Tupac Amaru. As the Peruvian government
proceeded to deal firmly with what it rightly viewed as serious threats
to social peace and order, the news media in the United States increasingly focused on the human rights abuses arising from government methods. Additional complications stemmed from the inter-
twining of the coca culture in Peru with the Sendero Luminoso and
the consequences of this development for a U.S. government that, at
the close of the 1980s, had put the war on drugs near the top of its
foreign policy agenda. In September 1989, the Bush administration
announced the Andean Initiative, a five-year strategy that concentrated on the coca producer countries and included military as well
as economic aid. By this time, Sendero Luminoso had consolidated
its position as the de facto government in the coca-ridden Upper Huallaga Valley and thus was a direct challenge to U.S. policy. Although

Sendero's exact relationship to the drug producers and traffickers
active in the region remained controversial, it appeared to be mostly
a marriage of convenience in which both parties shared an interest
in keeping government presence in the region to a minimum. Never
an advocate of the *narcotraficantes*, Sendero generated revenues by
levying a tax on coca paste shipments out of the area while also serv-
ing as a go-between for the region's coca farmers to ensure they
received fair prices for their product (Rudolph 1992: 120–125; Gonzales 1992: 106–125).

PERUVIAN RESPONSE

The economic policies of the García administration set the stage for
the 1990 presidential campaign. The gross domestic product of Peru
dropped by 28 percent from 1987 to 1989 and real wages fell by 60
percent. As the elections approached, government expenditures ran
three times the size of government revenues, and the annual rate of
inflation exceeded 3,500 percent. At the same time, the level of public debt swelled from $14 billion to $20 billion, with the government
unable to maintain even the limited repayment schedule of 10 percent of export earnings defiantly proclaimed in 1985. To make matters worse, by the end of the decade the Peruvian government had
defaulted on approximately $2 billion in loans from the IMF and
other international lending agencies, making it one of the leading
debtor nations in the world (Crabtree 1992: 138–151).

Running as a self-proclaimed political centrist, Alberto Keinya
Fujimori, founder of the Cambio '90 political movement, won a re-
sounding victory in the 1990 presidential elections, garnering almost
57 percent of the popular vote. The deplorable state of the Peruvian
economy was understandably the first priority of his new government. To deal with the problem, Fujimori launched an economic stabilization program, dubbed "Fujishock" by Peruvians, based in large
part on policies he had derided during the election campaign. The
program included liberalizing foreign trade policies through elimi-
nating exchange controls, lifting most import restrictions, and making deep cuts in tariff rates. Overnight the government ended price
controls and subsidies in place for decades, a decision that led to the
steepest one-day price increase in recent Peruvian history (Guillermoprieto 1990: 116–117; *Caretas* 1990: 10–19).

Thereafter, Fujimori pursued orthodox economic policies at
home and abroad in an effort to restore the international standing
of Peru. Domestically, the government moved to contain inflation,
reduce bureaucracy, privatize state companies, increase tax revenues,

and encourage investment. To liberalize commerce and stimulate free trade, it also eliminated tariffs, ended state monopolies, and relaxed restrictions on holding foreign currency. At the same time, it resumed interest payments on international obligations, moved to restore its external credit rating, and pursued new funding sources. Peruvian officials pressed in particular for the creation of a support group of creditor nations willing to make fresh loans to lift Peru out of the current crisis (St John 1992b: 214–215).

The economic policies of the Fujimori regime were largely—if not totally—successful. The far-reaching market reforms carried out after 1991 have led to solid economic growth rates in more recent years. The rate of inflation dropped, the size of the state bureaucracy declined, the labor market was more flexible, and interest rates lowered. In response, the level of foreign investment increased considerably. Peru cleared more than $1.7 billion in arrears to the IMF and the World Bank in the spring of 1993, which resulted in the IMF approving the country's 1993–1995 economic program. The ambitious program of privatization also picked up steam after a slow start with attractive offerings in such areas as mining, telecommunications, and energy. The export sector, however, continued to trail improvements elsewhere, a performance that reflected Peru's ongoing vulnerability to international raw materials prices (*Financial Times* 1994).

The Fujimori administration also pursued a broad policy of regional cooperation and development. President Fujimori attended the Andean Pact Summit in La Paz at the end of 1990, where dialogue centered on how best to reactivate the Andean process. In an upbeat assessment, Fujimori indicated that the participants had made substantive progress toward the common goal of greater Andean integration. With the removal of many trade barriers, trade among Andean Group members was expected to become almost free, with the exception of Ecuador, which was considered a special situation. Citizens of Andean Group states would be able to travel freely with no visa requirements, and tourists would be allowed to travel freely up to three months. Summit participants also agreed to open Andean skies by allowing the airlines of Andean Pact countries to operate freely on routes linking member countries. Finally, Fujimori suggested that the terms of the Andean code governing foreign capital would be modified to provide more equal treatment and thus reduce the concentration of capital in selected countries (U.S. Department of Commerce December 1990: 66–67; November 1990: 36).

The Peruvian president later joined his counterparts from Bolivia, Colombia, Ecuador, and Venezuela for a two-day Andean summit. In the ensuing Declaration of Caracas, the five heads of state agreed to establish a free trade zone beginning in January 1992 and a common market by 1995. They also called for a meeting with the U.S. government to discuss trade, investment, environmental, and drug trafficking questions. At the same time, the Andean leaders urged the U.S. Congress to pass the Andean Trade Preference Act, a ten-year program to grant duty-free access to the United States for goods from the coca-growing members of the Andean Group. Their call highlighted the importance the Andean governments in general and Peru in particular assigned to a broader approach to the drug war that addressed not only the issue of drug trafficking but also the economic development needs of the coca-growing areas (*Caretas* 1991: 26; *Le Monde* 1991).

In August 1991, Peru joined Chile and Mexico in renewing calls for active membership in the Asia-Pacific Economic Cooperation organization, a body rapidly becoming the preeminent forum for that dynamic region. A little over two months later, the five Andean countries, under open pressure from President Fujimori to increase the pace of Andean integration to coincide with Peruvian plans for a more active role in the international economy, agreed to set up a free trade zone and a customs union in 1992. About the same time, representatives of Peru joined other Amazonian nations in agreeing to a joint position before the forthcoming UN Conference on the Environment and Development. Finally, in late February 1992, President Fujimori joined President Bush and five other Latin American leaders in a so-called drug summit to seek new initiatives for regional attacks against the drug war. The Peruvian president had complained in the past that the United States had not provided the economic resources necessary for him to reverse his country's status as the world's leading grower of coca leaf. A related concern that again surfaced was U.S. policy to tie Peruvian aid to performance in meeting antinarcotics targets as well as improvements in human rights (Poole and Renique 1992: 198–202).

Given the increasingly active role of Peruvian diplomacy on both the continental and extracontinental scenes, President Fujimori shocked supporters and opponents alike in April 1992 when he suspended the 1979 constitution, padlocked congress, and dismantled the judiciary. His suppression of democracy, intended in part to stifle opposition to economic reforms and to facilitate a tougher campaign against terrorism, dealt a severe blow to the political credibility his administration had been building (McClintock 1984: 1–25). The ensuing political crisis also aggravated the growing rift among Andean Group members, which had been struggling to reach a broader consensus on economic matters. The impact of the so-called *autogolpe* was especially damaging to subregional relations because the Fujimori administration almost immediately withdrew from the

Andean Common Market's tariff reduction plan, a key element in regional trade integration efforts. Suspending the program to extend customs preferences for Andean products, the Peruvian government stated its intention to apply regular import tariffs of 15–25 percent to products from Bolivia, Colombia, Ecuador, and Venezuela (*Business Latin America* 1992).

The Colombian government responded to the change in import tariff policy with an announcement that it was canceling Andean trade preferences granted earlier to Peru. Diplomatic relations with Ecuador were already tense, as another flare-up in the eternal border dispute again raised the prospect of armed conflict. Trade relations between Peru and Ecuador were in limbo; and in part for this reason, Ecuador had earlier refused to commit itself to the common external tariff. The autogolpe did not result in an automatic suspension of commercial relations between Peru and its neighbors, but the Andean Group members were understandably reluctant to legitimize Fujimori's actions by concluding new economic agreements with Peru. The Peruvian crisis was thus a setback for group objectives to unify customs and trade regimes, and its effects threatened to damage future Andean integration efforts. The OAS urged a swift return to democracy but avoided imposing sanctions. In so doing, it lent a measure of support to the Peruvian president despite the widespread disapproval of the autogolpe voiced by OAS members (Poole and Renique 1992: 165).

At an August 1992 ministerial meeting of the Andean Group, the Fujimori government proposed that Peru withdraw from active group participation for a two-year period. The possibility of this step had been under discussion since late May, when the Peruvian minister of agriculture had suggested a temporary retreat on account of the adverse effects of preferential tariffs on the Peruvian agricultural sector. Less than one month later, the Peruvian government opposed a common external tariff at an Andean Group meeting in Quito. The withdrawal decision resulted in Peru losing most tariff advantages of the Andean market. It also delayed any possible Peruvian participation in other regional economic integration efforts such as the Southern Cone Common Market (U.S. Department of Commerce August 1992: 2; *Caretas* 1992: 21).

The Peruvian government tried to put a positive face on the decision to withdraw from the Andean Group. President Fujimori emphasized that the Peruvian decision to suspend its obligations was a temporary measure that did not signal a permanent policy change. He added that the decison to withdraw was taken only after consultation with Andean Group members and was largely due to the different rates of stabilization prevailing in member states. Other Peruvian officials argued that the agricultural sector of Peru, in particular, was in need of a transition period. The Peruvian minister of industry also attacked the notion that Peru was actually withdrawing from the Andean Group, because it remained an associate member. Acknowledging that Peru had suspended activities in important areas of integration, he argued that the total integration process was much broader than those few areas and would continue without Peruvian participation. At the same time, he emphasized that Andean trade had not markedly benefited Peru, as imports from the member states were growing much faster than Peruvian exports to them. The Andean Group later agreed in mid-1994, when common tariffs were scheduled to take effect, to allow Peru to rejoin the organization (*Wall Street Journal* 1994; U.S. Department of Commerce September 1992: 37).

Following its withdrawal from the Andean Pact, the Peruvian government negotiated new bilateral trade agreements with several neighboring states, including Colombia, Ecuador, and Venezuela. Negotiations with Bolivia resulted in an agreement in which Peru gave Bolivia a duty-free port and an industrial park at the Peruvian port of Ilo in return for similar facilities at Puerto Suarez on the Paraguay River. The two governments later concluded additional agreements to promote economic development in these areas as well as around Lake Titicaca. Elsewhere, economic integration in Latin America went forward at a surprising pace, with new trade pacts announced on a regular basis. Most Latin American governments argued that the proliferation of free trade areas, customs unions, and bilateral trade deals supported an open regionalism in which the Latin American states would intensify regional relationships while remaining open to the outside world. Other observers worried that the haphazard network of subregional trade alliances that were forming could become stumbling blocks as well as building blocks to a hemispheric free trade zone (St John 1994: 67; *El Comercio* 1994).

CONCLUSION

Over the past twenty-five years, Peruvian foreign policy appeared to move in totally new directions. A succession of administrations addressed new or unfamiliar issues, adopted fresh approaches, and consummated new bilateral and multilateral relationships. The Peruvian government expanded trade links, diversified arms transfers, pushed for enhanced subregional economic cooperation, and advocated radical reform of the inter-American economic and political system. In the process, intractable social, political, and economic problems, compounded by a prolonged insurgency, increasingly undermined any sustained redirection of Peruvian foreign policy. An examination of the current crisis in the light of historical experience highlights the remarkable extent to which the central concerns of contemporary Peruvian external policy remain core issues faced since independence.

In this sense, the past decade and a half can be seen as a historical high point in the evolution of Peruvian foreign policy but not as a time when there was a sharp break between past, present, and future. While there has been change in recent times, the extent and permanence of this change can be—and often has been—greatly overstated. Most of the policy developments after 1968—and this is especially true in the case of regionalism—have a clear parentage in earlier decades. To this degree, Peruvian foreign policy today is somewhat atypical for the region in that it is not experiencing the same degree of realignment and reorientation as is the external policy of some of its Latin American neighbors.

Many Peruvians in recent years welcomed a wider involvement in subregional, regional, and extraregional affairs as a concrete expression of enhanced independence, especially from the overall influence of the United States. At the same time, wider participation in international bodies carried with it new and sometimes unforeseen restraints to economic and political autonomy. Increasingly, the Peruvian government has been forced to accommodate the conflicting demands of domestic politics, Andean associations, and the inter-American system. This adjustment has been complicated both by the widening influence of the United States in and out of Latin America and by the growing involvement of the Peruvian government in the world beyond the inter-American system.

Trade barriers and other artificial trade restrictions are today tumbling throughout Latin America, but the full direction and extent of the change, as well as the degree to which it will be institutionalized, remains uncertain. The current period again brings mixed signals from Latin America in general and Peru in particular. The Peruvian government appears committed to a policy of freer trade as evidenced by the growing number of bilateral trade agreements it has recently negotiated. At the same time, it remains tied to a measured renewal of subregional integration in the traditional form such efforts took in the 1960s and 1970s. However, the degree of commitment to a higher level of transaction, involving the cultural, diplomatic, scientific, or security spheres, and possibly accompanied by limited institutional arrangements, is unclear but probably not high. There seems to be little consensus in Peru today to move in this direction and certainly none demanding movement at an accelerated pace. Equally important, given the enormous economic, social, and political problems still facing the Peruvian government, the development of a deeper form of regionalism is unlikely to be accorded a high priority in the immediate future. Consequently, Peru is most likely to accommodate the rising tide of hemispheric free trade agreements and regain full participation in the Andean Pact but remain wary of greater institutionalized ties in noneconomic spheres, in particular the political arena.

8

Brazil's Response to the "New Regionalism"

◆

Maria Regina Soares de Lima

Two different experiences in regionalism coexisted in Latin America into the 1980s: hemispheric, or inter-American, cooperation between the United States and the countries of Latin America and intraregional cooperation among the countries of South and Central America.

The former, born with the Monroe Doctrine's form of Pan-Americanism in the nineteenth century and modified by the Roosevelt Corollary at the beginning of the twentieth century, reached its peak with the formation of the postwar inter-American system, after the signing of the Inter-American Reciprocal Assistance Treaty in 1947 and the creation of the Organization of American States (OAS) in 1948.

From the late 1940s to the early 1980s, economics was of secondary importance in inter-American regionalism. The Alliance for Progress failed in the 1960s because of the lack of serious efforts by U.S. government elites and/or the contradictory combination of reformist rhetoric and counterreformist policies. During the Johnson administration, members of Congress and part of the business community allied with inter-American officials to advocate a free trade area in the Western Hemisphere, along with U.S. nonreciprocal trade concessions for Latin American manufactured goods. This proposal was scuttled by decisionmakers responsible for U.S. foreign economic policy; they were absolutely opposed to preferential trading arrangements with Latin America or any other region on account of the resultant discrimination for other developing countries outside the hemisphere and U.S. "worldwide interests and responsibilities."[1]

Intraregional cooperation was also political in nature when it first emerged as an expression of the Bolívarian current of Pan-Americanism early in the nineteenth century. Its aims included the creation of

137

an inter-American legal system—to make up for the legacy of political fragmentation left to the region by the process of political independence—as well as security objectives. By the end of that century, the Bolívarian current had merged with the Monroe Doctrine under the explicit hegemony of the latter; European influence thus gave way to incipient U.S. influence.

    U.S. predominance in Latin America in the twentieth century, initially economic and increasingly political and military, discouraged intraregional cooperation initiatives until the 1960s, a decade that witnessed the establishment of the Latin American Free Trade Association (LAFTA, 1960), the Central American Common Market (1960), and the Andean Pact (1969). Although intraregional in nature, these initiatives did enjoy Washington's blessings, given the prospect of growing regional trade opportunities for U.S. exports. However, the import substitution model adopted by Latin American countries—which penalized exports and virtually eliminated these countries' complementarities—together with economic imbalances among regional partners, led to limited successes and the early decline of the region's first attempt at economic integration. In 1980 LAFTA was replaced by the Latin American Integration Association (ALADI), which brought a greater degree of pragmatism and flexibility to intraregional economic cooperation and allowed for bilateral integration arrangements between member countries, whereby concessions did not necessarily have to be extended to all other members.

    Intraregional cooperation in the 1980s, while maintaining its economic objectives, highlighted the political dimension of Latin American consensus building around such issues as opposition to U.S. policies in Central America, coordination of common economic viewpoints vis-à-vis the United States, and the sharing of each nation's perspectives on the debt problem. The Contadora Group, organized in 1983 and complemented by the Contadora Support Group, the 1986 Group of Eight, which later became the Rio Group, and the Cartagena Consensus were all initiatives in this direction.

    Since the late 1980s and early 1990s, regionalism in the Americas has undergone profound changes. In the first place, political considerations have yielded to the prominence of economic objectives and motivations. In the second place, the progress of regionalism in the Americas has been increasingly regulated by U.S. actions and inactions.[2]

    The first section of this chapter presents the historical background to Brazilian regional cooperation. Then the Brazilian position in relation to the "new regionalism" in the Americas is discussed. The third section analyzes the evolution of regionalism in

Brazilian foreign policy since the mid-1980s. This is followed by an examination of regionalism from the perspective of Brazilian civil society. In the conclusion, the relationship between Brazilian foreign policy and regionalism is appraised in terms of global, regional, and domestic changes, as well as macroeconomic policy realignments.

BRAZIL AND REGIONAL COOPERATION: HISTORICAL BACKGROUND

During the nineteenth century, the Brazilian monarchy's foreign policy was clearly focused on Europe, and support for Pan-Americanism was, at best, discreet. Brazil's form of government, at variance with the republics in other Latin American countries, was another impediment to its participation in Pan-Americanism. The political realism of Brazil's imperial rulers put them at odds with Latin purposes they believed were idealistic, and Brazil showed no interest in participating in defense pacts, though its neutrality did not keep it from extending political support to other Latin Americans.

The advent of the Brazilian republic (1889) coincided with a period of U.S. hegemony through Pan-Americanism, which was becoming an instrument for U.S. economic expansion. Under the republic, Brazilian foreign policy came to revolve around Americanism, not to be confused with the North Americanization of the country's international relations, since Brazil's attention was also turned toward the rest of South America. During Baron Rio Branco's term as minister of foreign affairs (1902–1912), "the nexus of Brazilian diplomacy [shifted] definitively from London to Washington" (Cervo and Bueno 1992: 149–181). It was under Rio Branco that the "special alliance" with the United States was conceived as a paradigm that, with some variations in emphasis, would endure into the early 1960s. According to this outlook, the United States was seen as a global, hegemonic power in the Western Hemisphere and a focal point for Brazilian foreign policy. In particular, the United States was considered a tacit ally capable of enhancing Brazil's bargaining power with its Hispanic neighbors. This Americanist thrust under the republic suppressed any impulses toward intraregional cooperation. Relations with other Latin American countries were "subordinated" to the special relationship with the United States, or, as one observer put it, "In this context, the symmetric axis was clearly subordinate to the axis of asymmetry" (Ricupero 1993). Because of this orientation, there have been constant accusations, from Hispanic American foreign offices, of Brazilian hegemonic pretensions over the region. Early in the century, Rio Branco sought to neutralize these concerns by means of an *entente cordiale* involving Brazil, Argentina, and Chile. This pact was not a mechanism for counterbalancing North American influence, however, and was fully in tune with the U.S. government (Cervo and Bueno 1992: 177–178).

By virtue of the special alliance paradigm, intensified through close collaboration between Brazil and the United States during World War II, intraregional cooperation policies were subordinate to hemispheric cooperation. Brazil was an important ally for the United States in the piecing together of the political and military aspects of the inter-American system. Significantly, whenever Brazil chose to question the basis of this special relationship, for example during the periods of "independent foreign policy" (1961–1963) and "responsible pragmatism" (1974–1979), it strengthened its ties with Latin America within the framework of a more globalistic strategy for international relations.

Over the past three decades, Brazil's approach toward regional cooperation has been heavily influenced by the country's regional economic weight and strength and by the nature of the country's political regime. The scale of Brazil's economy compared with that of other countries in the region has historically been a factor inhibiting intraregional cooperation; other Latin American countries perceive a potential threat in Brazil's geoeconomic dimensions, and Brazil's own elite seems to nourish a belief that the country was "fated" to have its own independent destiny. Thus its vast land area and natural resources have, it seems, helped ground Brazil's behavior in two fundamental assumptions: the first is that sovereign, independent actions and policies grow out of a resource base strong enough for the country to "face the world on its own" and the second is that Brazil would have little to gain from relations with Latin American countries whose pace of economic and social development were similar to its own (Jaguaribe 1974: 116; Martins 1975).

The nature of its political regime has also influenced Brazil's outlook on regionalism. Until the political détente of the Ernesto Geisel government (1974–1979), policies toward Latin America were heavily conditioned by the military regime's definitions concerning "security." Behavior based on concepts of "ideological frontiers" set Brazil against countries like Mexico, Venezuela, and Peru, which advocated "ideological pluralism." Following the 1964 military coup and the return to automatic alignment with the United States and participation in the "hemispheric security system," Brazil came to be viewed by the other Latin countries as the region's "subimperialist" power and a "preferential ally" of the United States.

Brazil's rigorously bilateral behavior and the prevalence of a diplomacy based on ideological frontiers in Latin America concurred with the "economic miracle" years of the late 1960s and early 1970s, all of which heightened the mistrust of other Latin countries regarding Brazilian hegemonic designs over the region. The progressive decline of the economic situation, the foreign debt crisis, the oil price hikes, and the revival of protectionism in industrialized markets were decisive factors in changing foreign policy guidelines following the mid-1970s.

For the first sixty years of the twentieth century, Brazilian foreign policy systematically subordinated cooperation with South and Central American countries to cooperation with the United States. Despite the independent foreign policy that put this relationship into question during the early 1960s, and despite Brazil's distancing itself from the special alliance with the United States, twenty-one years of military rule, combined with the economic disparity between Brazil and the Spanish-speaking countries, kept regionalism out of the country's priorities from the late 1960s into the 1980s.

It took the consolidation of the democratization process and the aggravation of Brazil's international economic vulnerability to make closer ties with Latin America possible. During the 1980s the country was more active in Latin American consensus-building processes that, notwithstanding the vulnerability of most Latin American countries, pointed toward the emergence of a collective Latin American identity, one enhanced by the almost total return of democracy to the region. The transition from military to civilian government also fostered Brazil's wholehearted return to intraregional cooperation.

THE NEW LATIN AMERICAN REGIONALISM AND BRAZIL

Present-day regionalism in Latin America is based on proposals for economic cooperation and integration. A variety of factors, including political and economic processes at regional and global levels, have been flagged by way of explaining the advancement of regionalism in the 1990s. Structural changes in the world economy, particularly the globalization of markets and production, as well as the exponential leap in the rate of technological progress, have changed the map of competitive advantages in the global geoeconomic order. Together with the crisis of multilateralism and the end of bipolar politics at the end of the 1980s, these changes have given rise to various forms of economic regionalism and supranational arrangements.

In Latin America—in part because of these global changes and in part because of the fiscal crisis of the state, a corollary to the foreign debt crisis—the 1980s marked the exhaustion of import substitution. Behind this depletion were the loss of the state's inducement and financing capacity, the difficulty (partially due to foreign pressures) of sustaining closed and protected markets, and chronic macroeconomic imbalances. This was the setting in which Brazil, by the end of the decade, had to recognize the collapse of the development model that had carried it into industrialization.

Throughout Latin America, the negative outcome of the 1980s was perceived by policymakers and the interested public as a reason for the region's exclusion from the emerging geoeconomic order. Contributing to this outlook were a decline in Latin America's relative share of global trade, finance and investment outflows resulting from the region's decade-long macroeconomic instability, the resurgence of economic regionalism, and the end of the Cold War.

By the mid-1980s, economic regionalism had once again become a foreign policy priority in Latin America, a priority reflected in the establishment of the Program of Cooperation between Brazil and Argentina in 1986 and in the movements to revitalize the Central American Common Market and the Andean Pact. The turn of the decade brought a wave of trade agreements among Latin American countries. Import liberalization policies, following the crisis of earlier import substitution strategies, made it easier for these projects to flourish, their aim being to strengthen the global competitiveness of the participating countries. In addition to the existing Southern Cone Common Market (MERCOSUR) and the Andean Pact, the 1990s have brought about at least six concrete or projected free trade agreements among ALADI nations under the banner of intraregional cooperation (Pereira 1993: 32; Hurrell 1992; Bouzas and Lustig 1992).

The origins of Latin America's new economic regionalism can thus be traced to a defensive response to global and domestic changes. Yet it was the resurgence of hemispheric cooperation, with the Enterprise for the Americas Initiative in 1990 and the succession of developments beginning in 1989 and resulting in the Free Trade Agreement/North American Free Trade Agreement (FTA/NAFTA), that imposed a qualitative shift in the nature of Latin American regionalism. Following these U.S. initiatives, intraregional and hemispheric cooperation, which had advanced separately and even in conflict with each other since the postwar period, were once again brought together.

Since then, relations between the two forms of regionalism have become a key issue on Latin America's foreign policy agenda. With almost the sole exception of Brazil, Latin American countries have come to think of their respective subregional cooperation arrangements as steps toward hemispheric integration. Specifically, it was Mexico's 1990 decision to join a free trade agreement with the

United States that tipped the scales in favor of hemispheric cooperation. The foremost reason for this was that Mexico's new alignment rekindled the region's fears of economic exclusion and implied a "diversion of trade and investment towards Mexico." At the same time, "Mexico's 'defection' undercuts the political and economic viability of a purely Latin American form of regionalism . . . [by shifting] the balance of power between North and South America" (Hurrell 1992: 127).

From the Brazilian perspective, it has become more important to strengthen subregional and regional cooperative initiatives in trade and security issues. Thus, Brazil does not consider MERCOSUR necessarily a step toward hemispheric integration, nor does it view the Quadripartite Nuclear Agreement with Argentina and the International Atomic Energy Agency (IAEA) as a preliminary stage toward adhering to the Non-Proliferation Treaty (NPT). Brazil has also been uneasy with U.S. proposals for the enlargement of the interventionist instruments and powers of the OAS (Hirst and Soares de Lima 1994).

In light of the spectacular realignment of Latin American foreign policies vis-à-vis the United States and the inclusion of those countries in the current of hemispheric cooperation, the Brazilian exception can be explained both by structural factors and by certain features of its foreign policy. Several political and economic factors help clarify why regionalism is not Brazil's exclusive choice for foreign policy in general and foreign economic policy in particular.

There are two major structural factors at work. First, important transformations in Brazil's industrial structures during the thirty years that followed World War II have created a significant economic base, the most diversified in the region. Second, the country's trade flows, both imports and exports, have attained a relatively high degree of geographic diversification (see Table 8.1). This trade is, moreover, relatively diversified in terms of composition, as it covers a considerable range of production sectors.

Thanks to these fairly diversified markets—considering, in particular, the relative shares of Latin America, the United States, and the European Community—Brazil has come to be classified as a "global trader," although its share of world trade as a whole has historically remained around 1.0 percent or 1.5 percent. More noteworthy are the policy implications of being a global trader: a weaker preference for regional trade associations because of concerns about possible trade deviations in a clearly regionalistic strategy and the systematic defense of trade multilateralism (Barbosa and Panelli César 1994b: 308).

Foreign policy factors have complemented the structural conditions that underlie Brazil's placing a low priority on regionalism,

Table 8.1   Regional Distribution of Brazil's Foreign Trade, 1980 and 1992

	Exports		Imports	
	1980 (%)	1992 (%)	1980 (%)	1992 (%)
Latin America	17.9	22.3	12.0	18.3
European Economic Community	26.5	29.6	15.3	22.3
United States	17.1	19.3	17.8	23.8
Asia	9.9	15.5	6.8	8.4
Middle East	5.2	3.6	33.9	13.8

Source: Secretaria de Comércio Exterior/MIC, reproduced in Barbosa and Panelli César (1994b: 308).

particularly the lack of Brazilian involvement in the hemispheric current of Latin American regionalism.

The first such factor is the close link between economic development strategies and foreign policy guidelines in Brazil's postwar international relations. This relationship arose out of two historical trends that continue to influence the way Brazil thinks of itself in relation to the rest of the world. That there is room for economic development at the top of the foreign policy agenda is largely due to Brazil's having favorably resolved all its border conflicts and disputes with neighboring countries before the turn of the century. Thus, unhampered by territorial irritants, which tend to rigidify a country's diplomatic behavior, Brazil could better concentrate on industrialization. Furthermore, the establishment of a bureaucracy specialized in handling the country's international affairs during the first three decades of the twentieth century has allowed the country to take a more long-term view in its diplomatic policymaking and to focus on development priorities in its foreign policy agenda. The convergence of structural economic factors and political considerations has therefore been a cornerstone of contemporary Brazilian diplomacy.[3]

The other foreign policy factor resides in a trait of Brazil's diplomatic style, one that favors flexibility in policymaking and the broadening of available international options, such that the possibility of future choices is kept open. Of course, concerns about external constraints on a nation's freedom of choice are common to all states in the international system. Brazil's diplomatic style, however, has traditionally been guided by an excessive preoccupation with maintaining policy options and by a defensive commitment to cooperative arrangements. Although the defense of multilateralism in matters of foreign trade policy has been a pillar of Brazil's approach, in other affairs, such as Latin American control and security regimes, its adherence to multilateral principles and institutions has been much more restrictive and case-by-case.

Part of the explanation for this style, typical of the self-help logic of the state system, lies in the country's sheer vastness, which has strengthened the "inward orientation" prevalent in the political culture, along with a belief in "self-sufficiency." Specific historical circumstances in Latin America have given rise not only to a mutual mistrust between Brazil and its neighbors but also to the belief among Brazilian elites in the "uniqueness" of their country in relation to other countries of the region.[4] Until the 1970s, this uniqueness was valued by the diplomatic corps as an asset in bilateral relations with the United States. Since then it has been used to justify political and economic foreign policy stands taken independently by Brazil vis-à-vis the United States.

Yet if these economic and political factors illuminate Brazil as a quasi-exception in the context of the new Latin American regionalism, how can one explain that it was precisely an initiative by Brazil, along with Argentina, that produced this new cycle of regionalism?

First, the 1986 Program of Cooperation with Argentina, and all of Brazil's subsequent regional cooperation initiatives, were designed to complement its international strategy, which was centered on preserving and broadening the *multilateral* nature of its economic participation in the world order. Second, the regional cooperation initiative launched in 1985, though based on economic considerations, was more fundamentally political in its motivations. The aforementioned linkage between development strategies and foreign policy is not necessarily premised on economic determinism or the subordination of politics to economics. Economic regionalism was placed on the foreign policy agenda in the mid-1980s at the initiative of the government—specifically the Foreign Relations Ministry—for essentially political reasons.

THE EVOLUTION OF REGIONALISM
IN BRAZILIAN FOREIGN POLICY

In terms of the political and economic principles underlying Brazil's initiatives in regional cooperation, three major phases need to be discussed: the Program of Cooperation with Argentina begun during the José Sarney administration, the establishment of MERCOSUR during the Fernando Collor de Mello administration, and the move toward South American economic integration under President Itamar Franco. My objective is not to arrive at an exhaustive analysis of these historical moments but rather to point out, in the underlying

political and economic assumptions of each one, differences that reflect specific contextual constraints and factors—both global and regional—as well as various domestic political considerations.

Democratization and Cooperation with Argentina

On November 29, 1985, Raul Alfonsín and José Sarney, the two civilian presidents who succeeded the military regimes in Argentina and
Brazil, respectively, inaugurated the international bridge linking the
city of Porto Meira in Brazil to Puerto Iguaçú in Argentina. In the
history of the Southern Cone, that gesture symbolizes the end of
decades of tension and the beginning of unprecedented cooperation
between the two countries, developments made possible by their return to democratic regimes.

The Declaration of Iguaçú committed Argentina and Brazil to
participating jointly in multilateral forums, particularly in Latin
America; to reviving and expanding areas of political and economic
cooperation—including nuclear power—within the River Plate Basin;
and to accelerating the process of bilateral integration. The official
announcement of the Brazil-Argentina Economic Integration and
Cooperation Program (PICAB) came in July 1986 and included a
friendship declaration, twelve protocols, and a joint declaration on
nuclear policy. Over the following years, twelve more protocols were
signed, covering political, military, economic, technological, and cultural affairs.[5]

This unprecedented entry into cooperation in the River Plate
Basin was an initiative taken particularly by the two governments' foreign offices. On the Brazilian side, the diplomatic sector in charge of
coordinating official actions with other, notably economic, authorities was largely responsible for the PICAB's design and execution.
This intrabureaucratic coordination was enhanced, on the one hand,
by a political climate in which the purposes of the economic authorities were clearly identified with those of the diplomatic corps and,
on the other hand, by explicit support from the president's office.
Despite the initiative's major economic dimensions, business leaders
did not play a significant role in the program's formulation. Indeed,
here lies one of the differences between the Southern Cone process
of integration and the FTA/NAFTA process: in the Southern Cone,
little was heard at the outset from business interests about trade flows
between Brazil and Argentina (Tavares de Araújo 1990a); cooperation was much more the fruit of a political will to intensify bilateral
relations, with a view to leveraging the two countries' bargaining
powers in international negotiations. Diplomatic authorities saw the
return to democracy as both a guarantee of the initiative's success

and a means to propel the two countries into the international arena.

This very innovative, politically driven cooperation anticipated the post–Cold War trend toward a relaxation of regional tensions in several parts of the world. PICAB created the working group on nuclear policy, which gave rise to a permanent committee in April 1988. Joint initiatives in this field have gone beyond the simple coordination of international positions or scientific and technological cooperation; they now include mechanisms of confidence building that have begun a cycle of mutual trust on nuclear issues. Although cooperation in nuclear technology has not yet advanced significantly, these first steps toward establishing confidence-building measures gave Brazilian-Argentine cooperation a particular status among nuclear control and nonproliferation regimes. Furthermore, the arrival of civilian governments in both countries made it possible for the first time to institute mutual inspection mechanisms through the signing of a safeguards agreement in November 1990, their respective military establishments having long resisted full integration in the strategic military sphere (Hirst 1990b: 40–45).[6]

The economic component of this bilateral cooperation was somewhat less innovative. Initially, bilateral integration aimed for an intensification of bilateral trade preferences negotiated under the aegis of ALADI—in the context of closed economies—and sector-by-sector negotiations leading to greater trade and industrial complementarity in some sectors, particularly capital goods.[7] The years 1986 and 1987 were the peak period of PICAB activity, measured by both the number of specific initiatives and the actual growth of bilateral trade. In November 1988, when most of the protocols were still in the early stages of execution, the two governments moved to consolidate them in a Treaty of Integration, Cooperation, and Development, with the objective of creating a "common economic space" within ten years. The PICAB, however, was facing serious problems on account of the economic and political crises in both countries during the 1988–1990 period. The breakdown of the "Cruzado" stabilization plan in Brazil and the country's foreign reserve crisis brought back restrictive import policies; consequently, domestic support for a program of integration with Argentina was undermined. So by the end of the Sarney administration, both governments were clearly downplaying integration (Hirst 1990b: 5–20).

MERCOSUR and Hemispheric Cooperation

We have seen that regionalism was reintroduced into Brazilian foreign policy in the mid-1980s for political and economic reasons, mainly as the result of endogenous factors. But the Buenos Aires Declaration (July 1990), the decision to advance by five years the deadline set in the 1988 integration treaty for the inauguration of a free trade zone, and, in accordance with the March 1992 Asunción Treaty, Brazil's creation of MERCOSUR with Argentina, Uruguay, and Paraguay were events motivated by a combination of political and economic considerations rooted in both exogenous and endogenous factors.

The creation of MERCOSUR can thus be seen as a response to the potential effects of other regionalization processes, especially NAFTA, on the Southern Cone economies. The initiative also reflected the convergent political outlooks of Argentina's and Brazil's two new presidents, inaugurated, respectively, in mid-1989 and early 1990. In their determination to carry out a series of market-oriented reforms (and, in Brazil's case, to turn the page once and for all on the state-led model of a closed economy), the two leaders sought to link their foreign policies and foreign economic policies to domestic adjustment and restructuring policies. This intention was behind Brazil's efforts to clean up its bilateral agenda with Washington and its goal of making MERCOSUR compatible with trade liberalization policies. To this end, the focus and the tools of integration were reworked; hence, the replacement of sectoral protocols by an approach based on across-the-board trade liberalization (Pereira 1993; Hirst 1991; Camargo 1993).

But the agreements signed at that time went beyond the mere creation of a free trade area in the Southern Cone. The Asunción Treaty set December 31, 1994, as the deadline for the establishment of a common market that would have major implications: the free circulation of goods, people, services, and capital; the adoption of common external tariffs and trade policies by member states; and the harmonization of their national laws when necessary. The treaty also set up a relatively complex institutional structure comprising a higher deliberating body, the Common Market Council; an executive agency, the Common Market Group; several working groups for subareas; a political body, the Joint Parliamentary Commission; and an arbitration forum for dispute settlement (Almeida 1992, 1993; Fonseca 1994).

MERCOSUR's wide-ranging and ambitious goals were criticized at the time because of the prevalent macroeconomic imbalances in Brazil and Argentina. Objections were raised as to the short period of time set by the treaty to harmonize their respective economic policies. A similar process in Europe, in an environment of stable economies, had taken over three decades. According to critics, it would have made more economic sense to temporarily reduce the initiative's scope to a free trade treaty and set longer deadlines for the creation of a common market (Tavares de Araújo 1991: 177–178).

Hindsight, however, lends weight to the argument that what at the time appeared to be economically irrational was, on the contrary, the product of a political rationale. The idea was to preserve the "spirit" of the 1985 Declaration of Iguaçú: a multidimensional cooperation (political, economic, diplomatic, and cultural) between Brazil and Argentina, with the goal, among other things, of increasing the bargaining leverage of both countries in the international arena. The July 1990 meeting was in fact aimed at Brazil and Argentina achieving a joint position in the face of President Bush's Enterprise for the Americas Initiative (Nunes Amorim and Prata Saint-Clair Pimentel 1993: 22, 52–57).

In response to the potential attractions of the so-called Bush Plan, the concern of the Foreign Relations Ministry was how to avoid a "disorderly reaction by countries involved in the process of creating a sub-regional common market." Brazil's negotiating strategy had at least three objectives in mind: The first was to avoid Argentina's defection; an Argentine decision to go it alone in negotiations with the United States would considerably interfere with efforts at subregional integration. Brazil's second goal was to maintain the linkage between the three dimensions of the Bush Plan—debt, investments, and trade—while also introducing the issue of "access to technology." The third objective was to ensure that the four MERCOSUR countries presented a unified position in order to enhance their bargaining power with Washington. The institutional solution found was a "bilateral" agreement between the United States and the four countries, the so-called 4+1 Agreement, signed in Washington in June 1991 (Nunes Amorim and Prata Saint-Clair Pimentel 1993: 21–28, 58–66; Nunes Amorim 1991; Castrioto de Azambuja 1991).

Despite the Collor de Mello government's penchant for carrying liberal restructuring to an extreme and its desire to converge with U.S. positions in areas such as sensitive technology, intellectual property, and computer-industry policies, on the issue of regionalism, the political outlook of the Foreign Relations Ministry prevailed.

Apart from the designs of Brazilian foreign policy, however, proposals to create a hemispheric free trade area in the Americas have gained ground in the wake of NAFTA. Brazil's position has differed from that of the vast majority of Latin American countries, which have begun to conceive of their various plans for subregional integration as steps toward hemispheric integration. By contrast, discussions in Brazil involving diplomats, academics, politicians, business representatives, and bureaucrats have keyed in on two issues: (1) the advantages and, especially, the disadvantages of joining NAFTA and

(2) the consequent significance and role of MERCOSUR. The debate centers mainly on the following points: the considerable restraints on the country's capacity for international initiatives if it were to join NAFTA; a reduction or even loss of autonomy in policymaking on new issues emphasized by the United States, such as intellectual property, services, and investments and on issues such as the environment, science and technology, and macroeconomic policies; and, finally, given the lack of any institutional arrangements in this model for hemispheric integration, the asymmetric bargaining positions, weighted in favor of the United States (Departamento de Integração 1993; Abreu e Lima Florêncio 1992; Chaloult 1993).

The prevailing opinion on the role of MERCOSUR is that, in order to ensure a stronger position in hypothetical negotiations on a convergence with NAFTA, Brazil should make consolidating a subregional arrangement a priority. The point would be to preserve the intrinsic differences between the two approaches to integration. Those who share this skeptical assessment of the implications of joining NAFTA point to fallacies in the thesis that the world economy is inexorably moving toward a division into megablocs; they also dispute the inevitability of joining one of those blocs. They argue that Brazil is a "global trader" whose integration should be multifaceted and that the country therefore should not take part in regionalistic initiatives that might weaken a multilateral approach, which is still at the top of the agenda for economic diplomacy. Nevertheless, the potential advantages of MERCOSUR-NAFTA negotiations have not been forgotten: a better access to the North American market, the increased pull of direct investment, and external anchorage for stabilization policies.[8]

The issue of regionalism during the Collor de Mello administration suggests that the Itamaraty, the Department of Foreign Affairs, was not entirely alienated from foreign policymaking under that government (Nogueira Batista 1993; Lafer 1993b). Regarding subregional policy in particular, the new government's emphasis on trade did not mean abandoning the multidimensional approach to integration that was favored by its diplomats' "founding fathers"; at the same time, despite the catastrophe-ridden Collor de Mello presidency, a relative consensus reigned among domestic political and economic actors on the limits and, particularly, the costs of maintaining an autarkical approach within an ever more globalized economy. A new vision of economic integration as a springboard to better competitiveness in the world economy was clearly emerging among diplomatic and economic officials in the early 1990s, in contrast to the previous import substitution approach.

The Brazilian government's wait-and-see strategy proved correct in terms of foreign policy objectives.[9] On the one hand, uncertainties in the NAFTA process itself—such as the U.S. executive's difficulties in ratifying the agreement in Congress—confirmed Brazilian doubts as to the capacity of the United States to actually achieve a hemispheric free trade zone. In addition, the series of concessions made by Mexico in its negotiations with the United States strengthened the hand of those who, from the outset of the Enterprise for the Americas Initiative, had been skeptical about the intrinsic virtues of hemispheric cooperation.

South America and Beyond

Regarding the third key moment in Brazilian regionalism, it is clear that political motives overrode those of an economic nature.

The Amazon Initiative, announced in 1992, and, in particular, Brazil's intention to create a South American Free Trade Area (SAFTA), announced in October 1993, are clear indications of the importance that Itamar Franco's government attributed to intraregional cooperation. Experience with the "new regionalism" in the Americas has geographically redefined intraregional cooperation to cover South America as a continent. Both the extension of Brazil's regionalism beyond the MERCOSUR subregion so as to include South America as a whole and the renewed interest in the deepening of MERCOSUR–European Union economic cooperation in future negotiations have brought into relief Brazil's foreign policy agenda as to the "new regionalism": defense of multilateralism and multifaceted integration (Barbosa and Panelli César 1994a; Denot Medeiros 1994).

Notwithstanding the economic and trade potential of this movement toward the north of South America or the economic rationale for creating SAFTA, the Franco government's South American regionalism can only be understood in light of the political motivations that brought it into being. These motivations are both defensive and offensive in nature.

In terms of defense, the push into the rest of South America can be seen as a foreign policy strategy of "retreating forward" during what for Itamar Franco's government was a particularly troubled period marked by macroeconomic instability, a paralysis in executive decisionmaking, and an overcrowded agenda in congress. As post-impeachment unity waned, the resurgence of domestic problems was amplified by external difficulties, particularly in the new government's relations with the United States. There were two principal reasons for these difficulties: The first was the persistent instability of Brazil's economy and runaway inflation at a time when other Latin American countries had achieved relative macroeconomic stability. The second was Washington's initial skepticism regarding the Franco government's will and/or ability to pursue the former government's neoliberal platform and its commitment to "new issues," most notably the matter of intellectual property, so dear to the United States. The growing and systematic convergence of other Latin American countries (particularly Argentina) with the United States created two hazards for Brazil. One was the risk of becoming politically isolated in the region, a risk magnified by the economic attraction of a proposal for hemispheric cooperation. The other was the danger that its foreign policy initiatives might be severely constrained by the political and economic preferences and actions entertained by neighboring countries, Argentina in particular (Hirst and Soares de Lima 1994).

As a hypothetical formulation, the offensive component of Brazil's South American regionalism can be further broken down into two medium- to long-range aspects. The first has to do with the long-range creation of a regional alternative to the hemispheric model. In the eventuality of a failure to consolidate hemispheric integration, this option would indeed be an alternative, with SAFTA helping to strengthen the region's position on world markets. If, on the other hand, hemispheric integration were to advance, consolidation of SAFTA would enhance its members' bargaining power during future negotiations over conditions for joining a hemispheric arrangement.

The other strategic aspect of Brazil's South American regionalism relates directly to its aspirations for a permanent seat on the UN Security Council. Here, this regionalism is a key component in a broader international strategy, whereby the country "would not only broaden its economic presence and strengthen its 'global-trader' vocation, but would gradually gain recognition as a regional power as well, not only in South America but in the South Atlantic" ("Quais" 1994: 1).

REGIONALISM IN SOCIETY AND POLITICS

NAFTA and MERCOSUR are currently the most significant experiments in integration in the Americas. The MERCOSUR process, however, is not yet consolidated, and its results have so far fallen far short of its founders' ambitious integrationist objectives. The unequal pace of economic stabilization from one country to the next, difficulties in harmonizing and coordinating their respective sectoral and macroeconomic policies, delays in respecting the original timetable of goals and instruments, an unsatisfactory degree of institutional development, and different foreign policy approaches by its two main partners, Brazil and Argentina, have all kept MERCOSUR from advancing as expected toward its institutional objectives.

Yet, from the point of view of transnational relations between local economic players, MERCOSUR is a booming reality. Trade within MERCOSUR grew from U.S. $5.2 billion in 1991 to U.S. $7.2 billion in 1992 to U.S. $10.0 billion in 1993 (Hirst 1994: 75). Even greater growth was expected after January 1995, when the free trade zone took effect for the four countries. With its larger and more diversified economy, Brazil has been the most aggressive of the MERCOSUR partners. Over the past four years, Brazil's trade with its partners has tripled, from U.S. $3.6 billion in 1990 to an expected U.S. $10 billion in 1994. Brazil's trade surplus with its neighbors has grown, too, causing some delicate political problems. In 1992 more than half of Brazil's exports to MERCOSUR were industrial goods, whereas more than 65 percent of its imports from MERCOSUR partners were raw materials. Brazil has also begun to export capital; over the past four years Brazilian companies have invested approximately U.S. $1.5 billion in Argentina. Currently, nearly 500 Brazilian companies have offices in Argentina (Hirst 1992a; Caminoto and Pivetta 1994).

In the eyes of many analysts, the process of coordination has been privatized, mainly by large national and transnational companies, through what amounts to a de facto replacement of the fragile political coordination of public policies entrusted to the various governments. With greater private sector participation in negotiating bodies, by means of the working groups, the commercial side of integration has gained ground. In the absence of an industrial policy for any of the four MERCOSUR partners, trade liberalization has come to be seen more as an end in itself than as an industrial policy instrument. In any case, MERCOSUR has helped Brazilian business shift away from the excessively closed economy it was used to and thereby take an important step toward greater integration into world markets (Porta 1994; Sarti and Furtado 1993).

The greatest integrationist effects of MERCOSUR have been felt by the states of southern Brazil: Rio Grande do Sul, Santa Catarina, Paraná, and Mato Grosso do Sul. MERCOSUR generated 1992–1993 export growth rates of 18 percent, 23 percent, and 14 percent, respectively, for the first three of those states, compared with 11 percent for Rio de Janeiro's exports and 4 percent for Minas Gerais. Given this kind of dynamism, state economic agencies in the south have become more open, compared with federal economic agencies, to coordinating state government planning with a view toward sub-regional integration. Forums have also been created for interstate negotiations regarding joint initiatives with business, trade unions, politicians, and academics (Caminoto and Pivetta 1994; Hirst 1992a: 19–23; Hirst 1992b).

The interest shown by trade unions in the subregional integration process comes in response to real or anticipated losses. First of all, the unions apprehend the impact of integration on the labor market in terms of growing unemployment and reduced industrial wage levels. The second concern is that certain efforts to render labor relations more flexible, in Chile for example, may serve as models for legislative reforms in Brazil, where the Labor Code dates back to the 1930s. Actually, concerns over labor issues only emerged some years after MERCOSUR came into being, more specifically in 1992, when Subgroup No. 11 on Labor, Employment, and Social Security was created. Labor's fears and doubts about the Southern Cone integration process had already led to the formation of a Co-ordination of Southern Cone Labor Confederations in 1986, an unprecedented initiative in the Latin American trade union movement. Its common concern is that the prevalence of economic integration, dominated by the interests and strategies of big companies, will minimize social concerns, particularly in regard to the establishment of regional social policies and of workforce retraining programs (Candia Veiga 1993; Hirst 1992a: 23–26).

Despite the importance of regional integration for foreign policy and the interest shown by certain industrial sectors and southern states, integration is not a national priority. In a recent survey on the political culture of Brazil's strategic elites, only 2.5 percent of those interviewed identified as medium-term priorities for the country objectives concerning Brazil's international relations.[10] The concentration on domestic objectives and priorities observed in the study reflects the country's own economic, political, and social shortcomings. At the same time, it reveals an inward orientation among Brazilian elites, typical of the political culture in continent-spanning countries such as Brazil.

The diversified structure of Brazil's foreign trade also keeps regionalism from becoming a top priority in the country's foreign economic policy. Brazilian exports to MERCOSUR in 1992 were 11.4 percent of the total; 17 percent when manufactured exports alone are taken into account (Thorstensen, Nakano, and Lozardo 1994: 54, 59).

The salience of regionalism in foreign policy since the mid-1980s is based on political motivations, as has been recognized by diplomatic agents themselves (Barbosa and Panelli César 1994a: 302–303; Almeida 1994: 85–86). It is somewhat curious to see the Brazilian elites corroborating this orientation. Approximately 58 percent of the elite sectors interviewed in the survey previously cited agree with the statement that "Latin American integration is a goal to be pursued despite its difficulties." Of those in agreement, the percentage was higher among members of congress (63.3 percent) and business leaders (62.6 percent). On the other hand, 42 percent of the sampling of elites agreed with the statement that "Latin American integration should only be pursued as an answer to real economic needs." The highest percentages of answers emphasizing this economic rationale for integration were found among top-level bureaucrats (45 percent) and labor leaders (47 percent).

The survey's findings also reveal a certain affinity between the viewpoints of the Brazilian elite and the foreign policy current more favorable to intraregional than to hemispheric integration. For example, 66.2 percent of the total sample agreed with the statement that "Brazil should put a priority on sub-regional integration within the MERCOSUR." On the other hand, the statement "Brazil should put priority on a free-trade agreement with the United States" was chosen by only 16.4 percent of those interviewed. The majority of labor leaders (76 percent) prefer the MERCOSUR path to integration. Subregional integration is also preferred by 68.5 percent of top-level bureaucrats and 63 percent of the members of congress. Business leaders are more divided: 57.1 percent would set subregional integration via MERCOSUR as a priority; 21 percent prefer an agreement with the United States; and 22 percent indicated other choices. In the "other" category, answers ranged from those who consider both types of integration to be priorities to those who emphasize the country's role as a global trader, the general tendency being toward a more global participation rather than regional or subregional (Soares de Lima and Cheibub 1994: 20).

CONCLUSION

An appraisal of the relationship between foreign policy and regionalism in Brazil in the past ten years can be summarized as follows.

The Impact of Global, Regional, and Domestic Changes on Brazilian Foreign Policy Positions Concerning Regionalism

In the mid-1980s global and domestic changes intertwined to bring about Brazil's acceptance of multidimensional cooperation with Argentina. The first such change was the crisis brought on by the exhaustion of the import substitution strategy that had underpinned

Brazil's industrialization for half a century. Some of the principal reasons for this turn of events were changes in the world economy, particularly the globalization of markets and industrial production and technological changes; the debt crisis of the 1980s; the fiscal crisis of the state; and, last but not least, the hardening of international economic rules and procedures in trade and finance mostly as a result of U.S. postures and behavior. However, domestic political changes were also important causes. With the end of twenty-one years of military rule and the democratization of the political regime, Brazil's former "defensive positionalism" toward Argentina faded away.[11]

In the 1990s, Brazil's attitude toward regionalism has been affected by geostrategic changes brought on by the end of the Cold War and the regional trading bloc boom, particularly in the Americas. The shift, begun by the Collor de Mello administration, from closed markets toward liberalization of trade and import regimes also furthered Brazilian regional integration. Finally, defensive and offensive political objectives were behind Brazil's recently opening up to the rest of South America.

The Relationship Between Foreign Policy and Macroeconomic Policy Realignments

Brazil's multidimensional integration with Argentina in the mid-1980s was furthered by major foreign policy changes—the impact of democratization on its defensive positionalism in relation to Argentina—and hindered by the persistence of a protectionist economic policy. The foreign policy component of the country's approach toward regionalism outstripped its economic policy component. In the 1990s, however, foreign policy and foreign economic policy have become closely intertwined. Both have been used by the government to help implement other market-oriented reforms. Although Brazil's economic stabilization and restructuring had lagged behind those of other South and Central American countries, the gradual opening of its trade and import regimes did not stop after Collor de Mello's impeachment. The country's preference for intraregional integration has actually been furthered by the shift in foreign economic policy toward trade liberalization.

However, the relationship between foreign policy and macroeconomic policy realignments in Brazil differs from other experiences in the Americas, for example, in Canada and Mexico. In Canada, a shift from economic nationalism toward economic liberalism was *not* linked to a shift in foreign policy orientations from diversification to continentalism. By contrast, Brazil's approach toward regionalism in the 1990s constitutes an example of what might be termed the non-systemic convergence between politics and economics.

Brazil's Approach Toward Regionalism

Global, regional, and domestic political changes have affected Brazil's foreign policy realignment in the 1990s. One significant trend was the shift *away* from sovereignty-oriented options and actions in foreign policy and *toward* subregional, multidimensional cooperation. However, Brazil's relatively diversified trade relations have promoted a decided preference for multilateralism and for an all-out kind of integration. Besides consolidation of MERCOSUR and South American free trade arrangements, cooperative avenues with the European Union have been explored in both subregional and bilateral formats.

Growing systemic convergence of the other South American countries with the United States has been costly for Brazil. The foremost consequence of that process has been the vexing of the United States–Brazil–Argentina triangle, with its negative side effects for subregional cooperation. In fact, the projection of Brazil's regional influence depends as much on good relations with Argentina as on good relations with the United States.

NOTES

1. In the United States in the early 1960s, the issues of regional integration and hemispheric preferential arrangements were debated in the context of the idea of a special U.S. relationship with Latin America to face the rising tide of nationalism in the region. A telling argument against preferential trading arrangements with Latin America was presented by the assistant secretary of state for economic affairs in the Johnson administration, Anthony M. Solomon. See U.S. Congress (1965: 152–160).

2. For a discussion of the "new regionalism" of the Americas in the 1990s, see Hurrell (1992, 1993); Hirst (1994).

3. For the institutional features of Brazilian foreign policy, see Cheibub (1985) and Lafer (1993a). For the linkage between foreign policy and economic development strategies, see Camargo and Vásquez Ocampo (1988: 386–397); Soares de Lima (1992).

4. For the theme of Brazil's uniqueness within Latin America, see Amado (1982). This volume contains a collection of writings of Ambassador Araújo Castro, whose ideas were very influential in Brazilian foreign policy orientations as of the mid-1970s.

5. For an assessment of the Brazilian-Argentine integration program, see, in particular, Hirst (1990a); Tavares de Araújo (1988); Baumann and Lerda (1987); Hirst (1988a); Thompson-Flôres Netto (1989). For an analysis of the program's formulation and decisionmaking process, see Hirst (1988b). The political background of Brazilian-Argentine cooperation is discussed in Camargo (1985, 1993).

6. The Argentine-Brazilian safeguards agreement was approved in December 1991 by the IAEA. It has become a four-party nuclear safeguards agreement (Quadripartite Nuclear Agreement) that includes a full-scope nuclear safeguards system, jointly managed by a permanent bilateral committee and the IAEA. The Brazilian-Argentine security cooperation also resulted in full adherence to the Treaty of Tlatelolco and the Mendoza Accord on biological and chemical weapons control, first signed by both countries and Chile and adhered to by Uruguay, Paraguay, and Bolivia (Lamazière and Jaguaribe 1992).

7. It has been recalled that pragmatism, one significant feature of the integration program, allowed for the beginning of multidimensional cooperation with Argentina without changing the protectionist trade policy of Brazil (Tavares de Araújo 1990b: 221).

8. For distinct assessments on the Brazil/MERCOSUL-NAFTA agenda, see Bresser Pereira and Thorstensen (1992/1993); Paiva Abreu (1994); Almeida (1994); Motta Veiga (1994); Ricupero and Amaral (1993); Thorstensen, Nakano, and Lozardo (1994).

9. For the current government's posture vis-à-vis the Brazil/MERCOSUR-NAFTA agenda, see Barbosa and Panelli César (1994a: 301). To summarize: (1) there is no antagonism between the objectives of MERCOSUR and NAFTA; (2) both agreements are examples of the current process of trade liberalization in the Americas; (3) at the present time, it would be premature to start free trade negotiations between MERCOSUR and either NAFTA or the United States; (4) MERCOSUR is in the process of consolidation and it would be wise to wait for future developments in NAFTA.

10. The survey, carried out at Instituto Universitário de Pesquisas do Rio de Janeiro, was made possible through a grant from the North-South Center of the University of Miami. Interviews were conducted between October 1993 and June 1994 and encompassed a sample of 320 individuals, members of four elite sectors identified as key policy actors in the Brazilian political economy: top public officials, elected politicians, business leaders, and union leaders (Soares de Lima and Cheibub 1994: 8–9).

11. The concept was coined by Joseph M. Grieco. According to Grieco, because of anarchy, states are fundamentally concerned about their relative defensive capabilities, a concern that generates "a relative-gains problem for cooperation: a state will decline to join, will leave, or will sharply limit its commitment to a cooperative arrangement if it believes that gaps in otherwise mutually positive gains favor partners" (Grieco 1990: 10, 37–50). For Grieco, states are "defensive positionalists" because of a structural cause— the logic of anarchy that impedes the achievement of cooperation. However, I am arguing that Brazil's defensive positionalism toward Argentina can be attributed to a domestic-level variable: the military nature of its political regime.

9

Argentina:
The Great Opening Up

◆

Marc Hufty

Argentina has come a long way. Once a nationalist stronghold with a closed economy, Argentina over the past five years has undergone the most dramatic changes it has ever experienced in the realm of domestic and foreign policy. In the domestic sphere, a radical liberalization and privatization program has been implemented. As a result, inflation is low, the peso is linked to the dollar on a one-to-one basis, trade barriers are the lowest they have been in years, and foreign investment is once again welcome. The "Argentine cost," that is, the inefficient economic structure inherited from years of government intervention in economic life, is under siege: the budget deficit is now minimal, dozens of public concerns have been privatized, and a full battery of laws have been adopted that diminish the constraints on production and trade. The so-called *patria corporativa,* the organizations that have traditionally sustained government intervention, has lost ground: the army is smaller and military enterprises are being privatized; the once all-powerful labor unions have lost thousands of members; and, already severely affected by the 1976–1981 regime, the previously protected domestic-oriented enterprises on which the unions' strength relied now struggle to adapt.

In the foreign policy sphere, Argentina made peace with the international financial organizations—so well, in fact, that it has now regained access to international private credit and its treasury bonds have been given an investment rating. The black sheep has been transformed, and Argentina is now one of the most open economies in the world. Among Latin American countries, it is also one of the most favorable to U.S. interests. It has solved long-standing disputes with its neighbors and entered into a fast-lane integration program with three of them.

This chapter will try to provide an explanation for Argentina's transfiguration by examining the changes in the international environment as well as those in the country's domestic politics and foreign policy.

CHANGES IN THE INTERNATIONAL ENVIRONMENT

The international environment was determinant in Argentina's transformation. The turning point came with the deterioration of growth rates and balances of payments in the developing countries and their increasing indebtedness in the late 1970s. The deterioration was primarily due to the fiscal, monetary, and commercial policies of the industrialized countries, which, though they confronted the 1973 oil shock with expansionary policies, reacted to the 1978–1979 oil shock with restrictive monetary policies. What was called "the Volcker shock"—a radical increase in U.S. interest rates and consequently in international rates—had important effects on those developing countries that had contracted a large international debt at floating interest rates. At the beginning of the "debt crisis," middle-income countries, mainly Latin American, witnessed their debt stock soar from U.S. $31 billion in 1970 to U.S. $350 billion in 1981. In addition, these policies induced a world recession and a drop in the export revenues of developing countries. Their balances of payments deteriorated greatly, and many of them soon were unable to cope with the interests on their international debts.

These events should not obscure the domestic roots of the crisis. One important negative factor, especially in the case of Latin American countries, was the exhaustion of the "import substitution industrialization" model, which involved three basic elements: protectionism, state intervention, and external capital inflows. Despite strong growth until the late 1960s, the model was hampered by high inflationary tendencies, low productivity, and a dependency on imported technologies and capital. Its corrosion was temporarily hidden by massive borrowing on the international capital markets during the 1970s, but "with the debt crisis of 1982 and the net subsequent outflow of capital, one leg of the already rather rickety table was knocked out and the model collapsed" (Roxborough 1992: 422). Bad management, corruption, prestige spending, and the decay of populist policies might be added to this list of woes.

Argentina did not escape this crisis: its international debt rose from U.S. $5.5 billion in 1971 to U.S. $35 billion in 1981 to U.S. $63.7 billion in 1991. It had to allocate as much as 50 percent of its export revenues to cover the interest of its international debt in

1985–1986. Argentina's gross domestic product (GDP) growth rate fell from a yearly average of 2.6 percent between 1970 and 1979 to −1.5 percent between 1980 and 1989. Its annual inflation rate, which had already averaged 162 percent between 1970 and 1979, reached an impressive 577 percent average between 1980 and 1989, with a peak of 3,195 percent in 1989.

A second important change in the international environment was the emergence of the "international regime of development financing" (Hufty 1996). The world order created at the end of World War II was gradually replaced by an era of "complex interdependence," which, according to Keohane and Nye, was characterized by the end of the priority of security issues over other issues, the increasing inefficiency of military solutions to state problems, and the multiplication of formal and informal networks among nation-states (Keohane and Nye 1977). A direct effect was the increased importance of "international regimes," that is, the principles, norms, rules, and decisionmaking procedures (Krasner 1982) that orient the behavior of actors in the various spheres of international life.

Between 1945 and 1980 two international regimes related to credit availability for developing countries coexisted: the "balance-of-payments financing regime" (Cohen 1982) and the "international aid regime" (Wood 1986). They were clearly distinct, and at their core resided two international organizations, respectively, the International Monetary Fund (IMF) and the World Bank. After 1982 it became increasingly difficult to distinguish between these two regimes in their dealings with developing countries. In 1982 Benjamin Cohen had already observed:

> [W]e are witnessing a partial convergence of the roles of the Fund and the Bank—that is a partial overlapping of the regimes governing access to balance of payments financing and development assistance. Here, in the blurring of the jurisdictional boundary between these two regimes, is perhaps the most significant impact of the 1970s. In the 1980s it will be increasingly difficult to maintain a clear distinction between these two forms of lending. (Cohen 1982: 478)

At the core of this fusion process were the reactions of the actors involved in the resolution of the debt crisis. After 1982, the vulnerable commercial banks, mainly in the United States, went from a regime of massive, voluntary, and unregulated loans to one of limited, involuntary, and strictly conditioned loans. Faced with sovereign debtors and unable to pressure them adequately, they quickly left the management of the crisis to the IMF and the World Bank. The industrialized countries' governments, aid agencies, and central banks entirely backed the strategy of the commercial banks and international financial organizations. In an area where benign neglect reigned, the crisis gave rise to an intense, explicit, and remarkable cooperation between these actors and to a new international regime for development financing.

This cooperation led to two more changes in the international environment. One was a global ideological change. In response to inflationary pressures in the 1970s, the monetarist school gained ground in the industrialized countries. It focused on internal variables—bad management and excess demand—in order to explain the economic crisis. The solution was to correct the imbalances through "orthodox" or "neoliberal" policies: restrictive monetary policies, reduction of fiscal deficits and government intervention in the economic sphere, and the privatization and liberalization of business and trade. The whole set of recommendations aimed at fostering growth in the developing countries was labeled the "Washington Consensus" (Williamson 1990: 7–20). After 1982, it became dogma for the international financial organizations and the various participants in the regime.

This very ideological explanation not only dominated the regime but filled a void left by the disappearance of the socialist alternative in Eastern Europe and the failure of statist populism in Latin America. Moreover, the East Asian "miracle" and to a lesser degree the Chilean path were living examples demonstrating that only an export-oriented strategy could lead to growth and that domestic markets were too small to allow a sufficient economy of scale to be competitive at a world level. Attempts to find a middle ground between dirigisme and laissez-faire heterodox economic programs failed in Argentina as well as Brazil, leaving no choice but to accept orthodox economics.

The second change implemented by the new regime was that "structural adjustment" became the dominant strategy for development (Uvin 1993). Basically, a severely indebted country has three options to deal with its debt: finance it, default, or adjust its economy. After 1982, domestic financing possibilities were exhausted almost everywhere in Latin America, and external capital was no longer available. Defaulting was at times wielded as a threat but was in reality little more than a bargaining chip used to obtain better reimbursement conditions. The consequence of falling out with the world financial community was something few decisionmakers were ever willing to face, and cooperation among creditors rapidly eliminated this alternative.

Thus there remained the third option: to adjust the economy. As debt is in fact deferred trade, a debtor must import less or export more to pay back the debt. Reducing imports has clear limits: the maintenance and modernization of the productive apparatus requires investment and the importing of capital goods. Slowing down such imports sends a country into a vicious spiral of decline. Exports can be increased at the expense of internal consumption, a politically limited option, or they may be increased through an adjustment of the economy and resource reallocation, which is costly. For the latter option to work, the public and private sectors require financing, which may be provided by external sources, given the right circumstances. The country must be in good standing with its private and public creditors and must adopt an economic program designed according to the Washington Consensus and approved by the international financial organizations (the IMF and the World Bank).

Because of the conditional nature of the distribution of its financial resources, the international regime for development financing exerts considerable influence over the policy choices of developing countries. Frequently on the verge of bankruptcy and with little room to maneuver, indebted developing countries have to turn to the IMF and World Bank and to accept a system of constraints and the curtailment of their decisionmaking autonomy.

Argentina, a country with a low level of financial dependency before 1976, contracted massive debts in the 1977–1981 period, essentially for reasons of domestic policy choices.[1] This increased its sensitivity to external factors. From 1982 onward, it had to renegotiate its debt (which was "nationalized" by the authoritarian regime, with the Central Bank taking over responsibility for privately contracted debt) and face strong pressures from the regime to adopt orthodox policies. The Alfonsín government's refusal to accept this dictate rendered the negotiation process painful for creditors and Argentina alike. Argentina accepted IMF conditions, then turned to a confrontational strategy, and later tried what has been labeled a "heterodox program," the Austral Plan. Initial success was followed by tough times; Raul Alfonsín's presidency ended in the midst of a troubled economy and a hyperinflationary burst in 1989. The failure of the confrontation strategy helped persuade newly elected president Carlos Saúl Menem to accept the logic of the world political economy.

A fifth change in the international environment was linked to the new importance of trade in world affairs. Given the relative decline of Latin America in world trade—from 8 percent in 1970 to 3 percent in 1990—the move in the past fifteen years toward "bloc trading" and protectionism awoke fears in Latin America. Europe progressively closed ranks, in particular with the Common Agricultural Policy, and Japan achieved regional commercial preeminence through its investments in Asia. The negotiations for a free trade agreement involving the United States and Canada, and then Mexico a short time later, the North American Free Trade Agreement (NAFTA), reinforced Latin American fears of being left out.

The Enterprise for the Americas Initiative, announced by President George Bush on June 27, 1990, has been important in reassuring Latin American leaders. As symbolically significant as President John F. Kennedy's Alliance for Progress almost thirty years earlier, the Enterprise for the Americas Initiative lays out three goals: establishing step by step a hemisphere-wide free trade zone, increasing capital flows and investment, and providing support for debt stock and debt service reduction in Latin America and the Caribbean. Whereas the Alliance for Progress was based on government intervention and U.S. government funds, the Enterprise Initiative focuses on markets and "is built on the premise that no amount of official resources can offset inappropriate economic policies" (Porter 1991: 6). Despite its improvised aspect, it was perceived in Latin America as an encouragement to democratic and market-oriented regimes as well as a promise of access to the vast North American free trade zone, and it was warmly received as such. President Menem commented, "We are passing through the most brilliant moment in our relations with the United States" (Pastor 1991: 23).

According to official discourse, neither NAFTA nor the Enterprise for the Americas Initiative actually constitute a renouncing of multilateralism on the part of the United States. But through the initiative, the U.S. government nevertheless pursues a variable geometry commercial strategy, encouraging both regionalism and multilateralism. Regionalism can be seen as either a first step toward multilateral arrangements or "a fall-back option if the industrialized world retreats into regional blocs" and "a device for developing a competitive edge" (Pastor 1991: 3). The two systems actually coexist. Moreover, by emphasizing the private sector's role and restricting access to supplementary debt reduction financing to those countries that have implemented IMF- and World Bank–approved adjustment programs and have settled their differences with commercial creditors, the Enterprise for the Americas Initiative complements both the international financial organizations' strategy and the Washington Consensus.

Finally, the sixth significant change in the international environment was the democratic wave that swept Latin America in the 1980s. Without entering into a debate as to its origins (there is no single, satisfactory explanation for this change) one can observe, as in previous waves of this type, an emulation effect among Latin American states. The harshness of the last authoritarian regimes provoked a reaction of "never again" and a desire on the part of elected governments to stabilize democracy by diminishing the power of their armies and by creating strong links with neighboring countries; hence, the resolution of territorial conflicts that had justified the magnitude of their armies and the conclusion of international arrangements, especially those proscribing nuclear and chemical weaponry. Added to the continental acceptance of the liberal solution, the democratic spirit made possible a certain "community of basic values" that helped reinforce integration projects.

HOW DID ARGENTINA RESPOND TO THESE CHANGES?

It is almost impossible to understand how Argentina reacted to changes in the international environment without diagnosing the situation inside the country and being aware of domestic changes that occurred in tandem with international ones. But before focusing on domestic responses, it would be useful to establish a historical perspective.

What Was Wrong in Argentina?

Between 1880 and 1950 Argentina enjoyed steady growth based on a model of agricultural exports that complemented the British economy and functioned under the hegemony of the agrarian elite. Later it modernized, under both conservative and populist leaders, by following a model of industrial growth oriented toward the domestic market. But one has to admit that "Argentina has failed to realize its economic potential. Its ranking among countries in terms of GDP per capita has fallen steadily from among the most developed to close to the median" (World Bank 1987: xi). At the end of the 1980s, the country's economy was characterized by chronic inflation, endemic capital flight, persistent internal and external deficits, a stagnating per capita revenue, a formidable external debt, an oversized and corrupt state apparatus, and a market deformed by protectionism as well as an infinity of abusive regulations. "Socialist without a plan, capitalist without a market," in the words of Adolfo Sturzenegger,[2] Argentina's economy had to be considered a failure.

Since 1930 (the time of the first military coup) the country has not succeeded in finding a growth model on which a majority of the elites can agree. Each group brought to the fore by historical developments has held a kind of veto power over the country's economic orientation and has used it against all models other than its own. The agrarian elite controlled export revenues; the unions had a power similar to that of British unions before Margaret Thatcher's tenure and represented the popular Peronist Party when it was prohibited (most of the time after 1955); industrialists produced the largest portion of the GDP; and politicians and technocrats controlled state resources as well as the mechanisms of resource allocation among the various sectors. No hegemonic coalition (in the Gramscian sense) could impose itself; alliances alternated regularly between, on the one hand, a limited liberalism backed by a coalition centered on the owners of the means of production and, on the other hand, a distributive populism based on a union-led coalition. In this game, the military became a sort of referee of the political system. Under civilian pressure, they intervened periodically, preventing the domination of any coalition and attempting in vain to reform the state and the political game (O'Donnell 1973).

This pendulum process resulted in the systematic looting of state resources through ad hoc regulations by every coalition that temporarily ruled the political system. As long as external resources (from export surpluses, foreign investments, and loans) were available, a relative prosperity was maintained in stop-and-go economic cycles that allowed alternating growth and distribution (Díaz Alejandro 1970). But the accumulated cost of these cycles and the overgrowth of the state apparatus gradually caused the economic engine to stall.

Several strongly motivated governments tried to put an end to this situation by reforming the political and economic systems (Erro 1993). But in Argentina will is a necessary but insufficient instrument for the implementation of reform; the capacity to do so depends on the domestic political economy. Even authoritarian regimes were powerless: the last military regime, from 1976 to 1983, which was determined to definitively reform the society, ended in miserable political and economic failure and left behind memories of horror. Paradoxically, this disaster permitted the structural domestic changes that were to lead to the fundamental economic and political reform of Argentina.

What Has Changed in Argentina's Domestic Policy?

One of these changes was the radical transformation of what has been called la patria corporativa, formed by the national-populist segments of the political system: the military, the Peronist labor unions, and the economic elite. First, the awful repression of 1976–1979 and the lamentable Falklands defeat discredited the military as a legitimate political actor. This justified radical cuts in military spending (from over 5 percent to 2 percent of gross national product [GNP]) and personnel, the privatization of the military-industrial complex, and the end of the unpopular *colimba,* the compulsory military service that takes its name from the words *correr, limpiar y barrer* (to run, clean, and sweep).

Second, the Peronist defeat in the first electoral contest after the military regime, in 1983, was a political earthquake. The Peronists had never been defeated in open elections before; the old party, union-based bureaucracy was deeply shaken. This led to the emergence of a new generation of "pragmatists," among them Carlos Menem.

Third, the Peronist unions were powerful enough between 1983 and 1989 to prevent reforms of the labor laws and to impose wage increases through systematic general strikes. They also played a decisive role in Alfonsín's fall. But once the Peronists returned to power, the unions ceased to be useful as the opposition spearhead; instead, they were a threat to the liberal program adopted by Menem. Using all the resources of the Peronist system, Menem managed to divide and weaken the unions. This allowed him a free hand to dismiss thousands of state employees and to sell public enterprises, actions that would have caused the government to fall only a few years earlier. It also allowed the government to adopt new labor and union laws and to diminish union power further by reforming the social security system.

One important factor of the change in domestic policy was a general public demand for basic reforms. Though accustomed to political and economic instability, Argentines were nevertheless frightened by the social disorder resulting from the violence of 1974–1979, the economy of speculation of 1979–1981, the lost Falklands war, the failure of the heterodox Austral Plan, and, above all, the hyperinflationary episodes of 1988–1989.[3] The feeling of panic caused by the threat to social cohesion and the disastrous state of the economy after decades of economic nationalism predisposed large segments of the population, in particular the popular classes and the industrialists, to accept economic policies that had previously seemed unthinkable. Among the elites, a consensus began to emerge whereby there was no choice but to accept liberalism in order to renew growth. This consensus was at the base of the political coalition that backed Menem after his election.

Since 1916 (when the first "universally" elected government was installed), Argentina had been confronted with a fundamental antagonism between two sources of government legitimacy. At the risk of oversimplifying,[4] elected governments, although politically legitimate, lacked economic legitimacy. They were supported by the union-based popular coalition and tended to follow populist distributive policies. Conversely, economically legitimate governments, those backed by the capitalist coalition, lacked popular support and were imposed by military coups. They tended to follow liberal policies. Apparently, only a Peronist government could be politically legitimate, and only a government following liberal policies could be economically legitimate. The international and domestic changes discussed earlier permitted Menem's government to accomplish what had seemed impossible until then; that is, to reconcile, for the first time in the twentieth century, political legitimacy with economic legitimacy. One can conclude that only a Peronist government possessing popular legitimacy could succeed in implementing such a deep market economy conversion program for Argentina.

A Macroeconomic Revolution

Contrary to all expectations, Menem, once elected, imposed upon his surprised electorate an alliance with the business establishment, represented by the country's only real transnational firm, Bunge & Born. The firm provided Menem with not only an economic plan but also two ministers of economy, Miguel Roig and Néstor Rapanelli, who were followed in 1990 by Erman González, a personal friend of Menem's. In an attempt to control inflation and balance accounts, the new government implemented an emergency liberalization program: it freed up private sector prices, suppressed many nontariff trade barriers, lowered import tariffs, liberalized the oil industry, and opened the country to foreign investment. But despite some progress, it did not succeed in controlling inflation.

In January 1991 Domingo Cavallo became Menem's fourth minister of economy. In February, he launched the Convertibility Plan with the help of a team from Córdoba's Fundación Mediterránea, an industry-subsidized think tank. The first objective of the plan was to eradicate inflation and stabilize the economy. Parity of the Argentine currency with the U.S. dollar was one of its basic assumptions. By law (specifically, the Ley de Convertibilidad), each peso (austral until January 1992) injected into the economy had to be backed by a dollar (or gold) in the Central Bank reserve, which was a break with past practice in Argentina. As a result, 95 percent of the fiscal deficit was financed through the printing of banknotes in the first semester of 1991.

Then every economic sector in turn was touched by the most radical and ambitious structural adjustment program ever undertaken in the Americas. The program was based on several laws (Ley de Reforma del Estado, 1989; Ley de Emergencia Económica, 1990) and decrees.[5] The State Reform Program, based on the State Reform Law, was partly financed by World Bank sectorial adjustment loans and Inter-American Development Bank loans. The first steps were to eliminate the public sector deficit, to implement an administrative reform, to deregulate, and, above all, to reduce state intervention in the economy.

The public sector deficit was reduced by selling or closing state enterprises, decreasing the number of state employees, and raising fiscal revenues by means of a value-added tax (40 percent of state revenues in 1994) and strict enforcement of the law. The Central Bank was given greater autonomy; it no longer finances fiscal and provincial deficits or those of state-owned companies. The far-reaching system of subsidies to private firms and regulation boards has been slashed. Privatizations, initiated by the authoritarian government of 1976–1983, and pursued by the Alfonsín government, were accelerated. They are the keystone of the deregulation program, and the government has announced its intention to withdraw from every economic activity that can be managed by the private sector: "Argentina's privatization program may prove to be among the most impressive in the world" (Alexander and Corti 1993: 1). Telephone companies, airlines, oil wells and oil companies, gas, water, and electricity companies, nuclear power plants, railroads, subways, chemical and steel plants, roads, harbor facilities, radio and television channels, buildings, military industries—no sacred cow has remained untouched; everything has been or will be sold.

Industrial production has recovered and is at a record level. (It is nevertheless important to point out that the most dynamic industrial sector, the automobile industry, has been partly protected from foreign competition by quotas.) The private investment rate is progressively increasing, and Argentine firms have had to adapt rapidly to trade liberalization. They commonly complain about the overvaluation of the peso, a consequence of internal inflation and the pegged exchange rate. Since a nominal devaluation has been ruled out, the government is promoting a reduction of costs: taxes and social security contributions have been reduced, capital goods (which constituted half of all imports in 1993–1994) can be imported tax free, and the labor market is being gradually deregulated. Union negotiations that used to be sectoral are now carried out within individual firms.

The successes of the program have been numerous. Inflation went down from an annual rate of over 3,000 percent in 1989 to less than 5 percent in 1994. Real GDP growth, negative in 1989, averaged 5.6 percent for 1991–1994. Industrial output, led by the automobile industry, grew by 4.5 percent in 1993. Foreign capital inflow, U.S. $12 billion in 1992 and U.S. $16.5 billion in 1993, has been impressive and has helped sustain the economic program.

The darker side of the current program must, however, be considered. The current-account balance has been negative for some years: it showed a deficit of U.S. $5.8 billion in 1994, although it became a surplus after April 1995. The unemployment rate climbed to over 18 percent, and some sectors—education, social security, and public health—are severely neglected. Argentina used to be a largely middle-class society, but it is heading toward a model of the Brazilian type, with both a large underclass and a struggling lower middle class excluded from the "economic miracle" reserved for the happy few. Many workers dismissed because of privatizations and industrial reconversions have been unable to reintegrate into the labor market and have had to join the hordes of *cuentapropistas*, self-employed people, who may now make up more than a third of the workforce. The looting of public retirement funds by previous governments brought the system to the verge of collapse, with the minimum monthly pension around U.S. $200 in a country with Swiss prices. Pensioners' movements, protesting loudly and incessantly, are becoming the most important social movements in Argentina. Another sign of impoverishment is observable in the ever-growing size of the *villas miserias*, the slums that now surround each city. More and more, Argentina resembles other Latin American countries.

ARGENTINA'S NEW FOREIGN POLICY

The bases of Argentine foreign policy have been paradoxical: on the one hand, a desire for greatness and for participation in the concert of nations through very active diplomacy; on the other hand, a desire for withdrawal and isolation. The geopolitical school, grounded in early military thinking (maximization of state power and territorial expansion), shaped the foreign policy of governments for decades and led to a strategy of confrontation with the country's neighbors and trade partners. The so-called Third Position, Juan Perón's doctrine postulating the possible existence of a system transcending capitalism and communism, continued to shape Argentina's foreign policy well into the 1980s. And the Doctrina de Seguridad Nacional (National Security Doctrine) adopted by military regimes led to interventions in the continental war against communism and to a disastrous human rights record of the 1976–1982 regime.

Now a wind of change has blown over Argentina's foreign policy. The most significant change has been the present government's willingness to accept the "new world order"—in fact, U.S. hegemony—and to orient the country's economy toward the mainstream. One of the most significant measures it took was to leave the Non-Aligned Movement in 1991; Argentina's voting record in the UN General Assembly since 1991 aptly reflects this new alignment. The basis of its new foreign policy is pragmatism and normality.[6] Menem's government began resolving many long-standing problems with neighboring states and the international community. Argentines now hope to be offered membership in the Organisation for Economic Co-operation and Development (OECD), along with Mexico and South Korea.

Commercial Policy: Participation in World Trade

Economic relationships and growth have been given priority, and the government's goal is *integrar el primer mundo* (to integrate the First World). Argentines have always believed that their country's economic potential could raise them to the level of the industrialized countries: "In comparison with most Third World countries, of course, Argentina's condition did not appear all that desperate. . . . But Argentines did not take much comfort from such indices; rather, they compared themselves with Austria, Italy, Spain and other European nations, and the contrast remained unfavorable" (Wynia 1981: 63).

From a more realistic perspective, it should be acknowledged that Argentina occupies a minor position in world trade. Its exports account for only 0.34 percent of world total[7] and consist mainly of products with a high raw material content (see Table 9.1). And despite all its natural wealth, Argentina does not possess any strategic resources that could give it some importance. Moreover, since 1930 it had applied self-centered economic policies, with a consequent decline of the openness rate (exports plus imports as a percentage of GDP) from 80 percent in 1915 to 25 percent in 1990 (GATT 1992).

In 1989, Argentina decided to do away with such policies, to integrate world trade according to its comparative advantages, and to liberalize its exchanges. Menem is inspired no longer by the ECLAC thesis but by Michael Porter and the other "economic gurus" of the 1980s.[8] The new assumptions are that national growth is driven by exports and that nations as a whole compete in the world market through the intermediary of private firms. Entrepreneurs, manpower, and educational and productive systems all participate in giving the nation a competitive edge. Therefore, states and firms need to be complementary. Accordingly, instead of penalizing exports by taxing them, Argentina must help its enterprises to face world markets. Hence, the apparently unlikely alliance of Peronists and a transnational firm (Bunge & Born) in 1989 can be seen as a step toward the modernization of Argentina.

The persistent taxes on exports have been eliminated, and nontraditional exports are being encouraged through tax incentives. As a result, exports increased from U.S. $9.5 billion to U.S. $13 billion in 1993. While trying to participate in world trade, Argentina has

Table 9.1   Argentina's Principal Trade Products

	1989		1992	
	U.S. $ (millions)	% of total	U.S. $ (millions)	% of total
Main exports				
Agricultural products	1,557	16.3	2,901	24.2
Processed foods	1,923	20.1	2,397	20.0
Oils and fats	880	9.2	1,131	9.5
Animal products	909	9.5	1,064	8.9
Mineral products	352	3.7	941	7.9
Metals and products	1,222	12.8	626	5.2
Chemicals	533	5.6	584	4.9
Skins, hides, and products	438	4.6	537	4.5
Machinery	427	4.5	502	4.2
Transport equipment	189	2.0	390	3.3
Main imports				
Machinery	1,079	25.7	4,772	32.2
Transport equipment	239	5.7	2,278	15.3
Chemicals	1,080	25.7	1,797	12.1
Metals and products	399	9.5	1,055	7.1
Plastics	224	5.3	803	5.4
Textiles	74	1.8	785	5.3
Mineral products	554	13.2	601	4.1

Source: INDEC, quoted by the Economist Intelligence Unit (1994).

opened up considerably to foreign trade and capital. The commercial and financial open door program is almost as impressive as the state reform. Tariffs are at their lowest, averaging under 10 percent, and imports have jumped from U.S. $3.8 billion in 1989 to U.S. $15.7 billion in 1993.

Relations with External Creditors

The new Argentina has been one of the IMF's best pupils; Michel Camdessus, the IMF's director, has lauded its economic program. The country is now in step with the international financial organizations. Argentina received more than U.S. $12 billion in loans from the IMF and the World Bank in recent years. It renegotiated its debt with the Paris Club and commercial banks and qualified for the Brady Plan, saving U.S. $10 billion on its commercial debt repayments in the future.

The international capital market is once again open to Argentina, and as much as U.S. $30 billion in capital flowed into the country during the years 1991–1993, much of it from Argentines who had been hiding their savings. The Buenos Aires stock exchange has been one of the most profitable in the world in recent years. Despite a debt stock of around U.S. $70 billion in June 1994, Standard & Poor's gave Argentina's long-term debt bonds (in pesos) a BBB– rating in August 1994. It is the third Latin American country to receive a rating authorizing U.S. pension fund investment.

Turning Toward the United States

It has been said that Argentines suffered from anti-Americanism. This opinion is a remnant of the World War II period and the days of Perón, when Argentina flirted with the Axis powers. Except for the Peronists, the majority of Argentines always felt either neutral or positive about the United States. This was documented long ago by Jeane Kirkpatrick (1971: Chap. 8) and confirmed by recent polls (Turner and Carballo de Cilley 1989). Anti-Americanism has at times been an instrument in the hands of demagogic leaders, most notably when Perón used U.S. ambassador Spruille Braden unwittingly to help him win the 1946 elections (Tulchin 1990: Chap. 8). Argentina's governments used to be critical of the United States in international forums, and U.S.-Argentine relations reached a low point following the Falklands war and the debt crisis. But in a complete policy reversal, Menem's government has made its relations with the United States the central axis of its foreign policy. Since 1989 Argentina has been "emphasizing the elimination of each and every possible area of conflict on their joint policy agenda" (Russell and Zuvanic 1991: 121) and following a foreign policy closely aligned with U.S. interests.

When Menem was elected president in 1989, the Bush administration was very skeptical of a man described in the international press as a provincial caudillo in the Peronist tradition. The U.S. government therefore waited for the newly elected President Menem to demonstrate his goodwill before encouraging warmer relations. The demonstration of goodwill was not long in coming: Menem sent warships to the Persian Gulf during the Gulf War, scrapped the Condor II ballistic missile program (Santoro 1992),[9] began a struggle against drug trafficking when it was a top priority on the U.S. agenda, gave guarantees on the peaceful use of nuclear power,[10] and entered into negotiations to solve a major dispute over pharmaceutical patents.

At the cabinet level, the dispatching of Argentine troops during the Gulf War gave rise to a hot debate on foreign policy. The troop deployment was Menem's idea, and he had to win Cavallo, then chancellor (foreign minister), over to it. This military action had three functions: to demonstrate symbolically Argentina's new foreign policy and alignment, to promote the participation of Argentine companies in Kuwait's reconstruction (a hope that was not to be ful-filled), and to help give the military a new role, oriented toward peacekeeping.

Menem's relations with President Bush went beyond the usual courtesy between statesmen, and their friendship left its mark on Argentina's foreign policy. This harmony is not surprising given that some of Menem's closest advisers have close links with the United States. Cavallo and Guido di Tella—perhaps the most influential members of the cabinet in terms of foreign policy development—both studied in the United States, Cavallo at Harvard and di Tella at MIT. Even before the 1989 elections, Bob Felder, political adviser at the U.S. embassy in Argentina, had established close ties with members of the Menem circle: Alberto Kahan, Eduardo Bauzá, Eduardo Menem, and Diego Guelar. He had predicted Menem's victory in Peronist internal elections and in the presidential contest. Felder was one of the few and first to recognize Menem's pragmatism, when Menem was still considered a populist (Granovsky 1991). Jorge Triaca, trade unionist and labor minister in 1989, was known for his close friendship with U.S. ambassador Frank Ortiz. Some members of the "court" also had tight links with Terence Todman, Ortiz's successor from 1989 to 1993 (and now chairman of Aerolíneas Argentinas), who was so influential in Argentina that he was dubbed *el Vice Rey* (viceroy).

Despite these promising relations, it should be pointed out that Argentina is a middle-sized country and not of central interest to the United States, in terms either of gains or losses. It can make itself as attractive as possible and offer concessions without demands, but the risk is that any benefits accrued may be more symbolic than real. Argentina is, in sum, a minor partner in U.S. trade relations, representing about 0.2 percent of total U.S. trade. By contrast, the United States is Argentina's primary individual commercial partner, absorbing 11.7 percent of its exports and providing 21.6 percent of its imports (Makuc 1990).[11] Argentina is, then, in a vulnerable commercial position vis-à-vis the United States and protectionist tendencies there.

Disagreements between the two countries still occur, as, for example, when the United States decided to sell subsidized wheat to Brazil, a traditional Argentine market. While the Argentine government was complaining, U.S. representatives sent the ball into the European court by declaring that the United States would stop subsidizing agricultural exports if the Europeans scrapped their Common Agricultural Policy (CAP). Despite these frictions, the level of tension between the United States and Argentina is nowhere near where it had been previously, and a general climate of trust has been established. A case in point is a series of successes in the financial sector:

Argentina obtained the rescheduling of debts due to Eximbank and the U.S. Agency for International Development (USAID) and was able to make a comeback on the U.S. commercial capital market.

Relations with Great Britain

Whereas Alfonsín's government and its foreign minister, Dante Caputo, failed to normalize relations with Great Britain, the foreign ministers who followed, Cavallo and di Tella, took on this task with vigor. As an illustration of this administration's characteristically pragmatic attitude (a far cry from Menem's election campaign promise to take back the Falkland Islands at any cost), the Argentines initiated a series of unilateral concessions, lifting trade restrictions and special measures against British enterprises, disbanding the commission in charge of the surveillance of British property, offering consular exchange and diplomatic normalization, and seeking an agreement on fishing rights around the Falklands.

Relations with Great Britain progressively improved. While Britain itself no longer has the same importance for Argentina, the importance of the European market and Britain's capacity to veto trade agreements with the European Union have proved to be good reasons to seek an arrangement. Moreover, the previous situation no longer coincided with the international image Argentina hoped to project.

Relations with the European Union

Relations with Europe are highly emotional. A majority of Argentines have Spanish or Italian ancestry. For a long time, Britain was its primary trading partner and France its cultural model. Europe absorbed over 30 percent of Argentina's exports in 1990 (53 percent in 1970), mostly raw materials, and provided it with 27 percent of its imports (33 percent in 1970), mostly manufactured goods (GATT 1992) (see Table 9.2). The main obstacles between Argentina and Europe lie in the closure of European markets following the CAP and in the subsidies granted to common agricultural exports.[12] Not only have the Europeans deprived Argentina of its traditional markets, but they are dumping their own products on the world market. During the Uruguay Round negotiations, Argentina, a member of the Cairns Group, linked its approval of other agreements to the reduction of subsidies in the industrialized countries.

Still, with the British obstacles out of the way, Argentina could develop its trade relations with the Europeans by making some profitable trade agreements. These included an agreement that authorizes European boats to fish in Argentine waters in return for the cutting

**Table 9.2   Argentina's Principal Trading Partners
(percentage of total trade)**

	1988	1990	1992
Exports to			
Brazil	7.2	11.5	13.3
United States	15.3	13.5	11.7
Netherlands	5.1	11.1	10.1
Germany	8.8	5.2	6.0
Chile	2.6	2.6	4.5
Italy	4.4	4.2	4.3
Spain	2.1	2.5	4.0
Japan	4.8	3.2	3.1
USSR	8.3	4.0	0.8
Imports from			
United States	18.8	21.1	21.6
Brazil	17.3	17.6	18.8
Germany	10.7	9.9	7.3
Italy	6.1	4.9	5.2
Japan	5.3	3.3	4.7
Chile	2.7	2.7	4.4
France	4.7	3.5	3.9

Source: INDEC, quoted by the Economist Intelligence Unit (1994).

in half of European taxes on Argentine fish exports and some funds to refurbish its harbors. European businesses have also invested heavily in privatized Argentine enterprises.

Relations with Brazil, Paraguay, and Uruguay

Argentina's relations with Brazil were traditionally marked by mistrust because of their rivalry for subcontinental hegemony. More advanced than Brazil early in the century, Argentina progressively lost demographic and economic ground. Brazil is now the eleventh world economic power in terms of absolute GDP, whereas Argentina is seventieth (World Bank 1994). But in reality this competition has faded away. Brazil is a giant more concerned with the conquest of its domestic frontiers than with continental hegemony (Turner 1991). The changes in the international environment discussed previously made this competition even more anachronous, and the convergence of their interests brought the two countries closer together.

A new form of cooperation between Brazil and Argentina started in 1986 when Alfonsín and Brazilian president José Sarney concluded several protocols and an agreement on the creation of a common economic zone. The project was developed further by Menem and Brazilian president Fernando Collor de Mello with the creation of a free trade zone between Brazil and Argentina (MERCOSUR).

Bilateral agreements have already accelerated trade between Brazil and Argentina to the point where Brazil will soon be Argentina's most important trading partner. Uruguay and Paraguay joined in the process early on, having soon understood the disadvantage of being left out of an agreement between their main trading partners. The treaty creating MERCOSUR was signed on March 26, 1991. It provided for a freer circulation of capital, goods, and manpower; common external tariffs; and a convergence of macroeconomic policies.[13] It also provided for the inauguration of a free trade area among the four countries on January 1, 1995.

One sensitive point of this treaty is the convergence of macroeconomic policies. From 1991 through 1994, Brazil's economic policies were chaotic and inflation remained a structural problem. The Real Plan (the stabilization plan devised and implemented by Enrique Cardoso) has not fully succeeded in taming it. Revenue disparity is also a problem: Argentina has an annual per capita GDP of U.S. $7,220, compared with U.S. $2,930 for Brazil, U.S. $1,510 for Paraguay, and U.S. $3,830 for Uruguay (World Bank 1995). However, market size gives a clear advantage to Brazilian firms. In many sectors, Argentine firms are unable to compete and will have to make severe adjustments. This is offset, however, by the economy of scale that the most competitive industries will be able to realize and by the fact that MERCOSUR will increase the strength of its members in international trade negotiations.

Brazil and Argentina have also alleviated old political tensions in the area of nuclear power. They concluded a treaty in July 1991 on the peaceful use of nuclear energy.[14] The agreement stipulates reciprocal access to nuclear power plants and the control of fissionable material. It was accompanied by a reform of the 1967 Tlatelolco Treaty and its ratification by Argentina.

Argentina and Chile

Argentina's relations with Chile, like those with Brazil, used to be strained, to the extent that they almost went to war over the delimitation of the Beagle Strait. This dispute was eventually resolved through Pope John Paul II's mediation, which led to a treaty in 1984. The return to democracy gave the relations between these two countries a new start, and the primacy of economic issues allowed them to resolve age-old territorial disputes. In 1991, in accordance with the recommendations of a bilateral commission, and to the great displeasure of their respective military and nationalist circles, Menem and Chilean president Patricio Aylwin signed a treaty putting an end to twenty-four territorial disputes and definitively establishing the border between the two countries.[15]

The same year, within the framework of the Latin American Integration Association, the foreign ministers of both countries signed an important agreement whose objectives are a reinforcement of bilateral trade and the realization of an "enlarged commercial space" for the end of 1995.[16] It was accompanied by a series of protocols on investment protection, energy exchanges, and the development of physical links between the two countries, in particular the digging of a tunnel through the Andes.

Because Chilean and Argentine exports compete in external markets, their exchanges are relatively limited. Moreover, Chilean participation in NAFTA could be prejudicial for Argentine exports to NAFTA members. This is likely to be a major concern for Argentina's foreign policy elites in the coming years. At the same time, Chile's recent rapprochement with MERCOSUR is likely to be viewed favorably by Argentine authorities.

CONCLUSION

In contrast to the 1960s and 1970s, regionalism in Latin America is now seen as an instrument of negotiation within the global political economy. Regionalism no longer supports import substitution schemes for industrial development but is based on export promotion, a concept shared by Argentina.

The "great opening up" now taking place in Argentina can be understood as a huge step toward "modernization," that is, Argentina's inclusion as a reliable partner in the global political economy. This evolution reflects not only a fundamental adjustment of the economic structures but also a profound cultural and political change. Those who believed that the country was condemned to perpetual decline, including many Argentines, now have to admit that something has truly changed. Compelled by the international environment and exhausted by decades of disastrous public policies, Argentines have been wise enough not to delay these necessary changes.

Much remains to be done, but Argentina is now a "normal" country, and this is perhaps a little bit sad for the generations of scholars who made a specialty of explaining the "Argentine paradox."

NOTES

1. Argentina's debt was contracted during an attempt to solve its political problems through an economic open door approach that led to massive fraud, speculation, and capital flight.

2. Personal communication, 1991.

3. See the imaginary dialogue with an Argentine in Wynia (1992).

4. For a fuller development of this thesis, see O'Donnell (1973). This is also a point I develop in my doctoral thesis (Hufty 1996).

5. In fact, Menem has governed mostly by decree, taking advantage of the constitution's Article 5, which gives the president the power to issue decrees in cases of emergency. He justifies the intensive use of this supposedly exceptional procedure by invoking the urgency of the situation and the need to bypass congress, with its slowness and the inevitable compromises imposed by the legislative game.

6. Domingo Cavallo, then minister of foreign affairs, quoted by Russell and Zuvanic (1991: 113).

7. It was 0.42 percent in 1980 (Cárdenas 1994).

8. See, for example, Guadani (1991: 10), secretary of international economic relations at the Ministry of External Relations.

9. The cancellation of this program was enacted under Executive Decree No. 995/91.

10. Decree No. 603/92.

11. Argentine exports to the United States consist mainly of metal products, hides, meat, combustibles, and fish. Manufactured goods account for more than 50 percent of the total. Imports from the United States are mostly consumer goods, chemicals, machines, and transport equipment. Forty-seven percent of Argentine exports enter the U.S. market free of taxes, but 28 percent are limited by quotas.

12. Nontariff trade restrictions affect 27 percent of Argentine exports to Europe, mainly textiles, food products, cereals, oils, combustibles, and metal products (De la Guardia and Sánchez 1992).

13. "Tratado para la constitución de un mercado común entre la República Argentina, la República Federativa de Brasil, la República de Paraguay y la República Oriental del Uruguay," known as the Asunción Treaty. The text of the treaty can be found in *Integración Latinoamericana* (May 1991).

14. "Acuerdo entre la República Argentina y la República Federativa de Brasil para el uso exclusivamente pacífico de la energía nuclear," known as the Treaty of Guadalajara. The text of the treaty can be found in *Integración Latinoamericana* (August 1991).

15. The text of the agreement can be found in *Integración Latinoamericana* (September–October 1991).

16. "Acuerdo de Complementación Económica entre la República Argentina y la República de Chile." The text of the agreement can be found in *Integración Latinoamericana* (September–October 1991).

10

Democracy and Regional Multilateralism in Chile

◆

Roberto Duran

SETTING OUT THEMES

Latin American governments and their ministries of foreign affairs have invoked various rationales for their respective foreign policies in the context of regional multilateralism. Perhaps the rationale that is most frequently used is that of the necessity of expanding the influence of the region in the area of diplomatic and economic trade negotiations with more powerful countries. In this regard, the history of the modern inter-American system is a case in point.

Indeed, the history of the Pan-American Union was marked by an almost constant series of confrontations between the State Department in Washington and several Latin American ministries of foreign affairs, including Chile's, from the end of the nineteenth century and throughout the first three decades of the twentieth. Moreover, these differences of opinion would only increase with the creation of the Organization of American States (OAS) in 1948. The Guatemalan crisis of 1954, the events in the Dominican Republic in 1965, and the frustrated attempts of Brazil, Mexico, Chile, and Uruguay to introduce substantial reforms to the structure of the OAS between 1966 and 1974 were all moments of serious diplomatic conflict between the United States and Latin America (Atkins 1980: 175–219, 297–331). Finally, the U.S. military interventions of Grenada (1983), Panama (1989), and Haiti (1994) served as a warning that the discrepancies in the priorities of U.S. and Latin American foreign policy would ensure that conflict would continue to be a dominant theme in inter-American relations well into the 1990s. The preference of many Latin American governments for a policy of non-intervention in the domestic affairs of the countries of the region, among other issues, could not make this otherwise.

While inter-American conflicts have persisted over time, their reference points have changed. Presently, the hemispheric system is at a decisive turning point, brought on by a shift in global politics that is challenging its very viability. The effects of the end of the Cold War have signified important readjustments on the regional level for Latin America and have prompted a re-examination of the current inter-American system. There are three arguments in favor of reconsidering the nature of hemispheric relations, all of which point to fundamental changes that require new political and economic arrangements.

First, from the perspective of Latin America, there is the question of the compatibility of the double aspect of the role of the United States in global politics: its status as the only superpower, on the one hand, and its position as the most powerful player in the region, on the other. In fact, it is often suggested that these two positions are not compatible and that this has consequences for Latin America.

A second argument relates to levels of economic development of several Latin American countries and how these have been favorably influenced by multilateralism. There is empirical evidence that regional organizations have both increased the amount and improved the quality of technical cooperative links between developed and underdeveloped countries. In the end, of course, international cooperation is essentially a bilateral affair; nevertheless, it is clear that a significant proportion of these arrangements come as a result of complex multilateral efforts. The importance of these endeavors is that they facilitate concerted action on the part of donor countries and define the needs of recipient countries.

A third argument arises out of the positive effects of foreign trade diversification and the demands associated with sustained economic growth. This argument can assume one of two forms. First, it can be translated into the reinforcement of the trade relations of individual countries with those of a bloc of countries, which has been the position adopted by Chile over the past twelve years. Second, it can mean the grouping together of regional economies into a bloc, which then establishes trading links with other country blocs. This has been the path taken by the member countries of the Southern Cone Common Market (MERCOSUR). How can we explain Chile's course of action within the framework of regional multilateralism? Constant rates of growth of 5 percent of gross domestic product (GDP) from 1984 until the present and the favorable consequences for the national economy of extensive trade diversification have meant that Chile has pursued a path somewhat distinct from that of its neighbors, especially with regard to economic-commercial relations with the rest of Latin America.

THE IMPACT OF GLOBAL POLITICS
FOR CHILE'S FOREIGN RELATIONS

The diffusion of changes in the global arena has resounded asynchronously in countries such as Chile. Generally speaking, these changes will assume different forms and intensities depending on the sphere of activity they are affecting. For the principal world powers, their political and international economic relations are adapting only very slowly to these changes. But for the developing world, Latin America included, their domestic and foreign policies are oscillating in an anarchic manner, unable to adjust themselves immediately to the new global reality.

For this second group of countries, it is the commercial effects of these changes that hold the greatest significance, since they have substantially altered the structure and functioning of these developing economies. Moreover, the effects of these changes are felt even in countries with relatively high levels of economic prosperity. Consider that if the impact of changes in the global economy strikes during a period of crisis, the cumulative effect of these changes amounts to more profound social and political instability for underdeveloped countries. If, by contrast, these changes arrive during a period of economic prosperity, they will never generate sufficient resources to solve fundamental socioeconomic problems, nor will they produce even a stable level of minimum resources that would allow for the progressive resolution of problems of underdevelopment.

The asymmetrical character of the changes occurring in the international order is felt not only at the global level; asymmetry exists within the developing world itself, since developing nations have different degrees of foreign relations with the principal powers. Some countries, for example, have greater cultural or historical affinities with developed powers than others. In the same way, the economic links between some peripheral economies and developed nations are very crucial for the former, but this does not follow for all nations of Latin America. Asymmetry is in evidence at the national level as well, if one considers how Chile's own economic performance has varied with the times. The country's economic history in the twentieth century has been conditioned by two events. The first is the status attained by Argentina during the first three decades of this century, which forced Chile to relinquish its position of prominence in South America. This position was due to a period of economic prosperity in the mid-nineteenth century that was guaranteed politically by a bellicose victory in a border war between 1879 and 1882. Second, Chile's economic fortunes were seriously compromised by the devastating consequences of the world crisis of 1929–1931, which forestalled economic recovery until after World War II.

The events of the postwar period marked a turning point in the development of multilateralism in the context of Chile's foreign policy priorities in three important ways. First, Chilean diplomacy was confronted with several pressures emanating from the U.S. State Department between 1948 and 1962. The U.S. posture was most successfully wielded within the OAS, but it was also applied to its bilateral relations, where it occasionally managed to realize some of its objectives. Two examples are the negotiations for the Inter-American Treaty of Reciprocal Assistance in 1947 and the Cold War period, for each of which the U.S. government tried to obtain ideological backing—and eventually strategic political backing, too—for its foreign policy position. The highly consolidated nature of the Chilean state structure and the consistency of its diplomacy compared with that of its neighbors in Latin America made its support especially valuable from the U.S. perspective. Notwithstanding the official rhetoric of successive Chilean governments during this period, Chile maintained, in the broadest sense, a double standard. On the one hand, it kept a prudent distance between itself and the demands of the United States, and on the other, it assumed a position that could be understood as one of support for the Western side in the Cold War (Boye 1994). Overall, Chile was clearly in favor of multilateralism during this period, supporting the creation of the OAS just as it had earlier backed the founding of the UN in 1945.

Second, Chile's foreign relations with its immediate neighbors constituted another reason for its involvement in multilateral efforts. The changing circumstances of the regional context from the beginning of the twentieth century obliged Chile to modify its previous strategy. Chile's inability to wield an offensive deterrent in the border disagreements with Argentina, Bolivia, and Peru has been an extremely sensitive aspect in its foreign policy over the course of this century. Because of this inability, Chilean diplomacy has resorted to a deepening of its multilateral relations, adopting the perspective that this would make it possible to counterbalance politically the pressures from more powerful countries in the Latin American region, whether these were bordering nations or not. The basic supposition was that multilateral activity would help partially to overcome the shortage of political resources, opening up a new course of action for Chilean foreign policy and the defense of national interests.

A third explanation relates to certain bureaucratic considerations, namely, the existence of a professional foreign service. Indeed, multilateralism has always been a favorable environment for the development of a professional diplomatic bureaucracy, one that displays the attributes of political will and a capacity for negotiation. The definition of precise and attainable objectives constitutes the departure point for this political will, which, moreover, is required in order to implement a coherent foreign policy. For less powerful countries, these objectives are most easily fulfilled at the level of multilateral initiatives. The exigencies of multilateral negotiations emphasize the need for diplomatic expertise and experience, two features that are not as intensely visible at the bilateral level.

The effects of multilateralism can be stated in the form of a hypothesis: multilateralism can mitigate the asynchronous effects of global changes by permitting countries to anticipate particular circumstances and to advance a position in reaction to these. As I have presented it, this is one of the motives used by Chile and the rest of Latin America in opting to pursue a strategy of multilateral diplomacy, which is reflected in the region's political relations but also at the level of economic-commercial negotiations. In what follows, I will attempt to demonstrate this hypothesis by referring to the example of Chile's multilateral policy, particularly as it operates at the regional level. To achieve this objective, I will compare the orientation of Chile's regional policy during the period of military dictatorship (1973–1990) and in the democratic government that came to power in March 1990.

THE DOMESTIC EFFECTS OF MACROECONOMIC POLICIES

In the early 1980s there was every indication that the effects of Chilean economic growth that were in evidence after 1977 were seriously threatened by the debt crisis of 1982. Indeed, for the period 1977–1980, GDP grew at an average annual rate of 8 percent, a figure that easily surpassed the growth rate during the 1960s and early 1970s, which was situated between 3 and 4.6 percent (Banco Central de Chile 1975). Moreover, at the end of 1979, Chile's fiscal deficit had been reduced considerably, which contrasted markedly with the situation in the rest of Latin America. In addition, by 1980 inflation bordered on 30 percent, which was a considerable improvement over an inflation rate of 84 percent in 1977 (De Vylder 1989). These positive economic indicators were proof of the beneficial results of the iron-will application of a market economy, although these results had to be considered alongside the enormous social and political costs engendered by neoliberal reforms.

The prosperity of the period 1977–1980 was essentially due to two factors. First, the restrictive nature of the monetary and fiscal policies exerted a strong downward pressure on inflation and, at the same time, severely controlled public spending. Technically, it was believed that the introduction of a market economy in Chile could come only via a shock program, a measure justified as being the only means by which Chile could respond to the exigencies of a world economy that was beginning to overcome the economic delays caused by the energy crisis of 1973–1974. Second, prosperity came on the heels of a revitalized international image for the regime, which paid handsome dividends in the area of foreign investment. The neoliberal reforms guaranteed domestic economic stability and generated a positive external benefit in that they improved somewhat the international image of the military dictatorship. Following its gross human rights abuses and its proscription of the basic political rights of Chilean citizens, the military regime had suffered international condemnation. This new international image and the adoption of an exchange rate that guaranteed certain rates of interests attracted a massive increase in foreign capital investment. The take-off of the financial sector in the country's economy altered notably the behavior of domestic economic actors. The expanded presence and influence of financial institutions created an economic environment that was marked by speculation, which had the effect of expanding consumer expectations to a point previously unknown in Chile. These expectations led to an increase in the public and private debt that later would suffer the consequences of the financial crisis of 1982. Finally, and on a smaller scale, the growth expansion and the stability of the exchange rate affected several export sectors, such as mining and fruit (De Vylder 1989).

There is every indication that the prosperity of the period 1977–1981 left a lasting impression on Chilean economic actors. In spite of the recession in 1982 and 1983, during which GDP fell by 14.5 and 2.2 percent, respectively, financial activity continued apace, but with the support of the state. The military government was under no illusion that the viability of the economic model depended on creating a climate of confidence around the financial system, and for this reason any debt that was contracted by Chilean private financial institutions—either at home or abroad—would be settled by the Central Bank. The government's actions were designed to win the support of domestic actors but, more important, to guarantee the credibility of the Chilean economy for foreign investors from developed countries and for the most powerful international financial institutions. The way that the state and the private sector handled the external debt was diametrically opposite to the position taken by other Latin American countries, which were much less accommodating of international actors and institutions.

Chile's autonomous behavior was in response to two factors. First, it was a psychological reaction on the part of an authoritarian regime to pressures from the international community and was intended to moderate the effects of its virtual diplomatic isolation. These international pressures were prominent in the multilateral arena, especially in the annual reports of the UN Human Rights Commission in Geneva, which issued yearly condemnations of the Chilean regime (Muñoz 1986; Duran 1992). These pressures also emanated from certain governments, some of which consistently censured the military regime for its human rights abuses (Muñoz 1986; Duran 1992). Second, Chile's position can also be seen as an attempt to re-establish its nationalist character, a rather common feature of the foreign policies of other military regimes in the 1970s. But the Chilean nationalist thrust acquired a second motivating factor after the mid-1980s that was related to its successful management of the economy. Between 1984 and 1989, the Chilean economy enjoyed a constant growth of 6.2 percent, whereas the average for the rest of Latin America was –4.8 percent (Büchi et al. 1992: 11–19). The consequence of the rhythm and magnitude of this growth is that increasingly it distinguished the Chilean economy and society from those of the rest of the region, a tendency that sustained itself into the first years of the 1990s.

This double rationalization for the particular foreign policy of the military regime reduced the importance of regionalism for the Chilean government. The political pressures of the UN and of certain organizations associated with the European Union (EU) reinforced the aversion of the regime to engage in multilateral activities (Duran 1992). Clearly, then, there was little that the regime could expect from a foreign policy that emphasized regionalist initiatives, especially if such a policy would have brought the regime into contact with international censure (Muñoz 1986). Moreover, there was some evidence that this would have been the case. In a very concrete way, the growth of the Chilean economy and the subsequent emulation of its economic model by other countries in the region into the 1990s was interpreted as a foreign policy success for the military regime, and such an achievement had come about without the need to engage in regional initiatives.

By contrast, regionalism assumed a different meaning for the democratic government, at least at the beginning of its mandate. Just as ideological reasons, reinforced by certain objective goals, had been responsible for the low profile given to regionalism during the military dictatorship, so these very same reasons were used to support a directly opposite position under democracy. The recovery of a Latin American mission in Chilean foreign policy raised the importance of regionalism; however, this new policy direction did not assume full force until the end of the 1990–1994 presidential period and, paradoxically, it was through the medium of foreign trade. The new posture on regional co-operation was intended to support the Economic Commission for Latin America and the Caribbean (ECLAC) and Latin American Integration Association (ALADI), just as the emergence of MERCOSUR had done, but during the first two years of the democratic government, this posture was less effective than had been hoped essentially because of certain tensions between economic and political realities.

On the economic front, the policies of the government during the democratic phase were basically the same as those of the military government during the second half of the 1980s, especially regarding domestic matters and foreign trade. The democratic government was not at all concerned with establishing the validity or relevance of a market economy for an underdeveloped nation and instead accepted the preeminence of a market economy for the functioning of the world economy, especially for international trade. In this way, the democratic government stayed the course by continuing to adjust the domestic economy so that it conformed to the strict exigencies of the monetary and fiscal policies introduced by the previous military government. It rationalized this course by promoting the idea that such policies would assist Chile's foreign trade in today's increasingly competitive global economy. In fact, during its first two years in office, the democratic government pursued a policy of focusing on economic and political cooperation at the regional level. This was consonant with the priority given to Chile's international reintegration into important global and regional economic and political networks.

Chile's reintegration into these cooperative structures occurred simultaneously with two important international events. First, the Chilean transition to democracy was contemporaneous with the disappearance of the East-West confrontation at the international level, which reduced ideological conflicts in Chilean politics through the initiation of certain pragmatic political agreements. The ideological disputes of the 1960s and the political polarization of the years 1970–1973 continued to resonate in the Chilean political system, and for that reason pragmatism became a key feature of the transition. There was an important consensus among the majority of political actors regarding the principal attributes of representative democracy and the primacy of the market economy.

Second, there was the internationalization of traditionally domestic political and economic processes. The far-reaching process of democratization that struck military regimes in Latin America, Asia, and Central Europe from the mid-1980s onward returned some meaning to the distinction between domestic and international affairs. However, such a distinction does not mean that the two spheres cannot sometimes be interdependent, especially when one considers the conditions that guarantee socioeconomic growth and development. At least this was the perspective of the Chilean democratic government, which saw a clear link between the country's prosperity and the international arena. This link was reflected in a policy that created a series of rules and procedures aimed at securing the viability of a system of free trade by the second half of the 1990s. In this way, multilateral negotiations and agreements reflected a double process that, first, strongly linked regionalism with the development and defense of the democratic regime and, second, connected regionalism with a system of free trade in the area of goods and services.

Chile's first democratic government was firm about the connection between regionalism and democracy, maintaining that the former would encourage and perfect the latter, but it was not convinced at the outset about the link between regional concertation and the implementation of a regional framework for free trade. This doubt was due, in part, to the disappointing results from the efforts at integration during the 1960s and 1970s, the positive foreign trade balance for the period 1984–1989, and the vigor with which the Bush administration had introduced the Enterprise for the Americas Initiative in 1990. These economic realities and potential hemispheric developments were all arguments that weighed heavily on the pragmatic approach toward regionalism on the part of Chilean diplomacy.

There is no doubt that Chilean society in the late twentieth century has been marked profoundly by the experience of the military regime. The neoliberal experiments of this government shifted the reference point for the majority of political and social actors, especially those most closely connected to the professional and intellectual elite. Besides initiating a shift in the socioeconomic expectations of this elite and of the middle sectors in general, neoliberalism also affected the approach to decisionmaking and governing in both the domestic and international spheres. This means that the legitimacy of free trade did not issue only from the positive economic results that it produced in the second half of the 1980s but also from a changed cultural predisposition toward this form of economic activity on the part of the elite. Free trade, because it appeared to be so successful economically, began to be perceived in a positive light by social and political elites, and this sentiment extended into the governing class that assumed power in March 1990. This new perception can explain how regionalism acquired renewed importance in Chilean foreign affairs in the 1990s, both in an economic and political sense. Moreover, the democratic government had fewer fears than the previous government did in considering regionalism from a political perspective. It was conscious that the change in government was in fact a change in regime; therefore, a regional policy could improve Chile's international reputation, especially in multilateral forums.

As was the case in other Latin American countries, the mode of the transition was the product of a conjuncture of pressures and commitments. Following the results of the plebiscite of 1988 and the subsequent elections of December 1989, the balance swung toward the side of those forces that opposed the military regime. Moreover, the regime transition had the plebiscitary support of the population after it approved, in July 1989, important constitutional reforms. But it was only a practical combination of commitment and conviction on the part of political actors that ensured that the democratic government would maintain the political economy of the previous regime, at least in a general way. This policy stance had the positive effect of smoothing the rough edges in the relations between those participating in and those opposing the military regime and therefore facilitated the transition.

However, in the area of foreign policy, the new government was challenged by the need to render compatible the political profile of multilateralism with the preservation of a successful system of free trade. In response to this challenge, Chile's multilateralism took on a hybrid form. On the one hand, it responded to the political objective of multilateralism, which consisted of offering unconditional support to political democratization and promoting human rights in the region; on the other hand, the government pursued its strategy of export diversification inherited from the military regime, making only minor modifications to the system.

The policy of export diversification allowed Chile to pursue various strategies. For example, in 1993 Chile signed and ratified a basic agreement with the EU at the same time that Chilean-U.S. relations were tightening in anticipation of Chile's integration into the North American Free Trade Agreement. In a parallel process, Chile signed bilateral agreements covering a broad range of areas with Mexico and Venezuela, which raised the possibility of its eventually signing trade agreements with Argentina and Peru. By all indications, Chile was opting for bilateral commercial arrangements at the expense of multilateral ones. The rationale for this preference could be found in the very real economic benefits that these types of arrangements provided: GDP growth was at 2.1 percent in 1990, climbed to more than 5 percent in 1991, and reached just over 10 percent in 1992. This performance was markedly better than the historic average of 6.4 percent for the period 1950 to 1970, and 't situated Chile at the vanguard of Latin American development. C rtainly, these growth rates cannot be attributed entirely to foreign trade, but qualitative and quantitative increases in exports have caused an increase in foreign exchange, and this has had a positive impact on international reserves and the capitalization of the Chilean economy.

A second strategy for export diversification was the search for foreign markets for industrial and financial investments. This marked a new phase in the internationalization of the Chilean economy after 1990. Opportunities for investment abroad were stimulated by the high levels of capitalization attained by some firms that had been privatized during the mid-1980s, as well as by the difficulties experienced by various economies in the region. These conditions gave Chilean businesses the opportunity to push into more extensive markets and to respond to a wider range of demands for services. This strategy has been most successfully pursued in Argentina and Peru, where Chilean capital is an important percentage of foreign investment. However, Chile has not limited itself to investing in Latin American markets; it has also made important financial investments in the United States.

As a response to the economic crisis of 1982, Chile's financial sector committed itself to ameliorating its institutions by adopting some of the practices of the financial markets and stock exchanges of the United States, Japan, and Europe. These efforts and the growth of Chile's GDP guaranteed that within only a few years the country's markets and financial institutions would acquire a sophisticated expertise. By the beginning of the 1990s, this expertise propelled Chilean businesses to take advantage of alternative opportunities in the markets of developed economies. The employment of American Depository Receipts by Chilean financial institutions and firms not only increased their relative profitability but also strengthened the internationalization of the country's economy, which had an eventual impact on regionalism.

The examination of export diversification shows that the promotion of regionalism is not the exclusive prerogative of government; it also depends on how government efforts are perceived in other circles. It is a rather complex procedure that links decisions that simultaneously affect state interests and those of actors situated at other levels of the economy. Increasingly in Chile, the decisionmaking and feedback processes associated with regional multilateralism are not subordinated to government requests because the economy has acquired a certain amount of autonomy from government and nonstate actors have expanded their range of activity in Chilean society. Although the state does retain the capacity to initiate policy and leads the way in foreign affairs, other actors are no longer dependent on government institutions in order to engage in multilateral efforts, especially at the regional level. Because Chile's economy is a complex of networks at the domestic level and is very interdependent at the external level, some consensual decisionmaking is required, especially in foreign trade. So although the effective implementation of macroeconomic policy remains the purview of government, the design of this policy requires the input of a variety of actors and must respond to certain societal needs. Moreover, there are precedents for this type of societal intervention in other Latin American countries, although it is not without opposition in some sectors. One need only recall the iron-will opposition of associations of Venezuelan employers who participated in the subregional Andean market at the beginning of the 1970s, an attitude that postponed for years Venezuela's integration into the Andean Common Market.

The Venezuelan experience has an echo in Chile, where just prior to the transition to democracy, an influential group of employers did not support the integration of the country's economy into the trading circuit at the regional level. This opposition was influenced by the failure of previous attempts at regional integration in the 1960s and 1970s. The ideological skepticism of this sector toward such processes was deepened by its belief that the state had assumed a strong role in these earlier efforts. This group therefore adopted a discourse that emphasized the errors of these experiments and their total failure in the weak economies of Latin America. The position of this group was summarized in its judgments that what was most essential for Chile was to keep all of its trading options open and that the Latin American market represented only one option out of many. In any event, there were no significant changes made to the orientation of Chile's foreign trade between 1990 and 1993; the strategy of diversifying markets adopted in 1985–1986 was simply extended. Accordingly, overtures were made to the EU and the Asia-Pacific Economic Cooperation (APEC).

Chile had developed trading links with the EU under the military regime that were not insignificant: for the period 1987–1991, trade with EU member states represented approximately one-third of total Chilean trade, reaching 37.3 percent in 1990. Countries such as West Germany remained among Chile's top three trading partners for the period 1985–1989. The notable position of the Chilean economy within Latin America, as well as the change in regime, created

favorable conditions for the signing of a broad trade agreement between Chile and the EU at the end of 1990, referred to as a "third
generation" agreement. Politically, this agreement enhanced certain
privileges that the EU was willing to grant Chile, privileges from
which very few countries in Latin America had benefited. However,
the vagaries of world trade and the economic effects of political
changes in Europe between 1988 and 1990 restricted the applicabil-
ity of the agreement and moved several members of the EU to impose protectionist measures that affected Chilean exports. These
measures reduced the flow of Chilean exports to Europe, with the result that by the end of 1992 these exports represented less than 30
percent of total Chilean exports. European imports, however, did not
decline appreciably, moving from 21 percent of total imports in 1990
to 19.2 in 1992.

A significant proportion of Chile's loss in the European market
was recovered through a sustained increase in the amount of trade
with Latin America. Specifically, in 1990 trade with the member
countries of MERCOSUR represented 7.6 percent of total Chilean
trade but by 1992 had reached almost 10 percent. Based on trends
and predictions, trade with MERCOSUR for the period 1993–1995
should reach 13 percent of total Chilean trade, which would represent a doubling of Chilean-MERCOSUR trade in only five years. This
upward trend has been duplicated on the import side: imports from
MERCOSUR represented 15.5 percent of total imports in 1990 and
reached 18 percent by the end of 1992. Since 1990, MERCOSUR has
shown itself to be a vital force in the complex web of regional relations, which has forced the Chilean government to revise its initial
indifference toward MERCOSUR's development. The prospect of a
common tariff and the implementation of various institutional projects will force Chile to solicit a formal association with MERCOSUR,
a status that Chilean diplomats should negotiate by paying careful attention to certain conditions. It is possible to speculate on the inevitability of Chile becoming a full member, but before this could
happen, Chile would have to overcome its extreme pragmatism and
particularism regarding the way it envisions its regional policy.

Trade with Latin American countries is not the only aspect of
Chilean regionalism that is experiencing upward shifts. Recent data
reveal a constant flow of investment from Latin America into the
Chilean economy. A study by the Central Bank showed that from
1974 to 1994 Latin American investment increased fourfold, reaching 7.7 percent of projects in progress by mid-1994. Compared with
investments from the United States and Canada (51 percent of projects in progress), this figure is not very significant. Nevertheless,
what is interesting for our purposes is to detect the short- and/or

medium-term trend of Latin American investments. According to the Central Bank study, the trend is toward increasing investments (Banco Central de Chile 1994). As long as this projection proves to be correct, Latin American investment will contribute toward the global diversification of the Chilean economy.

Moving to the Asia Pacific region, Chile's trade with the countries in that part of the world has increased measurably. At the end of 1990, Chilean trade with APEC represented almost 26 percent of total trade, and this figure increased to approximately 31 percent in 1992. Chile's admission to APEC in 1993 must be seen as one of the most important successes of the country's multilateral diplomacy under the first democratic government, especially if one considers the short- and medium-term implications of this admission for Chile's political and commercial presence in the region. It is expected that by the end of 1995, or by mid-1996 at the latest, trade with APEC will represent 34 percent of total Chilean trade. Aside from the comparative advantages for trade, the Asia Pacific region is one of the spheres toward which Chile's foreign policy is seeking to gravitate. For this reason, it is highly probable that for the next few years, Chile will assign significant diplomatic resources to this area in order to develop a high-profile policy for the region.

EXPECTED PROJECTIONS IN CHILE'S REGIONAL POLICY

Chilean regional multilateralism is similar to that of other Latin American countries in that it has two institutional channels. The first and oldest of these functions is at the regional, or inter-American, level and has as its organizational reference point the OAS. Not only was Chile one of the founding members of the OAS, it has also been, since the end of the 1960s, a principal actor in its various component units. During the 1960s, and especially after the U.S. invasion of the Dominican Republic, the Chilean delegation was among those that promoted noninterventionism while advocating a substantial reform of both the structure and the purpose of the OAS. Chile's relations with the OAS changed substantially under the military regime. After 1973, Chile was harshly censured by the Interamerican Commission on Human Rights. While these charges did not manage to isolate Chile to the same extent as those emanating from the UN, they nevertheless further stigmatized the international reputation of the regime and lessened Chile's influence within the OAS. (Among other things, this loss of status provided Bolivia with the opportunity to have a historical grievance against Chile addressed by the 1979 Annual Assembly of the OAS. The grievance centered on Bolivia's loss of territory on the Pacific coast as a result of a military occupation by Chile during a nineteenth-century war.)

The return to democracy in 1990 reaffirmed the importance of the hemispheric democratization process for Chile's foreign policy and made democratic consolidation its most important objective. In 1990 the Annual Assembly of the OAS approved the Declaration of Santiago de Chile, with the intention of renovating the organization's agenda and defining a concrete role for the OAS in the changed political context of the region. This declaration highlighted the importance of democracy and proposed certain preventive actions in order to assist in the process of democratic consolidation. Among its many principles, the declaration emphasized the necessity of politically isolating governments that opposed or violated democratic principles. Taking its cue from these criteria, the Chilean government determinedly supported the auspices of the new Program for the Consolidation of Democracy, which falls under the purview of the secretariat of the OAS.

Chile's involvement in multilateral regionalism at times conflicts with its bilateral relations, and in this respect the Peruvian case is illustrative. At this point, it is not clear whether the eventual restoration of democracy in Peru will come as a response to internal or external pressures, including, among the latter, the injunctions of the General Assembly of the OAS. Although for historical and political-strategic reasons, maintaining cordial relations with Peru has been a priority in Chilean diplomacy, Chile's open support of these external pressures from the OAS may have negative repercussions for already fragile bilateral relations between the countries.

The problem of merging bilateral considerations with hemispheric multilateralism was also evident in the complex relations between Chile and Argentina during the 1980s. One only need remember the extraordinary May 1982 session of the OAS, during the middle of the Falklands war, convoked by Argentina in accordance with the Inter-American Treaty of Reciprocal Assistance. While the majority of countries supported Argentina, Chile preferred to abstain; this position was taken because of some border tensions between the two countries during this period that had caused strong resentment in Chilean-Argentine relations. Chile's posture in the OAS on this occasion, therefore, conformed to a strategy that consisted of mutual political and diplomatic pressures.

During this century, border crises have provoked serious conflicts of interest between Latin American countries, and even some wars. To the extent that these differences, or others that might emerge, will persist in endangering national interests, the potential for conflict between neighboring countries will require the complete vigilance of hemispheric multilateralism. The necessity, and sometimes the urgency, of maintaining a practical modus vivendi between neighbors will condition the political objectives of regional multilateralism. Such has been, and will continue to be, the case with Chile.

Political concertatión is the second most relevant area of activity for Chilean regional multilateralism. Here, however, it is necessary to distinguish between the position taken by the military regime and that of the democratic government because they appear to be antagonistic. For the military regime, regional concertatión was almost entirely irrelevant. The very notion of multilateralism did not conform to the style of a military regime's foreign policy. Since the central assumptions of the dictatorship's foreign policy rested on its convergence with a strict conception of realism, any form or instance of negotiation that did not involve a redistribution of international power was considered irrelevant.

The reticence displayed by the military regime toward regional multilateralism also had an ideological root. At the beginning of the 1980s a group of Latin American countries, principally the Contadora Group and the Contadora Support Group, attempted to draw a purely Latin American outline of hemispheric security, but one that did not rely on the support of Chile. From a global perspective, this regional policy conformed to the logic of the East-West conflict, the same logic that ran through all aspects of international relations at that time. Within this framework, no degree of autonomy was conceivable, not in the Central American imbroglio or in any other regional process.

Without a doubt, Chile's return to democracy progressively altered the conception and extent of multilateralism in its foreign relations. As I have already noted, the priorities of its hemispheric policy consisted in promoting democracy in the Americas, and toward that end it relied on the institutional structure of the OAS. This facilitated, moreover, obtaining the sometimes wayward support of the United States on this front. But it was Chile's incorporation into the Rio Group in mid-1990 that marked the return of its traditional regional posture that since 1940 had represented an important aspect of its foreign policy but that, for ideological reasons, had been abandoned between 1974 and 1989 (Duran 1992). Strictly speaking, the origin of Chile's regional policy was the Pan-American Union conferences of the late nineteenth and early twentieth centuries. This policy acquired a new force at the end of the 1960s, when Chile's Ministry of Foreign Affairs assumed a preeminent role in hemispheric political affairs with the Viña del Mar Consensus of 1969. In a chronological sense, this was the first expression of political concertation between Latin American countries, and its objective consisted of making certain propositions to the United States regarding a new style of hemispheric relations (Yopo 1993).

Considering that for over fifteen years not one Chilean proposal for regional political cooperation was ever made or debated, its admission to the Rio Group was a sign that this omission would soon be redressed. Still, Chile's membership does not mean that the country's multilateral diplomacy will change profoundly; since 1990, Chilean pragmatism and particularism has not been altered substantially.

Essentially, Chile's pragmatism consists in extending the logic of comparative advantage from the commercial sphere to the political one. Thus there is a twofold explanation for Chile's membership in an organization such as the Rio Group: First, the political cost of remaining outside such an organization is greater than being inside, even if Chile maintains a low profile. Despite its limitations, the Rio Group is in a position to articulate an effective regional posture that opens up the opportunity to each member country, and to the group acting together, to attain a position of greater prominence in world politics. Second, regional concertation is not a substitute for Latin American integrationalism, certainly not when the experiences of the late 1960s and early 1970s are considered. To achieve a consensus on certain fundamental issues does not preclude the emergence of other objectives that eventually might become as, or even more, relevant, depending on certain circumstances. From the Chilean perspective, the Rio Group should be a flexible organization, one that will facilitate the articulation of a conjuncture of propositions regarding the political effects of economic-commercial interdependence and globalization. Chile is also interested in promoting the evolution of an organization that will encourage the debate of common political concerns, above all those that are related to the consolidation of democracy and the respect for human rights.

Particularism is a second aspect of Chile's multilateral diplomacy. By this I mean that the country's participation in regional forums is understood as a process in itself, relatively autonomous in both its functional and demand structure. It should be obvious that from the perspective of Chilean diplomacy, instances of political multilateralism (the annual meetings of the Rio Group and the meetings of heads of state of Latin America) are not homologous with mechanisms for commercial cooperation (ECLAC, ALADI, and MERCO-SUR), since each of these has distinct institutional priorities. But above all else, they are not homologous in a factual sense, because each generates certain processes that cannot be extended from one to the other, nor can they be compared. This is not to say that political concertation and regional cooperation do not have a global meaning. What can be said, by contrast, is that each is imbued with its own dynamism, reinforced by the particular institutions of each of its organizations. We need, therefore, to understand them as "international regimes" in the strictest sense.

It is evident that institutional autonomy at the regional level is subsumed under global processes. These tend to manifest themselves in the medium and long term at that moment when a conjuncture of international events obliges a reconsideration of the system that had been in operation until then. What remains to be seen is what will become of this re-examination of Latin American regionalism and what impact it will have on countries such as Chile.

11

Conclusion:
External Forces, State Strategies,
and Regionalism in the Americas

◆

W. Andrew Axline

The preceding chapters provide an analysis of the factors underlying the emergence of a dominant vision of regionalism in the Americas over the past few years. They offer an explanation of how the vision inspired by Bolívar has succumbed to the vision embodied in the Monroe Doctrine as the dominant organizing force in Latin America today. The purpose of this chapter is to draw some broad conclusions from the foregoing analyses in order to contribute to the understanding of the larger processes leading to the emerging form of regionalism in the Americas at the end of the twentieth century. The chapter is divided into two parts. The first section contains a synthesis of the evolution of the domestic and foreign policies (state strategies) of the countries of the hemisphere as a response to the changes in their external environment. The second draws conclusions about the overall structure of regionalism in the Americas that may emerge by the end of the century.

NAFTA, STATE STRATEGIES, AND THE NEW REGIONALISM

The emergence of regional blocs represents a new and different form of regionalism, characterized by its major objective of guaranteeing bloc members greater security in their international economic relations in a context of increasing vulnerability. It is the product of the pursuit of strategic trade policy through domestic and foreign policy, including regional policies and institutions. "Strategic regionalism" is the term applied to this new form of regionalism, which distinguishes it from the earlier examples of integration in Europe and other parts of the world. The North American Free Trade Agreement (NAFTA) can be seen as the manifestation of strategic regionalism in the North American context (Deblock and Brunelle 1993). It is primarily outwardly oriented, providing the United States, Canada, and Mexico a way of reducing their external constraints and facilitating the attainment of their international economic policies. NAFTA affords the United States the means to redefine the rules governing international economic relations in a trilateral configuration with Japan and the European Union and adds another tool to those of unilateral protectionism, bilateralism, and multilateral negotiations in attempting to retain its hegemonic position in international markets (Deblock and Brunelle 1993: 605–607).

The shift of perspective from neoclassical customs union theory to neomercantilist strategic trade theory also contributes to our understanding of the new regionalism, with NAFTA providing the key element in the determination of the direction of regionalism in the Americas in the 1990s. Understood as an example of strategic regionalism, NAFTA is not about freeing trade. Rather, it is part of a system of management whereby the state can intervene in the economy to promote the interests of its corporations ("Implications" 1993). As such, it represents a response to globalization in the post–Cold War period, in which the loss of strategic importance, the decline of U.S. hegemony, and the regionalization of policies combine to lead the United States to seek a regional dominance in place of lost global hegemony. The policies of the other countries of the Americas can in turn be understood as responses to the U.S. policy of strategic regionalism.

Domestic Reform and Foreign Policy

The analysis in the preceding chapters of the specific domestic and foreign policy responses of countries to the impact of globalization provides an insight into the eventual form that regionalism in the Americas will take. The patterns described in those chapters will in turn determine the architecture of the Americas as reflected in the institutions and policies at the hemispheric, regional, and subregional levels, including the established organizations of regional cooperation such as the Central American Common Market (CACM), the Andean Group, and the Caribbean Community and Common Market (CARICOM), as well as new initiatives such as the Association of Caribbean States (ACS), the Group of Three (G-3), the Southern Cone Common Market (MERCOSUR), and a potential South American Free Trade Area (SAFTA).

The three original signatories of NAFTA, the United States, Canada, and Mexico, have chosen this path as part of their broader domestic and foreign policy objectives in response to the imperatives of the new world order. Although Louis Balthazar places the NAFTA initiative within the historical continuity of U.S. policy toward Latin America from Kennedy to Bush, it clearly represents a response to the new position occupied by the United States in the post–Cold War order (Chapter 1). Similarly, Canada's decision to embrace NAFTA reflects the convergence of a failed "Third Option," a shift in domestic policy according to the globalized neoliberal agenda, and the desire to protect the gains from the Canadian-U.S. Free Trade Agreement (Chapter 3). For Mexico, adherence to NAFTA involved a more radical shift in domestic and foreign policy, based on extensive domestic reforms and implying a new commitment to an open trade regime that will more fundamentally affect economic, social, and political change than in the two other partner states (Chapter 2).

As the dominant power in the hemisphere, the United States sets the parameters for regionalism in the Americas. The rules embodied in NAFTA and the framework agreements signed under the Enterprise for the Americas Initiative, inter alia, provide the institutional context for these parameters, which will in turn determine the opportunities and conditions for participation in regional processes by other countries of the hemisphere. Mexico will also play a key role in the eventual form that regionalism in the Americas will take, depending in part on its ability to benefit from membership in NAFTA and in part on its ability to occupy the role of intermediary through which other Latin American and Caribbean countries may define their access to the larger North American market.

The impact of NAFTA on Mexico's economic well-being is crucial because NAFTA represents the first time that an economic integration agreement has been concluded between partners of such different levels of economic development. Although traditional customs union theory suggests that "spread" effects will benefit the lesser developed partner, the experience of regional integration among developing countries with great disparities of wealth provides a less sanguine outlook (Axline 1994). Failure to produce the anticipated gains or, still worse, significant negative effects from NAFTA could result in a shift in the perceived desirability of participation on the part of other countries. Having said that, it is apparent that virtually all Latin American and Caribbean countries see some form of access to the North American market as key to the success of their domestic reforms and foreign trade policies.

If Canada chose NAFTA as a means to consolidate gains achieved in the Free Trade Agreement with the United States, Mexico took a bold step seizing on the opportunity for a closer relationship with the United States over one with its Latin neighbors, in large measure as a means to consolidate hard-won domestic reforms. The choice is not so clear for other countries of the hemisphere, and the eventual available options will depend on several factors. First, there must be a willingness and capability to make the domestic reforms and trade policy changes necessary for insertion into the regional processes. Second, the particular paths chosen will depend on the level of development and capacity to benefit from freer trade, as well as the alternative options available to a given country. Third, and not least important, will be the acceptability and desirability on the part of the United States to enter into arrangements with a given country. This last factor is closely related to the previous two, as the more economically "stabilized" and the more politically "reformed" a given country, the more likely it will be acceptable as a partner in NAFTA.

The previous chapters show that virtually all the countries of the region have undertaken domestic economic and political reforms to some degree. These reforms reflect unambiguously the redefinition of state-market relations that correspond to the neoliberal ideology of globalization underlying the open approach required by the strategic regionalism of the United States. The analysis in the preceding chapters of the new policy directions chosen by the countries of the region shows, however, that the extent of the reforms varies considerably from country to country and that it may not be possible to maintain a strong thrust in this direction indefinitely.[1]

Anthony Payne's analysis illustrates the dilemma produced by the transition from the Cold War to the new world order as Jamaica finds itself poised between the old world and the new, facing new challenges in the Americas as European ties are redefined by globalization and the new regionalism. Provided direction by the redefinition of its domestic and external policies from the early 1980s, Jamaica has assumed the role of leader of the Commonwealth Caribbean countries' shift within the new regionalism. As the most important CARICOM country, Jamaica is eager to sign a framework agreement under the Enterprise for the Americas Initiative; this readiness set a direction for a redefined Caribbean regional arrangement, with a closer connection between CARICOM and the Central American countries within the ACS (Chapter 4). This shift provided the foundation for a new definition of the Caribbean Basin based on the mercantilist imperatives of the new regionalism rather than the strategic concerns of the Cold War (Axline 1988).

The three Andean countries of Venezuela, Colombia, and Peru have also adopted new policy directions in response to the challenges of globalization and regionalization. The *apertura* of Colombia involved opening and modernization of the international trade regime, a new impulse toward multilateral policies, and support of a variety of subregional trade initiatives, including the Rio Group, the G-3, and the Andean Group. A commitment to freer trade with Mexico and Venezuela also opens up the possibility of access to the larger network of trade encompassing all of the Americas (Chapter 6). Colombian policy reveals an additional consideration in the eventual pattern of regionalism, raising concerns that too intensive integration with subregional partners may become an impediment to eventual broader integration into the open regionalism of the Americas. It also raises an issue that has largely been ignored in the new regionalism but that remains an important obstacle to broader integration: asymmetry among partners. This issue is relevant also to Venezuela and is of even greater significance to Peru. With the failures that have marked the later history of the Andean Group, bilateral ties with Venezuela have assumed a greater role in Colombia's strategy.

Andrés Serbin's analysis provides a clear example of the combination of external pressures of globalization and internal crises leading to the *gran viraje* in Venezuela's foreign policy. Domestic reforms —involving traditional economic restructuring based on fiscal and monetary adjustments, deregulation, and privatization—have been pursued jointly with a policy of outwardly oriented growth based on an opening up of commercial policy (Chapter 5). On the foreign policy side, Venezuela's position in the regional economy provides it with the possibility of pursuing regional relations on a number of different fronts. While direct access to NAFTA through relations with the United States has not been ruled out, various subregional possibilities are being pursued in the bilateral relationship with Colombia, the creation of the G-3 and its key relationship with Mexico, greater cooperation with Central America and the Caribbean through the ACS, and a greater emphasis on the Andean Group.

Peru's diplomacy has been more active on a subregional, regional, and extraregional basis, although the domestic and foreign policy shifts have shown less realignment than some of the other countries of the region (Chapter 7). As one of the less advantaged members of the Andean Group, Peru finds itself faced with more limited opportunities than Colombia or Venezuela. Peru's ability to achieve a satisfactory insertion into the regional economy is more likely to depend on a collective approach through subregional organizations such as the Andean Group, in which Peru's negotiating strength vis-à-vis the United States may be enhanced by regional solidarity, or through eventual access to the G-3 as a means of creating links with NAFTA via Mexico.

The Southern Cone presents a somewhat different picture, and it is likely that the pattern of regionalism there will play a major role in determining the overall structure of regionalism in the Americas. With the election of President Fernando Cardoso in Brazil, there is some indication that the subregional grouping of MERCOSUR may assume the lines of "open regionalism" now promoted by the Economic Commission for Latin America and the Caribbean (ECLAC), but this will depend on the position adopted by Argentina, Uruguay, and Paraguay toward the Brazilian initiatives. Recent changes in the domestic policies of Brazil, Chile, and Argentina offer important insights into the relationship between domestic and foreign policies, globalization, and the new regionalism.

The sheer scale of the Brazilian economy places this country in a unique position. Its size contributes to its perception as a potential threat by Latin American neighbors, enhances its self-perception of having opportunities and even an independent destiny, and has allowed it to retain a more inward orientation than its neighbors. This perception of greater self-sufficiency has allowed it to pursue a pace of restructuring and reform less dictated by outside forces and has given it greater latitude in pursuing different regional options (Chapter 8). The decision to redefine its relationship with Argentina in a way that eventually led to the creation of MERCOSUR was an important foreign policy choice. This decision was based as much on the self-perception of Brazil as a "global trader" as it was on the recognition that NAFTA provided a very uncertain basis for the creation of a hemispheric regionalism. MERCOSUR could provide the institutional focus for enhancing the bargaining strength of Argentina, Brazil, Uruguay, and Paraguay vis-à-vis the United States, it could provide a framework for locking in domestic reform, and it could provide the platform for diversification of trade.

Chile's situation is in stark contrast to that of Brazil. Lacking any delusions of potential self-sufficiency, Chile is a middle-level country with several viable options, the most preferred one being accepted as a full member of NAFTA. Domestic policies of restructuring and stabilization have been in place for years and have made Chile the most "eligible" candidate for accession. However, this has not prevented Chile from pursuing bilateral and regional agreements with other Latin American countries, including affiliation with MERCOSUR on a basis less than that of full membership. The domestic policy response of Chile to the challenge of globalization is unambiguous, whereas the foreign policy response represents a form of "pragmatic regionalism," with much hope being placed on membership in NAFTA (Chapter 10).

Argentina, however, reflects the true ambivalence of a country that has neither the opportunity for full integration into NAFTA, such as Chile, nor the size and viability of a potential global trader, such as Brazil. The analysis by Marc Hufty shows that Argentina represents the archetype of the processes underlying the new directions of regionalism in the Americas (Chapter 9). It has undergone the most dramatic changes in the realm of domestic and foreign policy in response to its global and regional environments. The response in terms of domestic policies included the acceptance of an orthodox approach to economic development to replace a vacillation between dirigisme and laissez-faire approaches and a strong commitment to structural economic reform, involving an emergency liberalization program and a fully backed currency, which led to a dramatic improvement in the rate of inflation. Commercial policy shifted from a protectionist approach based on the earlier Economic Commission for Latin America (ECLA) doctrine to one of insertion into the globalized economy that included the acceptance of the United States as the central axis of foreign policy. It also took a new approach to regionalism, involving cooperating with Chile on a bilateral basis under the Latin American Integration Association (ALADI) and with Brazil in MERCOSUR. Although clearly not as prepared for membership in NAFTA as Chile, Argentina wavers between the open regionalism of hemispheric free trade and closer integration with Brazil in MERCOSUR. It has already committed itself to MERCOSUR (with which it has had a not always smooth relationship) and has negotiated the 4+1, or "Rose Garden," Agreement under the Enterprise for the Americas Initiative. The vitality and dynamism of MERCOSUR will be a key factor in determining the eventual direction of Argentina's regional policy.

It is through the policies pursued by these individual states of the region that the broad changes in the global political economy will have a significant influence on the direction of regionalism in the Americas. As indicated above, the most direct influence flows from NAFTA, the Enterprise for the Americas Initiative, and the possibilities of a free trade agreement of the Americas, uniting all of the Western Hemisphere. This influence will have a direct impact on the established subregional organizations (CACM, CARICOM, Andean Group) as well as on the emerging forms of regional cooperation in Latin America (MERCOSUR, G-3, ACS), which in turn will define the overall structure of regionalism in the Americas into the next century. The various strategies analyzed in the preceding chapters provide the basis for outlining the broad features of an eventual architecture of the Americas.

NEW DIRECTIONS IN REGIONALISM

Latin American and Caribbean countries face several options in their efforts to seek access to the U.S. market as the central element of their attempts at insertion into the globalized political economy. The first option is to seek a direct bilateral agreement with the United States. This option holds little hope for smaller, less developed economies that provide virtually no incentive for the United States to enter into negotiations. The second option is to seek unilateral accession to NAFTA, joining Mexico and Canada in a multilateral free trade agreement with the United States. The possibilities of this are also limited, as all three original parties must agree to accept any new signatories; Mexico may be reluctant to grant equal access to potential Latin American competitors, and the United States may prefer to deal with potential partners through bilateral arrangements. Moreover, the United States has indicated that only those countries that meet its standards of domestic reform and international trade policy will be candidates for admittance, thus reducing the field significantly (perhaps limiting it only to Chile, which began negotiations for accession in 1995). The third possibility is for Latin American and Caribbean countries to join with their subregional partners in signing a "framework agreement" under the Enterprise for the Americas Initiative as a preliminary step in negotiating liberalized trade with the United States. The fourth option is for Latin American countries to seek bilateral or subregional agreements with Mexico as a springboard to the larger North American market. These options are not mutually exclusive, and in fact a number of countries are pursuing several of them simultaneously. The choices that the various Latin American countries make will ultimately determine the structure of regionalism in the Americas.

Based on the examples of new directions in domestic and foreign policy analyzed previously, it is possible to summarize in three scenarios the possible directions that Latin American integration may be taking. Each scenario represents the consequences of a strategy of insertion into the globalized and regionalized economy on the part of individual countries. The three scenarios result from a two-level choice process on the part of a country: First, there is a choice between, on the one hand, seeking direct membership or access to the North American market through full membership in NAFTA or a bilateral agreement with one of the signatories of NAFTA and, on the other hand, seeking a subregional approach in collaboration with regional partners. Second, if a subregional approach is adopted, a choice is to be made between a regional strategy as a preparatory step to seeking a collective negotiated entry to NAFTA and a subregional strategy that seeks to create a strong regional counterweight to NAFTA. In the latter case the subregional organization would bargain bilaterally with NAFTA over potential mutual concessions. The choice of policies by the various countries would result in three possible scenarios of subregional cooperation:[2]

1.   A unilateral direct approach to NAFTA would be likely to lead to subregional disintegration in the face of strong attraction of NAFTA. Each member state would attempt to negotiate its best bilateral deal with NAFTA at the expense of intraregional cooperation. Other forms of bilateral and subregional cooperation would be subordinated to this option.

2.   Subregional integration could be adopted as a preparatory step to entering NAFTA. This approach would see the creation of subregional organizations as a means to adopt intraregional policies that would prepare them better for accession to NAFTA as a group and provide greater negotiating weight through a common front. These subregional policies would likely be quite different from the past experiences of regional integration in Latin America.

3.   Subregional integration could be pursued as a strategy to produce a counterweight to NAFTA. Member countries of subregional organizations would attempt to solidify their intraregional ties to strengthen their negotiating position vis-à-vis NAFTA on a region-to-region bilateral basis.

Which of these scenarios is most likely will depend upon the various factors that influence the processes of regional integration, including domestic economic and political factors, the distribution of regional benefits, and extraregional opportunities available to each of the member countries (Axline 1977). Larger, more developed countries with greater bargaining weight and wider opportunities for trade and investment will be more likely to pursue unilateral approaches in gaining access to the North American market, whereas smaller, less developed countries with fewer alternative opportunities will be constrained to pursue a subregional approach. For most countries this subregional approach will be aimed at an eventual incorporation into the NAFTA arrangements as a group, and the subregional arrangements will be designed to achieve this end. Only the most important Latin American countries will be able to conceive of creating a Latin American subregional counterweight to NAFTA, and these subregional arrangements will differ significantly from those designed for negotiating entry into NAFTA. Thus the scenario chosen as a response to the strategic regionalism of NAFTA will determine both the future direction of subregional integration in

Latin America and the larger architecture of the regionalism of the Americas.

Subregional Cooperation

By the 1980s it was clear that regional integration in Latin America was moribund. The ambitious plans that had marked the efforts of the Andean Group had been abandoned; an attempt had been made to resurrect ALADI out of the ashes of the Latin American Free Trade Association on the basis of a bilateral set of arrangements; the CACM was struggling to relaunch the Central American efforts; and CARICOM plodded forward in the face of successive crises. The new efforts at integration in Latin America and the Caribbean under-taken in the wake of these earlier experiences clearly reflect the im-pact of globalization and the new regionalism. The goals of regional cooperation had shifted from those of import substitution, integra-tion of production, and collective self-reliance to those of solidifying domestic reforms and ensuring future access to the larger North American and global markets as a means of stimulating growth through increased foreign investment, greater competition, and more rapid diffusion of technology (De Melo and Panagariya 1992: 25; Mytelka 1992). The new direction chosen by existing integration schemes as well as the newly launched projects can be understood in the light of this new regionalism, which is reflected in the dramatic contrast between the thrust of ECLA's efforts at promoting regional integration as part of the new international economic order in the 1970s and its new promotion of "open regionalism" in the new world order of the 1990s.[3]

The position taken by Jamaica and the other small countries of the Caribbean suggests the emergence of a subregional integration movement as a basis for collective negotiated access for the Com-monwealth Caribbean countries to the larger North American mar-ket, either on their own or in coordination with the countries of Central America. The expression of interest on the part of non-Caribbean countries, including Colombia, Venezuela, Suriname, and Mexico, also provides the possibility of access to the wider North American market through the ACS. Here the role of Mexico will be important in determining the nature of the relationship to NAFTA and the eventual larger architecture of regionalism in the Americas. On the other side of the Caribbean, Costa Rica provides an example of the situation of the Central American countries as they develop strategies for insertion into the global and regional political econ-omy (Salazar-Xirinachs 1993). The CACM and CARICOM reflect the need for smaller countries to negotiate collectively to gain access to the larger American bloc, using the subregional institutions to adopt domestic and intraregional policies that will both help them adapt to the conditions of the larger regionalism and better prepare them for acceptance into the NAFTA arrangements. The alternative opportunities available to the countries of Central America and the Caribbean are so limited as to make any unilateral approach to NAFTA, even on the part of the largest among them, unfeasible. The creation of the ACS is the tangible manifestation of this reality.

Venezuela, Colombia, and Peru provide examples of middle-level Latin American countries that find themselves between the pull of greater access to NAFTA and the existing and new ties with subregional partners. The eventual policy directions that these countries will follow may well determine the larger pattern of regionalism in the Americas that will emerge. Without the economic potential of Brazil, and lacking the basis for greater integration with the United States that Mexico enjoys or the acceptability to NAFTA that Chile possesses, these countries have adopted strategies that represent a variety of approaches to insertion into the global and regional economies. The middle-level status of the Andean countries puts them in an ambivalent position, with inevitable consequences for the future of the Andean Group. Significant enough to entertain some possibility of gaining access to NAFTA or of concluding a bilateral arrangement with the United States but uncertain about the success of achieving either one, these countries see a subregional approach as a reasonable alternative. Centrifugal forces work against strong subregional solidarity, however, which is exemplified by Chile's negotiations for full membership in NAFTA and Venezuela's simultaneously pursuing a number of regional alternatives and keeping open bilateral ties with the United States.

The new regionalism is likely to have an impact on all the existing regional integration schemes in Latin America, undermining regional institutions of a strong dirigiste character, whether they are for industrial allocation, redistribution of benefits, or regulation of foreign investment. Preparation for insertion into the larger regionalism of the Americas requires an openness to trade and investment, with a minimum role for the state, which contradicts long-standing trends in regional integration among developing countries. The G-3, the ACS, and MERCOSUR are examples of new subregional cooperation that illustrate different scenarios in response to the challenge of the new regionalism in the Americas. The first and second are examples of groups that may eventually be incorporated into NAFTA, whereas the third could form the basis of a counterweight to NAFTA.

With the G-3, Colombia and Venezuela have negotiated an agreement with Mexico designed to open up trade among themselves with the dual purpose of consolidating the impetus of domestic and foreign trade reforms and of providing access to the larger market of NAFTA through specific arrangements with Mexico. If Colombia and Venezuela do not eventually attain direct access to the U.S. market, Mexico may still serve as an intermediary via the G-3. Trade agreements with other Andean countries, either on a bilateral basis with Mexico or as adherents to the G-3, would enhance Mexico's role as a crucial link between Latin American countries and NAFTA. Such agreements would be attractive even for countries that aspired to full accession to NAFTA, either as a preparatory step or as a fallback position if unilateral accession was not achieved. Thus the emergence of Mexico as a central link between NAFTA and the rest of the Americas will have a significant influence on the larger pattern of regionalism in the Americas.

Venezuela's policy also provides insights into the larger pattern that regionalism in the Americas may assume. First of all, the possibility exists for *some* countries to pursue direct ties bilaterally with the United States. Second, bilateral or multilateral agreements with Mexico may offer alternative access to NAFTA. A third possibility is a regional approach to access to the broader North American market through negotiations with such subregional organizations as the Andean Group. A fourth possibility, not clearly evident in present Venezuelan policy, is revealed through an examination of Brazil's policy toward regionalism in the Americas, particularly as it relates to MERCOSUR.

MERCOSUR provides the basis for a very different form of regionalism in the Americas, and Brazil occupies a key place in the determination of the eventual pattern of inter-American organization. By virtue of the size of Brazil's domestic market, augmented by that of other potential MERCOSUR partners, the Southern Cone offers the only plausible nucleus of a counterweight with the capability to negotiate concessions with NAFTA on a bilateral region-to-region basis. MERCOSUR's aim of going beyond trade liberalization to a customs union and eventually a common market also offers the policy basis for eventual one-on-one negotiations with NAFTA. Brazil's policy toward MERCOSUR reflects this orientation. Unlike virtually every other Latin American country, Brazil does not see this example of subregional integration as a step toward inevitable hemispheric integration. It is at odds with the "open regionalism" approach of ECLAC, and provides the institutional basis for a counterweight to NAFTA, perhaps through the creation of a SAFTA, proposed by Brazil in October 1993.

The realization of a potential SAFTA will depend in great measure on the interaction between two factors: the relative opportunity that MERCOSUR offers to other South American countries, particularly the Andean countries, and the likelihood that accession to NAFTA as full multilateral partners will be available to these countries. The first factor is directly related to the domestic situation in Brazil and the second is greatly dependent on the attitude of NAFTA partners (particularly U.S. policy) with respect to the way links with other American countries will be pursued, bilaterally or through NAFTA.

The election of President Cardoso in Brazil, attributed in no small measure to the success of his stabilization policies, suggests that domestic reforms will proceed apace in that country. Yet structural reforms have progressed more slowly in Brazil than in other countries, and although there has been a dramatic retreat from the persistent hyperinflation, Brazil's inflation still outstrips that of its Southern Cone and potential Andean partners. These differences pose obstacles to a closer economic relationship between Brazil and these countries, especially one that goes beyond the simple liberalization of trade and opening of markets implied by the "deeper" integration measures envisaged by MERCOSUR. This approach is further reinforced by the priority accorded by Brazilian elites to subregional cooperation over hemispheric cooperation.

Chile's attitude toward MERCOSUR will also have a significant influence on the possibility of the development of a counterweight to NAFTA. If the cautious examination of the option of greater integration in the Southern Cone gives way to a willingness to join MERCOSUR as a full partner, the potential for a stronger counterweight will be increased. Chile's desire to join NAFTA, however, is unambiguous. The extent of Chilean domestic restructuring, under way much longer than in other countries, eliminated most of the structural obstacles, and with the announcement of the initiation of negotiations for Chilean accession to NAFTA at the Summit of the Americas in December 1994, Chile's accession becomes almost a certainty. In spite of the prohibition against belonging to another integration grouping expressed in the accession provisions of MERCOSUR, it is possible to envisage derogations from that proscription, although technical complications would need to be overcome.

Chile's accession to NAFTA can only increase Argentina's ambivalence, expressed in the wavering between commitment to MERCOSUR and hopes for accession to NAFTA on a unilateral basis. With Chile as a participant to some degree in MERCOSUR and limited opportunities for membership in NAFTA, MERCOSUR becomes a more viable option for Argentina. With Chile in NAFTA and its reluctance to develop closer ties with MERCOSUR, Argentina may be more tempted to follow the unilateral path to NAFTA, although it is not clear whether NAFTA members would consider that Argentina had made sufficient progress toward eligibility in terms of domestic reform and economic stabilization.

It is too early to judge whether the policies being pursued by Brazil indicate a clear trend toward a consolidation of a southern core to counter NAFTA. Brazil has led initiatives to associate Chile, Venezuela, and Bolivia with MERCOSUR and has proposed the formation of SAFTA as a possible counterweight to NAFTA (Chaloult 1994). A further indication of developments in this direction is the decision of the European Union to deal with the Southern Cone countries only as a regional grouping through MERCOSUR in their negotiations beginning in 1995. Although the North American market might be much more attractive, some countries may not be able to accede to NAFTA individually or may not wish to meet the conditions for collective negotiated access through a framework agreement. The counterweight strategy would also allow for the continuation of a role for the state at the national level and the regional level that is incompatible with the neoliberal ideology embodied in the strategic regionalism of NAFTA.

The older organizations of the CACM, CARICOM, and the Andean Group have also embarked on a new path in response to the new regionalism. The CACM and CARICOM see regional cooperation as a tool for insertion of national economies into the regional and global markets, and their policies reflect this conception. As stepping-stones to access to NAFTA, these organizations serve as a basis for new domestic and regional policies suitable to open regionalism. These policies are diametrically opposed to the general trend of dirigisme that marked the evolution of regional cooperation in Latin America in the 1960s and 1970s. The Andean Group, which was the archetype of this form of collective self-reliance, with its regime for foreign investment and regional programming, most dramatically reflects this new thrust (Mace 1994: 61–64). The new direction adopted by this organization in the 1980s corresponds to the shift to open regionalism, but it is unlikely that the Andean Group will provide the institutional framework for accession to NAFTA that the CACM, CARICOM, or ACS may provide for the Caribbean countries. This is mainly because some Andean countries may have the alternative of direct access to the North American market through admission as a full partner to NAFTA such as envisaged by Chile, through linkage to the United States via Mexico as in the case of Colombia and Venezuela, or through eventual association with MERCOSUR.

The situation is most difficult for the smaller economies of Latin America that are unable to gain unilateral accession or to participate in a framework agreement with NAFTA. They may still succeed in participating in bilateral or multilateral agreements on a subregional basis, but their relative weakness will prove to their disadvantage in the emerging new form of regionalism. One of the major problems related to regional cooperation among developing countries is asymmetries in development among partners, which has inevitably led to conflict over unequal distribution of benefits and polarization in integration schemes and has required significant redistributive policies to redress these inequalities. Discussions of the new regionalism have remained silent on this issue, which is likely to become a major problem as regionalism in the Americas progresses along the present lines. The neoliberal ideology of globalization that underlies the thrust toward open regionalism will limit the ability to address asymmetries on two levels: between rich and poor countries of the Americas and between the more and less advanced countries within subregional integration schemes.

First of all, there is the problem of asymmetries within NAFTA between, on the one hand, the wealthy industrialized countries of the United States and Canada and, on the other hand, the less developed countries such as Mexico, Chile, and regional partners through framework agreements under the Enterprise for the Americas Initiative (Central American and Caribbean countries). A central element of the new regionalism as embodied in NAFTA is the principle of reciprocity, which is in direct conflict with the concessionary arrangements that characterized relations between rich and poor countries under the Generalized System of Preferences, established by the General Agreement on Tariffs and Trade or the Lomé Convention. It remains to be seen if the poorer countries of Latin America will be willing or able to participate in the new regionalism of the Americas on a basis of full reciprocity. The Caribbean countries provide a clear example of this question, as they replace the European ties of the concessionary arrangements of Lomé with the concessionary ties of the Caribbean Basin Initiative (CBI), only to see them superseded by the less concessionary arrangements of the Enterprise for the Americas Initiative and eventually to submit to the reciprocal arrangements of a framework agreement with NAFTA.[4]

The ability of subregional institutions to address intraregional inequalities will also be compromised by the new regionalism. The requirement of domestic reforms to reduce the role of the state at the national and regional levels deprives regional cooperation schemes of the ability to undertake direct intervention to offset the market forces leading to unequal distribution of benefits and polarization. The overall effect of this neoliberal thrust on subregional cooperation will effectively turn back the clock to the early days of Latin

American and Caribbean integration involving laissez-faire approaches to market integration based on traditional customs union theory. The effect of this is likely to be the erosion of regional solidarity, which, when combined with the centrifugal pull of NAFTA, is likely to result in the disintegration of these subregional arrangements.

The Architecture of the Americas

The larger structure of regionalism in the Americas will depend on the policy directions reflected in the domestic reforms and external relations of the countries of the hemisphere as discussed in the preceding chapters. The form of the new architecture has hardly begun to emerge, and it is too early to know the patterns that it will eventually reflect. It is possible, however, to suggest potential patterns and to indicate the factors that will influence the most likely form that they will assume.

It is clear that regionalism in the Americas in the year 2000 will not reflect the traditional patterns of regionalism of the 1970s or 1980s. It will be a function of the national policies of the countries of the hemisphere and the various strategies toward regionalism and subregionalism that they represent. These strategies, in turn, will be related to their positions in the larger hierarchy of power and trade in the Americas. It is possible to characterize the positions of the various states, ranging from the most central to the most marginal actors, with respect to their importance in the determination of the patterns of regionalism. Let us start with the United States as the most important "maker" of the regional architecture and move on to the other "takers" in order of their importance to the eventual form of regionalism.

The United States is clearly the central actor in the determination of the eventual form of regionalism. As the surviving superpower in the post–Cold War era, the United States sees its regional policy as the centerpiece of a hemispheric strategy to achieve global ends. Its most formalized element, NAFTA, provides institutionalized ties with its most important hemispheric partners, Canada and Mexico. These ties, in the form of full partnership in NAFTA, may be extended to other important partners, such as Chile, that are able to conform most closely to the required neoliberal reforms. Other countries that are less important to the U.S. policy of strategic regionalism are more likely to be dealt with on a mediated basis by the United States, through ties that may take one of two forms. Countries that are not accepted as full members in NAFTA may be incorporated into the larger regional trade regime either through framework agreements under the Enterprise for the Americas Initiative or through bilateral or subregional arrangements with Mexico or other NAFTA partners (Canada and eventually Chile). Clearly, the United States will have the dominant role in determining which countries will accede to NAFTA and which ones will rely on different mechanisms of insertion into the new regional structures. As such, it will be the major determinant of the form of regionalism in the Americas. The policies of Canada and Mexico already reflect the strong influence of the options defined by the United States.

Mexico, although a taker rather than a maker in the overall regional process, will also play a pivotal role in the determination of the eventual form of hemispheric regionalism. To the extent that full accession to NAFTA will not be available to all countries of Latin America and the Caribbean, Mexico offers a link to the larger North American market that will both be easier to attain and involve fewer constraints to achieve. A bilateral trade agreement with Mexico or membership in a subregional project such as the G-3 offers an attractive alternative to NAFTA. The degree of attractiveness will depend on the relative difficulty of gaining full membership in NAFTA as well as on the ability of the third parties to benefit under the rules of origin requirements of NAFTA and under additional bilateral or subregional arrangements with Mexico. For its part, Mexico will want to take advantage of its position as mediator between NAFTA and its subregional neighbors to create economic and trade benefits for itself. This will ensure that Mexico does not become simply an entrepôt for exports from these countries to the North American market but rather plays the central role as a regional hub for investment and value-added transformation with its accompanying economic benefits. With Chile as a full member of NAFTA, Mexico will find a rival for its role as a link to NAFTA. Although it does not possess the strategic advantage of geographical contiguity with the United States, in many ways Chile is better prepared to meet the exigencies of NAFTA participation and has become the platform for significant investments aiming to export to the North American market.

Brazil, because of its size and economic importance, will also exert significant influence on the eventual form of hemispheric regionalism. Brazil's role as an alternative pole for economic cooperation in South America puts it in a position to make a difference in the overall pattern of regional processes by offering a secondary center for regional trade and investment. MERCOSUR is the institutional framework through which such a center could develop as a counterweight to NAFTA, according to the scenario discussed above. The emergence of such a counterweight will depend both on Brazil's willingness and ability to pursue this alternative to direct accession to NAFTA and on the cooperation of other Southern Cone and Andean countries to join Brazil in such an enterprise. One of the advantages of this approach would be the ability to retain national policies that permit a greater role for the state and therefore require less extensive domestic restructuring than membership in NAFTA. A disadvantage would be the need to engage in hard bargaining with NAFTA to gain concessions that are likely to be less comprehensive than the benefits of full accession to NAFTA. An effective counterweight strategy would also depend on the ability to attract a significant number of Latin American countries to the subregional organization, extending it beyond the original Southern Cone to middle-level Andean countries. The ability of Brazil to play the role as a key actor in a counterweight strategy gives it some significance as a maker of the overall regional architecture.

The Andean countries, because of their middle-level status, find themselves in a position of having to "cover all bets": keeping open the hope of eventual accession to NAFTA through pushing toward more extensive domestic reforms; developing bilateral or subregional ties with Mexico as an alternative point of entry to the North American market; and examining the possibility of strengthening ties with Brazil as a counterweight strategy. These countries are more takers than makers in the regional processes, with their eventual choices being determined more by the opportunities available to them than by their autonomous preferences. This is particularly true for the smaller countries because their relative lack of economic importance and, in some cases, the less extensive nature of their domestic restructuring make them marginal players in the process. For the less advantaged Andean countries, a revitalized Andean Group may well be the most feasible (perhaps the only possible) means of a subregional, collectively negotiated access to NAFTA.

The very small countries of Central America and the Caribbean are takers all the way. Their choices are limited by their relative lack of importance to the United States, which makes unilateral accession to NAFTA unlikely. To the extent that they are able to use subregional cooperation to promote domestic reforms, to develop trade regimes that serve as a stepping-stone to freeing trade on a broader basis, and to coordinate a common front in negotiating with NAFTA, they may be able to achieve an arrangement that provides them with a means of insertion into the larger regional economy. The desirability of doing this will also depend on the ability to negotiate access on something less than a fully reciprocal basis, retaining some of the concessionary elements that marked the CARIBCAN agreement, between Canada and the CARICOM, and the CBI. Failing this, ties with Mexico represent an alternative to the subregional collective approach to NAFTA, with geographical proximity and previous trade agreements providing a basis for further cooperation and the means for access to the larger North American market.

This brief survey of the makers and takers suggests the broad outlines of the eventual architecture of the Americas. The first possibility, that of a hemispheric regionalism in which virtually all the countries of the Americas are incorporated into an enlarged NAFTA, is unlikely. NAFTA is not likely to embrace even the majority of Latin American and Caribbean countries for a number of reasons. First, they are not important enough to motivate the United States to bring them into the fold. Second, it is not at all clear that the generally recognized trend toward domestic reform, restructuring, and liberalization is deep enough or sustained enough to satisfy the requirements of accession to NAFTA. Third, it has not been convincingly demonstrated that accession to NAFTA on its principles of reciprocity will carry positive rather than negative results for many of the countries of the hemisphere. In spite of great enthusiasm, the costs and advantages of NAFTA to Mexico are still to be determined, and for other countries the prospects are much less likely to offer an advantageous insertion into the regional and global economy.

The possibility of a bipolar structure of regionalism in the Americas represents a second possibility: one pole being a slightly enlarged NAFTA, the other pole centering on Brazil and providing a nucleus for a SAFTA emerging out of subregional ties like those being developed in MERCOSUR. The difficulties posed with respect to direct accession to NAFTA and the incomplete domestic restructuring of many of the Latin American countries may contribute to the likelihood of the emergence of this pattern. However, the necessity of a relatively high degree of subregional solidarity with respect to external policies in negotiations with NAFTA makes this type of cooperation difficult to achieve. If MERCOSUR evolves into SAFTA, the asymmetry among partners (manifest even among its present Southern Cone members) will loom larger, making it difficult to achieve solidarity or to agree on a common policy position with respect to external negotiations without significant redistributive measures. These factors, along with the inherent difficulties in resisting the great force of strong U.S. policies of strategic regionalism, make it difficult to envisage the emergence of this kind of bipolar structure of regionalism in the Americas.

The overall structure is more likely to represent a mixture of these patterns, with Mexico as a southern hub of ties to NAFTA and several subregional organizations with ties to either the United States or Mexico. Although this form of regionalism in the hemisphere may not be the preferred outcome for many individual countries (with the possible exception of Mexico), it is the second-best alternative for most countries under the dual constraints of domestic restructuring and globalization. The weakening of the subregional solidarity of the Andean Group, CACM, and CARICOM in response to the impetus of the new regionalism reduces their viability as sources for national developmental needs and provides no assurance that they will achieve access to NAFTA under the framework agreements of the Enterprise for the Americas Initiative. Bilateral ties with Mexico provide access with fewer requirements and constraints. The middle-level Southern Cone and Andean countries that are not able to gain full accession to NAFTA are likely to find that bilateral and subregional agreements with Mexico require fewer sacrifices and less effort to attain than the riskier counterweight to NAFTA centered on Brazil. The combination of costs, risks, and opportunities posed by each of these alternatives propels Mexico into the key position in the overall architecture of the Americas.

The form that this would take, then, would be a NAFTA, somewhat expanded in membership, providing a North American area of strategic regionalism around which are grouped the other countries of the Americas. Their ties with NAFTA would be in the form of bilateral and subregional arrangements with Mexico, such as the G-3 and the ACS, with the possibility of formal agreements with the existing subregional integration schemes such as the CACM and CARICOM, evolved to fit into the new regionalism of the Americas. Such an arrangement would fulfill the requirements of the United States in the new world order and provide a role for the other countries of the hemisphere in response to the forces of globalization.

NOTES

1. As the analysis in the preceding chapters indicates, the degree and stability of domestic reforms varies greatly from country to country. For a skeptical view on the extent to which these reforms reflect a reduction of state involvement, see Félix (1992).

2. A similar, though not identical, set of scenarios is suggested by Andras Inotai (1994: 70–72).

3. The tenets of open regionalism are spelled out in a document proclaiming the new ECLAC doctrine: (UN Economic 1994).

4. The difficulties faced by the Caribbean countries in this context are elaborated in Chapter 4 by Anthony Payne.

BIBLIOGRAPHY

◆

Abreu e Lima Florêncio, S. (1992) "Área Hemisférica de Livre Comércio: Dados para uma Reflexão," *Boletim de Integração Latino-Americana*, 5, April/June: 9–11.

Acosta, S. (1993) "Entre el boom de la apertura y las exportaciones que faltan," *Economía Hoy*, February 2: 18–19.

Aguilar, A. (1968) *Pan-Americanism from Monroe to the Present: A View from the Other Side*, New York and London, Monthly Review Press.

Alexander, M., and Corti, C. (1993) "Argentina's Privatization Program," CFS Discussion Paper, Washington, D.C., World Bank.

Alexander, R. J. (1968) "Economic Union and Political Reunion in Latin America," *Inter-American Economic Affairs*, 21, Spring: 19–33.

Almeida, P. R. (ed.) (1992) *MERCOSUL: Textos Básicos*, Brasília, Fundação Alexandre de Gusmão.

Almeida, P. R. (1993) *O MERCOSUL no Contexto Regional e Internacional*, São Paulo, Edições Aduaneiras.

Almeida, P. R. (1994) "O Brasil e o MERCOSUL em face do NAFTA," *Política Externa*, 3, June/August: 84–96.

Amado, R. (ed.) (1982) *Araújo Castro*, Brasília, Editora Universidade de Brasília.

Aragao, J. M. (1993) "La Integración en América Latina: Objectivos, Obstáculos y Oportunidades," *Integración Latinoamericana*, 18 (196), December: 45–56.

Ardila, M. (1991) *¿Cambio de norte? Momentos críticos de la política exterior colombiana*, Santafé de Bogotá, Tercer Mundo Editores/Instituto de Estudios Políticos y Relaciones Internacionales/Universidad Nacional.

Arias, M. F. (1991) "Colombia y el Grupo de los Tres," *Revista Cancillería de San Carlos*, 8, July: 14–20.

Arlacchi, P. (1988) *Mafia Business: The Mafia Ethic and the Spirit of Capitalism*, Oxford, Oxford University Press.

Arriola, C. (1994) *Tratado de Libre Comercio de América del Norte: Documentos Básicos*, México, Miguel Angel Porrua/Secretaría de Comercio y Fomento Industrial (selection and notes).

Ashby, T. (1989) *Missed Opportunities: The Rise and Fall of Jamaica's Edward Seaga*, Indianapolis, Hudson Institute.

"Assessment of Fernando Solana, Secretary of Foreign Affairs" (1989) in M. Anaya, L. Galaz, and F. Garfias, "Nada a costa de nuestros valores," *Excélsior*, August 8: 1.

Atkins, G. P. (1980) *América Latina en el Sistema Político Internacional*, Colección Política y Comunicación, México, Ediciones Gernika.

Axline, W. A. (1977) "Underdevelopment, Dependence, and Integration: The Politics of Regionalism in the Third World," *International Organization*, 31: 83–105.

Axline, W. A. (1988) "Regional Cooperation and National Security: External Forces in Caribbean Integration," *Journal of Common Market Studies*, 27, September: 1–25.

Axline, W. A. (1994) "Cross-Regional Comparisons and the Theory of Regional Cooperation: Lessons from Latin America, the Caribbean, Southeast Asia, and the South Pacific," in W. A. Axline (ed.), *The Political Economy of Regional Cooperation: Comparative Case Studies*, London, Pinter: 178–224.

Baer, M. D. (1991) "North American Free Trade," *Foreign Affairs*, 70 (4), Fall: 132–149.

Baer, M. D., and Weintraub, S. (eds.) (1994) *The NAFTA Debate: Grappling with Unconventional Trade Issues*, Boulder, Colo., Lynne Rienner.

Baer, W. (1962) "The Economics of Prebisch and ECLA," *Economic Development and Cultural Change*, 10, January: 169–182.

Bailey, N. (1992) "Venezuela and the United States: Putting Energy in the Enterprise," conference at the seminar "Lessons of the Venezuelan Experience," Washington, D.C., October.

Balze, F. A. de la (1991) *El comercio exterior argentino en la decada de 1990*, Buenos Aires, Ed. Manantial.

Banco Central de Chile (1975) *Boletines Mensuales*, October: 35–38.

Banco Central de Chile (1994) *Boletines Mensuales*, July: 27–29.

Barbosa, R. A., and Panelli César, L. F. (1994a) "A Integração Sub-Regional, Regional e Hemisférica: O Esforço Brasileiro," in G. Fonseca, Jr., and S. H. Nabuco de Castro (eds.), *Temas de Política Externa Brasileira II*, 1, São Paulo, Editora Paz e Terra: 285–304.

Barbosa, R. A., and Panelli César, L. F. (1994b) "O Brasil como 'Global Trader,'" in G. Fonseca, Jr., and S. H. Nabuco de Castro (eds.), *Temas de Política Externa Brasileira II*, 1, São Paulo, Editora Paz e Terra: 305–324.

Barrenechea y Raygada, O. (1942) *El congreso de Panamá, 1826*, Lima, Ministerio de Relaciones Exteriores.

Barrenechea y Raygada, O. (1947) *Congresos y conferencias internacionales celebrados en Lima, 1847–1894*, Buenos Aires, Peuser.

Baumann, R., and Lerda, J. C. (eds.) (1987) *A Integração em Debate*, São Paulo, Editora Marco Zero/UnB.

Behrman, J. N. (1972) *The Role of International Companies in Latin American Integration: Autos and Petrochemicals*, New York, Committee for Economic Development.

Belous, R. S., and Hartley, R. S. (eds.) (1990) *The Growth of Regional Trading Blocs in the Global Economy*, Washington, D.C., National Planning Association.

Bernal, R. L. (1992) *The Implications of the NAFTA for Jamaica and the CBI Region: A Policy Proposal*, statement by the ambassador of Jamaica to the United States before the U.S. House of Representatives Ways and Means Subcommittee on Trade, North American Free Trade Agreement Hearings, September 22, Washington, D.C. (mimeo).

Berrios, R. (1986) "The Search for Independence," *NACLA Report on the Americas*, 20 (3), June: 27–32.

Bhagwati, J. (1991) *The World Trading System at Risk*, Hemel Hempstead, Harvester Wheatsheaf.

Bhagwati, J. (1993) "Beyond NAFTA: Clinton's Trading Choices," *Foreign Policy*, 91, Summer: 155–163.

Blanco Mendoza, H. (1994) *Las negociaciones comerciales de México con el mundo*, México, Fondo de Cultura Económica.

Bloomfield, R. J. (1994) "Making the Western Hemisphere Safe for Democracy? The OAS Defense-of-Democracy Regime," *Washington Quarterly*, 17 (2), Spring: 157–169.

Bloomfield, R. J., and Treverton, G. F. (eds.) (1990) *Alternative to Intervention: A New U.S.–Latin American Security Relationship*, Boulder, Colo., Lynne Rienner.

Bouzas, R., and Lustig, N. (eds.) (1992) *Liberalización Comercial e Integración Regional—De NAFTA a MERCOSUR*, Buenos Aires, Grupo Editor Latinoamericano.

Bouzas, R., and Ros, J. (eds.) (1994) *Economic Integration in the Western Hemisphere*, Notre Dame, Ind., University of Notre Dame Press.

Boye, O. (1994) "Chile y el interamericanismo en las dos últimas décadas," *Chile y el Fin de la Guerra Fría*, Santiago, Instituto de Estudios Sociales, Económicos y Culturales (ISEC): 67–86.

Bradshe, K. (1994) "Mexico Seen as Barrier to a Broader Trade Pact," *New York Times*, March 1: 2D.

Brand, D. (1992) "Regional Bloc Formation and World Trade," *Intereconomics*, November/December: 274–281.

Braveboy-Wagner, J. A. (1989) *The Caribbean in World Affairs: The Foreign Policies of the English-speaking States*, Boulder, Colo., Westview Press.

Bresser Pereira, L. C., and Thorstensen, V. (1992/1993) "Do MERCOSUL à Integração Americana," *Política Externa*, 1, December/January/February.

Büchi, H., et al. (1992) *La transformación Económica de Chile*, Serie Debates Nr. 1, Santiago, Universidad Nacional Andrés Bello, Cuadernos Universitarios.

Buelens, F. (1992) "The Creation of Regional Blocs in the World Economy," *Intereconomics*, 27, May/June: 124–132.

Bulmer-Thomas, V.; Craske, N.; and Serrano, M. (1994) *Mexico and the North American Free Trade Agreement: Who Will Benefit?* New York, St. Martin's Press.

Business Latin America (1992) May 4: 142.

Buzan, B. (1991) "New Patterns of Global Security in the Twenty-first Century," *International Affairs*, 67 (3), July: 431–451.

Cafruny, A. W. (1990) "A Gramscian Concept of Declining Hegemony: Stages in U.S. Power and the Evolution of International Economic Relations," in D. P. Rapkin (ed.), *World Leadership and Hegemony*, Boulder, Colo., Lynne Rienner: 97–118.

Calleo, D. P. (1982) *The Imperious Economy*, Cambridge, Mass., Harvard University Press.

Calleo, D. P. (1987) *Beyond American Hegemony*, New York, Basic Books.

Calleo, D. P., and Rowland, B. M. (1973) *America and the World Political Economy: Atlantic Dreams and National Realities*, Bloomington, Indiana University Press.

Camargo, S. de (1985) "Os Novos Amigos: Brasil e Argentina Atravessam a Ponte," *Contexto Internacional*, 2, July/December: 63–80.

Camargo, S. de (1993) "A Integração do Cone Sul," *Textos IRI*, Rio de Janeiro, April: 1–58.

Camargo, S. de, and Vásquez Ocampo, J. M. (eds.) (1988) *Autoritarismo e Democracia na Argentina e Brasil (Uma Década de Política Exterior 1973–1984)*, São Paulo, Editora Convívio.

Caminoto, J. F., and Pivetta, M. (1994) "O Quintal do Vizinho dá Dinheiro," *Veja*, September 28.

Canadian Investment, Trade and Aid in Latin America (1981), *LAWG Letter,* 7 (1–2), August: 1–40.

Candia Veiga, J. P. (1993) "MERCOSUL: Evolução Institucional e Intervenção Sindical," in *MERCOSUL Integração na América Latina e Relações com a Comunidade Européia,* São Paulo, Instituto Cajamar and Departamento de Estudos Sócio-Econômicos e Políticos da CUT: 197–211.

Carasales, J. C. (1992) *National Security Concepts of States: Argentina,* New York, UNIDIR.

Cárdenas, F. (1994) "La competitividad de las exportaciones argentinas," *Bol-Informativo-Techint,* January–March: 81–96.

Cardona, D. (1990) *Evaluación de la política exterior de la administración Barco,* Documentos Ocasionales, Centro de Estudios Internacionales, 16, July–August.

Cardona, D. (1992) "El Grupo de los Tres: Una lectura política," *Colombia Internacional,* 17, January–March: 3–13.

Cardona, D., and Tokatlian, J. G. (1991) "El sistema mundial en los noventa," *Colombia Internacional,* 13, January–March: 16–21.

Cardona, D., and Tokatlian, J. G. (1993) "Colombia: Viejos desafíos, nuevas oportunidades," in J. Heine, *Enfrentando los cambios globales,* Santiago de Chile, Ediciones Dolmen: 143–168.

Cardona, D., et al. (1992) *Colombia-Venezuela: ¿Crisis o negociación?* Santafé de Bogotá, Centro de Estudios Internacionales, Universidad de los Andes/ FESCOL.

Cardozo de Da Silva, E. (1992a) "Las relaciones Venezuela-U.S.A. y el comercio: Evolución reciente, estado actual y perspectivas," first workshop on "Libre Comercio e Impacto Ambiental en Venezuela," Caracas, July 8–10.

Cardozo de Da Silva, E. (1992b) *Continuidad y consistencia en quince años de política exterior venezolana 1969–1984,* Caracas, UCV/CDCH.

Caretas (1990) June 24: 10–19.

Caretas (1991) May 20: 26.

Caretas (1992) July 13: 21.

Caribbean Basin Technical Advisory Group (CBTAG) (1992) *CBTAG Status Reports,* San Juan, Department of State, Commonwealth of Puerto Rico, January and September.

Caribbean Community and Common Market (CARICOM) (1991) "Preliminary Report of CARICOM on Enterprise for the Americas Initiative," *Caribbean Affairs,* 4 (3), July–September: 68–72.

Caribbean/Latin American Action (C/LAA) (1990/1991) *Caribbean Action (1990–1991),* Washington, D.C., Caribbean/Latin American Action, various issues.

Carmona Estanga, P. (1993) "Carrousel de reflexiones," *El Universal,* February 6: 2–3.

Carothers, T. (1991) *In the Name of Democracy: U.S. Policy Toward Latin America in the Reagan Years,* Berkeley and Los Angeles, University of California Press.

Carre, S. (1992) *Canada's Foreign Policy: Shifting Patterns of Influence,* Ottawa, Ontario, Policy Planning Staff.

Carvajal, L. (1993) "Neointegración, neoliberalismo y política exterior colombiana," *Colombia Internacional,* 22, April–June.

Castañeda, J. G. (1990) "Latinoamérica y el fin de la Guerra Fría," *Nexos*, 153, September: 31–43.

Castañeda, J. G. (1993) "Can NAFTA Change Mexico?" *Foreign Affairs*, 72 (4), September–October: 66–80.

Castañeda, J. G., and Heredia, C. (1992) "Another NAFTA: What a Good Agreement Should Offer," *World Policy Journal*, 9 (4), Fall/Winter: 673–685.

Castrioto de Azambuja, M. (1991) "Iniciativa para as Américas e Integração Latino-Americana: Convergência e Divergência de Interesses entre EUA e América Latina," in J. P. dos Reis Velloso (ed.), *O Brasil e o Plano Bush: Oportunidades e Riscos Numa Futura Integração das Américas*, São Paulo, Nobel: 21–30.

Cavallo, D., and Cottani, J. (1991) "Argentina," in D. Papageorgiou, M. Michaely, and A. M. Choski, *Liberalizing Foreign Trade*, Cambridge, Mass., IBRD–Basil Blackwell: 1–167.

CEPAL (1991a) "La integración económica en los años 90: perspectivas y opciones," LC/R 1024, August 24.

CEPAL (1991b) "Coordinación de políticas macroeconómicas en la integración latinoamericana: ¿Una necesidad o una utopía?" LC/R 1064, October 23.

CEPAL (1992a) "Los nuevos proyectos de integración económica en América Latina y el Caribe y la dinámica de la inversión," LC/R 1145, May 20.

CEPAL (1992b) "Convergencias de los esquemas de integración," LC/R 1192, October 2.

CEPAL (1992c) *Ensayos sobre coordinación de políticas macroeconómicas*, Santiago de Chile, CEPAL.

Cepeda Ulloa, F., and Pardo, R. (eds.) (1985) *Contadora: Desafío a la diplomacia tradicional*, Bogotá, Centro de Estudios Internacionales/Editorial Oveja Negra.

Cervo, A. L., and Bueno, C. (1992) *História da Política Exterior do Brasil*, São Paulo, Editora Ática.

Chabat, J. (1990) "Los instrumentos de la política exterior de Miguel de la Madrid," *Foro Internacional*, 119, 30 (3), January–March: 398–418.

Chabat, J. (1991) "Mexico's Foreign Policy in 1990: Electoral Sovereignty and Integration with the United States," *Journal of Interamerican Studies and World Affairs*, 33 (4), Winter: 1–25.

Chabat, J. (1993) "Mexico: So Close to the United States, So Far from Latin America," *Current History*, 92 (571), February: 55–58.

Chaloult, Y. (1993) "O Brasil e o NAFTA," *Boletim de Integração Latino-Americana*, 9, April/June: 103–108.

Chaloult, Y. (1994) "Le Brésil et la zone de libre-échange sud-américaine," paper presented at the annual conference of the Canadian Association for Latin American and Caribbean Studies, Ottawa, Ontario.

Chavez, C. R. (1992) "La economía venezolana perdió terreno," *El Universal*, November 6: 2–4.

Cheibub, Z. B. (1985) "Diplomacia e Construção Institucional: O Itamaraty em uma Perspectiva Histórica," *Dados*, 28 (1): 113–131.

Claps, A. (1991) "Más Nexos con Europa y AL Para Mantener el Equilibrio," *Excélsior*, December 20: 1-A, 39-A.

Clark, J. (1985) *Competitiveness and Security: Directions for Canada's International Relations*, Ottawa, Ontario, Minister of Supply and Services Canada.

Clark, J. (1989) *Notes for Remarks by the Right Honourable Joe Clark, P.C., M.P. Secretary of State for External Affairs, at the Meeting of the General Assembly of the Organization of American States, Washington, November 13, 1989,* Ottawa, Ontario, Department of Foreign Affairs.

Cobo, L. (1992) "Prioridades de la política exterior de Venezuela para el año 2000," in C. Romero, *Reforma y política exterior en Venezuela,* Caracas, COPRE/INVESP/Nueva Sociedad.

Cohen, B. J. (1982) "Balance-of-Payments Financing: Evolution of a Regime," *International Organization,* 36 (2): 457–478.

Colett, Raymond (1993) "Nuevo auge del Pacto Andino," en *Economía Hoy,* February 6: 32.

El Comercio (1994) February 13.

Commins, M. M. (1993) "De la seguridad al comercio en las relaciones entre Estados Unidos y América Latina: Cómo se explica el apoyo estadunidense al Tratado de Libre Comercio con México," *Estados Unidos: Informe Trimestral,* 3 (1), Spring: 5–30.

Connell-Smith, G. (1974) *The United States and Latin America, A Historical Analysis of Inter-American Relations,* London, Heinemann Educational Books.

Corbo, V., and Havrylyshin, O. (1980) *Les relations commerciales entre le Canada et les pays en développement,* Ottawa, Ontario, Ministre des Approvisionnements et Services.

CORDIPLÁN (1990) *El Gran Viraje: Lineamientos Generales del VIII Plan de la Nación,* Caracas, CORDIPLÁN.

Cornelius, W. A. (1994) "Mexico's Delayed Democratization," *Foreign Policy,* 95, Summer: 53–71.

Cox, R. (1990) "Dialectique de l'économie monde en fin de siècle," *Études internationales,* 21 (4), December: 693–704.

Crabtree, J. (1992) *Peru Under García: An Opportunity Lost,* Pittsburgh, Pa., University of Pittsburgh Press.

Crane, D. (1994) "Letting Others into NAFTA May Dilute American Power," *The Toronto Star,* July 16: C2.

Dallek, R. (1983) *The American Style of Foreign Policy: Cultural Politics and Foreign Affairs,* New York, Alfred A. Knopf, Inc.

Davis, D. E. (1992) "Mexico's New Politics: Changing Perspectives on Free Trade," *World Policy Journal,* 9 (4), Fall/Winter: 655–671.

Dawkins, K., and Brecher, J. (1994) *NAFTA, GATT and the World Trade Organization: The New Rules of Corporate Conquest,* Open Magazine Pamphlet Series No. 29, Open Media.

Deas, M., and Chernick, M. (1988) *Colombia durante el gobierno del Presidente Betancur: Las relaciones entre política exterior, crisis centroamericana y proceso de paz nacional: Dos enfoques,* Documentos Ocasionales, Centro de Estudios Internacionales, 5, September–October.

Deblock, C., and Brunelle, D. (1993) "Une intégration régionale stratégique: Le cas nord-américain," *Études internationales,* 24 (3), September: 595–629.

De la Guardia, E., and Sánchez, R. (1992) "Limitaciones al comercio exterior," *Boletín del Centro de Economía Internacional,* October: 4–20.

De Melo, J., and Panagariya, A. (1992) *The New Regionalism in Trade Policy,* Washington, D.C., World Bank.

Denot Medeiros, J. A. (1994) "A Área de Livre Comércio—Sul-Americana: O Imperativo e a Lógica da Cooperação Econômica Regional," *Boletim de Integração Latino-Americana,* 13, April/June: 1–3.

Departamento de Integração Latino-Americana/MRE (1993) "MERCOSUL-NAFTA: Perspectivas de Relacionamento," *Boletim de Integração Latino-Americana*, 8, January–March: 58–72.

De Vylder, S. (1989) "El cambio económico en Chile en los años 80," in R. García," *Economía y Política Durante el Gobierno Militar en Chile*, México, Editorial Siglo XXI: 89–99.

Dewitt, D. B., and Kirton, J. J. (1983) *Canada as a Principal Power*, Toronto, Ontario, John Wiley and Sons.

Díaz Alejandro, C. F. (1970) *Essays on the Economic History of the Argentine Republic*, New Haven, Conn., Yale University Press.

"Discurso de Fernando Solana, Secretario de Relaciones Exteriores," en la ceremonia del CLXXX Aniversario de la Independencia de México (1990), Mexico City, September 16 (mimeo).

Dosman, E. (1992) "Canada and Latin America: The New Look," *International Journal*, 47 (3), Summer: 529–554.

Drekonja, G. (1982) *Colombia: Política exterior*, Bogotá, Centro de Estudios Internacionales, Universidad de los Andes/FESCOL/La Editora Ltda.

Drekonja, G, (1983) *Retos de la política exterior colombiana*, Bogotá, Centro de Estudios Internacionales, Universidad de los Andes/CEREC.

Drekonja, G., and Tokatlian, J. G. (eds.) (1983) *Teoría y práctica de la política exterior latinoamericana*, Bogotá, Centro de Estudios Internacionales, Universidad de los Andes/CEREC.

Dresser, D. (1991) "La nueva política mexicana en Estados Unidos," *Estados Unidos: Informe trimestral*, 1 (4), October–December: 15–31.

Durán, M. (1992) "El Grupo de los Tres ratificará necesidad de adelantar procesos de libre comercio," *El Diario de Caracas*, June 11: 30–31.

Duran, R. (1992) "Changing State/Society Perspective on the United Nations System: Some Aspects Concerning the Chilean Case," conference on "Changing State/Society Perspectives on the United Nations System," United Nations University's Workshop, Centre for International and Strategic Studies, York University, Toronto: 15–23.

Eastman, J. M., and Cabra, M. G. (1987) *El diferendo colombo-venezolano*, Bogotá, Editorial Oveja Negra.

Echeverri-Carroll, E. (ed.) (1994) *NAFTA and Trade Liberalization in the Americas*, Austin, University of Texas at Austin, Bureau of Business Research.

Economía Hoy (1992) November 11: 19.

Economía Hoy (1993a) January 28: 9.

Economía Hoy (1993b) January 29: 18.

Economist Intelligence Unit (1994) *Argentina: Country Profile*.

Einsenstadt, T. (1993) "El TLC o los límites del cabildeo," *Este País*, 30, September: 10–15.

Epstein, E. C. (ed.) (1994) *The New Democracy in Argentina: The Search for a Successful Formula*, New York, Praeger.

Erro, D. (1993) *Resolving the Argentine Paradox: Politics and Development, 1966–1992*, Boulder, Colo., Lynne Rienner.

Erzan, R., and Yeats, A. (1992) "Free Trade Agreements with the United States: What's in It for Latin America?" *World Bank Working Papers Series*, 827, January.

Escudé, C. (1992) *Education, Political Culture and Foreign Policy: The Case of Argentina*, Durham, Duke University of North Carolina Program in Latin American Studies.

El Espectador (1992) August 30: 1, 5E.

Félix, D. (1992) "Privatizing and Rolling Back the Latin American State," *CEPAL Review*, 46, April: 31–46.

Fernández de Soto, G. (1992) *Reflexiones sobre política internacional*, Santafé de Bogotá, Editorial Kempres Ltda.

Ferrero Costa, E. (1979) *El Nuevo Derecho del Mar: El Perú y las 200 Millas*, Lima, Pontificia Universidad Católica del Perú.

Ferrero Costa, E. (1987) "Peruvian Foreign Policy: Current Trends, Constraints and Opportunities," *Journal of Interamerican Studies and World Affairs*, 29 (2), Summer: 55–78.

Ffrench-Davis, R., and Tironi, E. (1982) *Latin America and the New International Economic Order*, New York, St. Martin's Press.

El Financiero (1989) June 27.

Financial Times (1994) June 14.

Fiori, M. (1993) *Pasado, presente y futuro de la política exterior argentina*, Buenos Aires, Biblos.

Fonseca, J. R. F. da (1994) "MERCOSUL: Estrutura Institucional e Sistema de Solução de Controvérsias," in *MERCOSUL: Desafios a Vencer*, São Paulo, Conselho Brasileiro de Relações Internacionais: 79–87.

Frances, A. (1990) *Venezuela posible*, Caracas, Corimón/IESA.

Fry, E. H.; Taylor, S. A.; and Wood, R. S. (1994) *America, the Vincible: U.S. Foreign Policy for the Twenty-first Century*, Englewood Cliffs, N.J., Prentice-Hall.

FUNDAFUTURO (1992) *Cuando Venezuela perió el rumbo: Un análisis de la economía venezolana entre 1945 y 1991*, Caracas, Ediciones Cavendes.

Galbraith, J. K. (1994) "What Mexico—and the United States—Wants: What NAFTA Really Means," *World Policy Journal*, 11 (1), Spring: 29–32.

Gallardo, S. (1993) "El debate sobre el Acuerdo de Cooperación Ambiental," *Estados Unidos: Informe Trimestral*, 3 (4), Winter: 34–48.

Garay, L. J. (ed.) (1992) *Estrategia industrial e inserción internacional*, Santafé de Bogotá, FESCOL.

Garcia Muñiz, H. (1991) "Defence Policy and Planning in the Caribbean: The Case of Jamaica, 1962–88," in J. R. Beruff, J. P. Figueroa, and J. E. Greene (eds.), *Conflict, Peace and Development in the Caribbean*, London, Macmillan: 110–145.

Garciadiego, J.; Hernández, B.; del Rayo González, M.; Reta, E.; and Zepeda, B. (1994) *El TLC Día a Día: Crónica de una negociación*, México, Miguel Angel Porrúa/Secretaría de Comercio y Fomento Industrial.

GATT (General Agreement on Tariffs and Trade) (1992) *Examen des politiques commerciales: Argentine*, 2 vol., Geneva, GATT.

Gaviria Trujillo, C. (1992) *Política internacional: Discursos*, Santafé de Bogotá, Imprenta Nacional de Colombia.

Gherson, G. (1992) *Canadian Continentalism and Industrial Competitiveness*, in F. O. Hampson and C. J. Maule (eds.), *Canada Among Nations 1992–1993, A New World Order?* Ottawa, Ontario, Carleton University Press: 155–173.

Gill, S., and Law, D. (1988) *The Global Political Economy: Perspectives, Problems and Policies*, London, Harvester Wheatsheaf.

Gilpin, R. (1987) *The Political Economy of International Relations*, Princeton, N.J., Princeton University Press.

Golden, T. (1993) "As U.S. Vote on Trade Pact Nears, Mexicans Are Expressing Doubts," *New York Times*, November 8: 1A.

Golob, S. R. (1993) "¿Un nuevo orden internacional? La decisión de México respecto al libre comercio," *Estados Unidos: Informe Trimestral*, 3 (1), Spring: 31–56.

Gómez, M. M.; Drekonja, G.; Tokatlian, J. G.; and Carvajal, L. (1993) *Redefiniendo la autonomía en política internacional*, Documentos Ocasionales, Centro de Estudios Internacionales, 31, July–September.

Goodman, L., et al. (1995) *Lessons of the Venezuelan Experience*, Baltimore, Johns Hopkins University Press.

Gonzales, J. E. (1992) "Guerrillas and Coca in the Upper Huallaga Valley," in D. S. Palmer (ed.), *Shining Path of Peru*, New York, St. Martin's Press: 105–125.

González Aréchiga, B., and Ramírez, J. C. (1994) "La nueva frontera norte de México," *Estados Unidos: Informe Trimestral*, 4 (1), Spring: 24–34.

Gouvernement du Canada (1970) *Politique étrangère au service des Canadiens*, 6 booklets, Ottawa, Ontario, Imprimeur de la Reine.

Granatstein, J. L., and Bothwell, R. (1990) *Pirouette, Pierre Trudeau and Canadian Foreign Policy*, Toronto, Ontario, University of Toronto Press.

Granovsky, M. (1991) "Política exterior: las relaciones carnales," in O. Martínez, A. Borón et al., *El Menemato: Radiografía de dos años de gobierno de Carlos Menem*, Buenos Aires, Ediciones Buena Letra: 171–205.

Grieco, J. M. (1990) *Cooperation Among Nations*, Ithaca, N.Y., Cornell University Press.

Griffith, I. (ed.) (1991) *Strategy and Security in the Caribbean*, New York, Praeger.

Grupo de los Tres (1991) "Coordinar las acciones de cooperación e integración," *Comercio Exterior*, 41 (1), January: 30–31.

Guadani, A. (1991) "La reforma del Estado y la política exterior argentina," *Integración Latinoamericana*, 173: 3–13.

Guerón, C. (1991) "La política de Estado y el estado de la política," *Política Internacional*, 3, July–September.

Guillermoprieto, A. (1990) "Letter from Lima," *New Yorker*, October 29: 116–129.

Guy, J. J. (1976) "Canada and Latin America," *The World Today*, 32, October: 376–386.

Hakim, P. (1992) "President Bush's Southern Strategy: The Enterprise for the Americas Initiative," *Washington Quarterly*, 15 (12), Spring: 93–106.

Hall, K. G. (1994) "Mexico Denies It Seeks Limits on NAFTA Spread," *Journal of Commerce*, March 2: 3-A.

Hampson, F. O., and Maule, C. J. (eds.) (1991) *Canada Among Nations 1991–1992: After the Cold War*, Ottawa, Ontario, Carleton University Press.

Hart, M. (1991) *Canada Discovers Its Vocation as a Nation of the Americas*, in F. O. Hampson and C. J. Maule (eds.), *Canada Among Nations 1991–1992: After the Cold War*, Ottawa, Ontario, Carleton University Press: 81–107.

Hartmann, F., and Wendzel, R. L. (1985) *To Preserve the Republic*, New York, Macmillan.

Heine, J. (ed.) (1993) *¿Hacia Unas Relaciones Internacionales de Mercado? Anuario de Políticas Exteriores Latinoamericanas 1991–1992*, Santiago, Ediciones Dolmen/PROSPEL.

Hirst, M. (1988a) "Contexto e Estrátegia do Programa de Integração Argentina-Brasil," *Revista de Economia Política*, 8, July/September: 55–72.

Hirst, M. (1988b) "El Programa de Integración Argentina-Brasil: De la Formulación a la Implementación," *Documentos de Investigación*, 67, Buenos Aires, FLACSO, July: 1–27.

Hirst, M. (ed.) (1990a) *Argentina-Brasil: Perspectivas Comparativas y Ejes de Integración*, Buenos Aires, Editorial Tesis.

Hirst, M. (1990b) "Continuidad y Cambio del Programa de Integración Argentina-Brasil," *Documentos de Investigación*, 108, Buenos Aires, FLACSO, December.

Hirst, M. (1991) "O Programa de Integração Argentina-Brasil: Concepção Original e Ajustes Recentes," in P. da Motta Veiga (ed.), *Cone Sul: A Economia Política da Integração*, Rio de Janeiro, Fundação Centro de Estudos do Comércio Exterior: 71–88.

Hirst, M. (1992a) "La Participación de Brasil en el Proceso del MERCOSUR: Evaluando Costos y Benefícios," paper presented at the conference "Transformaciones Internacionales y Reestructuración Hemisférica," Santiago, FLACSO/Chile and University of Miami, December.

Hirst, M. (1992b) "Avances y Desafíos en la Formación del MERCOSUR," *Documentos de Investigación*, 130, Buenos Aires, FLACSO, July: 15–20.

Hirst, M. (1994) "Las Relaciones Internacionales de América Latina a Mediados de los '90: Nuevos Desafíos y Viejos Dilemas," *América Latina/Internacional*, 1, Fall–Winter: 65–84.

Hirst, M., and Soares de Lima, M. R. (1994) "Between Neo-Alignment and Neo-Autonomy: Is There a Third Way in U.S.-Brazilian Relations?" *Documentos de Investigación*, 164, Buenos Aires, FLACSO, July: 16–19.

Hoffmann, S. (1968) *Gulliver's Troubles or the Setting of American Foreign Policy*, New York, McGraw-Hill.

Hoffmann, S. (1978) *Primacy or World Order: American Foreign Policy Since the Cold War*, New York, McGraw-Hill.

Holmes, J. W. (1970) *The Better Part of Valour: Essays on Canadian Diplomacy*, Toronto, Ontario, McClelland and Stewart.

Holmes, J. W. (1976) *Canada: A Middle-aged Power*, Toronto, Ontario, McClelland and Stewart.

Hormats, R. D. (1994) "Making Regionalism Safe," *Foreign Affairs*, 73 (2), March–April: 97–108.

Hufbauer, G. C., and Schott, J. J. (1993/1994) "Prescription for Growth," *Foreign Policy*, 93, Winter: 104–114.

Hufbauer, G. C., and Schott, J. J. (1994) *NAFTA: An Assessment*, Washington, D.C., Institute for International Economics.

Hufty, M. (1996) *Un gouvernement sous influence: l'économie politique du programme de réformes du gouvernement Menem en Argentine*, doctoral thesis, IUHEI, Geneva.

Hunt, M. H. (1987) *Ideology and U.S. Foreign Policy*, New Haven, Conn., Yale University Press.

Huntington, S. P. (1988/1989), "The U.S.—Decline or Renewal," *Foreign Affairs*, 67 (2), Winter: 76–96.

Hurrell, A. (1992) "Latin America in the New World Order: A Regional Bloc of the Americas?" *International Affairs*, 68 (1), January: 121–139.

Hurrell, A. (1993) "Os Blocos Regionais nas Américas," *Revista Brasileira de Ciências Sociais*, 22, June: 98–118.

"The Implications of Free Trade and the NAFTA for Latin America" (1993), *Peace Research*, 25, February: 77.

Inotai, A. (1994) "The New Regionalism and Latin America," in B. Hettne and A. Inotai (eds.), *The New Regionalism: Implications for Global Development and International Security*, Helsinki, UNU World Institute for Development and Economic Research: 51–92.

Instituto de Estudios Políticos (IEP) (1983) *La agenda de la política exterior de Venezuela*, Caracas, EBUC.

"Integración económica y nacionalismo: Canadá, Estados Unidos y México" (1991) *Este País*, 1, April: 7.

Integración Lationamericana (1991) May, August, and September–October.

International Economic Review (1992) *Chartbook: Composition of U.S. Merchandise Trade 1987–1991*, Washington, D.C., U.S. International Trade Commission, March.

International Monetary Fund (1994), *Direction of Trade Statistics Yearbook*, Washington, D.C., IMF: 300.

IRELA (1992) *Venezuela en crisis: Raíces y consecuencias*, Dossier No. 39, Madrid, June.

Jaguaribe, H. (1974) *Brasil: Crise e Alternativas*, Rio de Janeiro, Editora Zahar.

Jaramillo, L. F. (1991a) "La política exterior colombiana," *Revista Cancillería de San Carlos*, 9, August: 3–31.

Jaramillo, L. F. (1991b) *Memorias al Congreso Nacional*, Santafé de Bogotá, Ministerio de Relaciones Exteriores.

"John McLaughlin's 'One on One' with Guest: Mexican President Carlos Salinas de Gortari." Taped: Monday, September 21, 1992. For Broadcast: Weekend of September 26–27, 1992 (mimeo): 4.

Josko de Guerón, E. (1992) "Cambio y continuidad en la política exterior de Venezuela: Una revisión," in C. Romero (ed.), *Reforma y política exterior en Venezuela*, Caracas, COPRE/INVESP/Nueva Sociedad.

Kennedy, P. (1987) *The Rise and Fall of the Great Powers: Economic Change and Military Conflict, 1500–2000*, New York, Random House.

Keohane, R. O., and Nye, J. S., Jr. (1977) *Power and Interdependence: World Politics in Transition*, Boston, Little, Brown and Company.

Keohane, R. O., and Nye, J. S., Jr. (1989) *Power and Interdependence*, 2d ed., Glenview, Ill., Scott, Foresman and Company.

Kirkpatrick, J. (1971) *Leader and Vanguard in Mass Society*, Cambridge, Mass., M.I.T. Press.

Knight, A. (1994) "México y Estados Unidos en el primer año del presidente Clinton: Una perspectiva histórica (o, al menos, de un historiador)," *Estados Unidos: Informe Trimestral*, 4 (1), Spring: 5–11.

Krasner, S. D. (1982) "Structural Causes and Regime Consequences: Regimes as Intervening Variables," *International Organization*, 36 (2): 185–205.

Krauthammer, C. (1991) "The Unipolar Moment," *Foreign Affairs*, 70 (1): 23–33.

Kryzanek, M. J. (1985) *U.S.–Latin American Relations*, New York, Praeger.

Kryzanek, M. J. (1992) *Leaders, Leadership and U.S. Policy in Latin America*, Boulder, Colo., Westview Press.

Lafer, C. (1993a) "A Autoridade do Itamaraty," in *Política Externa Brasileira: Três Momentos*, São Paulo, Fundação Konrad-Adenauer-Stiftung: 41–49.

Lafer, C. (1993b) "A Política Externa Brasileira no Governo Collor," *Política Externa*, 1, March.

Lamazière, G., and Jaguaribe, R. (1992) "Argentina and Brazil: Nuclear Non-Acquisition and Confidence-building," *Disarmament*, 15 (3): 102–117.

Langley, L. D. (1989) *America and the Americas: The United States in the Western Hemisphere*, Athens, The University of Georgia Press.

Lanús, J. A. (1984) *De Chapultepec al Beagle: Política exterior argentina: 1945–1980*, Buenos Aires, Editorial EMECE.

Latin American Economic System (1993) *The Implications for Caribbean Economies of Current International Changes*, Caracas, Latin American Economic System.

Latin American Weekly Report (LAWR) (1992) WR-92–35, September 10: 1.

Leal Buitrago, F., and Tokatlian, J. G. (1994) *Orden mundial y seguridad: Nuevos desafíos para Colombia y América Latina*, Santafé de Bogotá, Tercer Mundo Editores/Instituto de Estudios Políticos y Relaciones Internacionales, Universidad Nacional/Sociedad Internacional para el Desarrollo, Capítulo Colombia.

Lindberg, L., and Scheingold, S. (eds.) (1970) *Regional Integration: Theory and Research*, special issue of *International Organization*, 24 (4).

Loaeza, S. (1988) "Nacionalismo y democracia en México: tensión entre dos ficciones," in R. Cordera Campos, R. Trejo Delabre, and J. E. Vega (coord.), *El Reclamo Democrático*, México, D.F., ILET-Siglo XXI: 98.

Lodge, J. (ed.) (1993) *The European Community and the Challenge of the Future*, London, Pinter.

Lomas, E. (1990) "Alerta Solana sobre la democracia de exportación," *La Jornada*, September 17: 1, 8.

Lowenthal, A. F. (1987) "Estados Unidos y México," in G. M. Bueno, *México–Estados Unidos 1986*, México, El Colegio de México: 41–76.

Lowenthal, A. F. (1990) "Rediscovering Latin America," *Foreign Affairs*, 69 (4), Fall: 27–41.

Lowenthal, A. F. (1993) "Latin America: Ready for Partnership?" *Foreign Affairs*, 72 (1): 74–92.

Lujambio, A. (1993) "Presidentes y congresos: Estados Unidos, la experiencia latinoamericana y el futuro mexicano," *Foro Internacional*, 33 (3) July–September: 517–560.

Lyon, P. (1989) *The Evolution of Canadian Diplomacy Since 1945*, in P. Painchaud (ed.), *From Mackenzie King to Pierre Trudeau: Forty Years of Canadian Diplomacy*, Québec, Presses de l'Université Laval: 13–33.

Mace, G. (1989) *Les relations du Canada avec l'Amérique latine et les Caraïbes*, in P. Painchaud (ed.), *De Mackenzie King à Pierre Trudeau, Quarante ans de diplomatie canadienne*, Québec, Presses de l'Université Laval: 401–432.

Mace, G. (1994) "Consensus-building in the Andean Integration System," in W. A. Axline (ed.), *The Political Economy of Regional Cooperation: Comparative Case Studies*, London, Pinter: 34–71.

Mace, G., and Hervouet, G. (1989) "Canada's Third Option: A Complete Failure?" *Canadian Public Policy*, 15 (4), December: 387–404.

Mace, G.; Bélanger, L.; and Thérien, J.-P. (1993) *Regionalism in the Americas: The International Trade Component*, unpublished manuscript.

McClintock, C. (1984) *The Breakdown of Constitutional Democracy in Peru*, paper presented at the 18th Congress of the Latin American Studies Association, Atlanta, Ga., March 10–12.

Makuc, A. J. (1990) "Estados Unidos y Argentina: Una relación difícil: Un análisis de las relaciones comerciales bilaterales," *Boletín Informativo Techint*, 264: 73–107.

Manley, M. (1982) *Jamaica: Struggle in the Periphery*, London, Third World Media in Association with Writers and Readers Publishing Cooperative Society.

Martins, C. E. (1975) "A Evolução da Política Externa Brasileira na Década 64/74," *Estudos Cebrap*, 12, April/May/June: 91–92.

Martner, G. (1992) *América Latina: el precio de vivir de las materias primas*, Caracas, PROFAL/Nueva Sociedad.

"Mexico: Free Trade Efforts in High Gear" (1991) *Interpress Service*, April 19 (mimeo).

"México y el mundo, por un comercio más intenso y más benéfico" (1990), conclusiones sobre el Foro de Consulta sobre las Relaciones Comerciales de México con el Mundo, *La Jornada*, May 27: 18, 23.

"Mexico's Serra Sees Concerns on Widening NAFTA" (1994) *Reuters*, May 2 (mimeo).

Ministerio de Relaciones Exteriores (1993a) *Colombia-Venezuela: Un nuevo esquema bilateral*, Santafé de Bogotá, Puntos Gráficos.

Ministerio de Relaciones Exteriores (1993b) *Grupo de los Tres*, Santafé de Bogotá, Puntos Gráficos.

Ministerio de Relaciones Exteriores (1994) *Actuar en el mundo*, Santafé de Bogotá, Interlínea Editores.

Mitchell, C. (1967) "The Role of Technocrats in Latin American Integration," *Inter-American Economic Affairs*, 21: 3–39.

Moffett, M. (1990) "Moves by Mexico Toward U.S. Free Trade Pact Means Salinas Must Walk Domestic Tightrope," *Wall Street Journal*, March 30: A14.

Molina Duarte, S. (1992) "Venezuela y el CARICOM: una relación comercial paradójica," *El Universal*, December 11.

Molineu, H. (1986) *U.S. Policy Toward Latin America: From Regionalism to Globalism*, Boulder, Colo., Westview Press.

Le Monde (1991) May 8.

Moran, R. T., and Abbot, J. D. (1994) *NAFTA: Managing the Cultural Differences*, Houston, Gulf Publishing Co.

Morici, P. (1992) "Free Trade with Mexico," *Foreign Policy*, 87, Summer: 88–104.

Morici, P. (1993) "Grasping the Benefits of NAFTA," *Current History*, 92 (571), February: 50–54.

Morrison, A. J., and Roth, K. (1992) "The Regional Solution: An Alternative to Globalization," *Transnational Corporations*, 1 (2), August: 37–55.

Moss, A. H., Jr. (ed.) (1994) *NAFTA: Assessments of the North American Free Trade Agreement*, Miami, University of Miami, North-South Center, Transaction Publishers.

Motta Veiga, P. da (1994) "Relações Comerciais Estados Unidos–MERCOSUL: A Agenda Minilateral: O caso do Brasil," *Documentos de Investigación*, 165, Buenos Aires, FLACSO, July.

Muñoz, H. (1986) *Las Relaciones exteriores del Gobierno Militar Chileno*, Santiago, Las Ediciones del Ornitorrinco/PROSPEL-CERC: 35–83, 135–200.

Muñoz, H. (ed.) (1989) *A la Espera de una Nueva Etapa: Anuario de Políticas Exteriores Latinoamericanas 1988–1989*, Caracas, Editorial Nueva Sociedad/PROSPEL.

Mytelka, L. K. (1992) *South-South Co-operation in a Global Perspective*, Paris, OECD.

Naim, M. (1993) *Paper Tigers and Minotaurs: The Politics of Venezuela's Economic Reforms*, Washington, D.C., Carnegie Endowment.

Nettleford, R. (ed.) (1989) *Jamaica in Independence: Essays on the Early Years*, Kingston/London, Heinemann Caribbean/James Currey.

Nogueira Batista, P. (1993) "A Política Externa de Collor: Modernização ou Retrocesso?" *Política Externa*, 1, March: 106–135.

Nogués, J. J. (1994) "Argentine Exports Affected by the Implementation of the NAFTA and Chile's Accession," *Fundación Mediterránea Newsletter*, 9 (7): 4–7.

Nunes Amorim, C. L. (1991) "O Pano de Fundo Regional and Global," in J. P. dos Reis Velloso (ed.), *O Brasil e o Plano Bush: Oportunidades e Riscos Numa Futura Integração das Américas*, São Paulo, Nobel.

Nunes Amorim, C. L., and Prata Saint-Clair Pimentel, R. (1993) "Iniciativa Para as Américas: 'O Acordo do Jardim das Rosas,'" in Instituto de Pesquisas de Relações Internacionais (IPRI), Ministério das Relações Exteriores and Programa de Política Internacional e Comparada, *60 Anos de Política Externa*, São Paulo, University of São Paulo.

Nye, J. S., Jr. (1990) *Bound to Lead: The Changing Nature of American Power*, New York, Basic Books.

Nye, J. S., Jr. (1992) "What New World Order?" *Foreign Affairs*, 71 (2), Spring: 83–96.

Nye, J. S., Jr.; Biedenkopf, K.; and Shiina, M. (1991) *Global Cooperation After the Cold War: A Reassessment of Trilateralism*, New York, Paris, Tokyo, The Trilateral Commission.

Obregón, L., and Nasi, C. (1990), *Colombia-Venezuela: ¿Conflicto o integración?* Bogotá, Centro de Estudios Internacionales, Universidad de los Andes/ FESCOL.

Ochoa Antich, F. (1993) Entrevista en *El Diario de Caracas*, February 3: 31.

O'Donnell, G. (1973) *Modernization and Bureaucratic-Authoritarianism: Studies in South American Politics*, Berkeley, University of California Press.

Ogelsby, J. C. M. (1976) *Gringos from the Far North*, Toronto, Macmillan.

Ogelsby, J. C. M. (1979) "A Trudeau Decade: Canadian–Latin American Relations, 1968–1978," *Journal of Interamerican Studies and World Affairs*, 21 (2), May: 187–205.

Oman, C. (1994) *Globalisation and Regionalisation: The Challenge for Developing Countries*, Paris, OECD.

Opinión sobre EU y México (1992) *Este País*, 14, May: 22.

Organisation des Nations Unies (ONU) (1992) *Étude sur l'économie mondiale 1992*, New York, United Nations.

Orme, W. A., Jr. (1993) *Continental Shift: Free Trade and the New North America*, Washington, D.C., The Washington Post Company.

Ortiz de Zevallos Paz Soldán, C. (ed.) (1972) *Confederación Perú-Boliviana*, Vol. I: *Estado Nor Peruano—Estado Sud Peruano—Bolivia (1835–1839)*, Vol. 9 of *Archivo diplomático Peruano*, Lima, Ministerio de Relaciones Exteriores.

Ortiz Ramirez, E. (1992) *La política comercial de Venezuela*, Colección Estudios Económicos No. 16, Banco Central de Venezuela, Caracas.

Ortiz Ramirez, E. (1993) "Apertura y comercio en América Latina," *Economía Hoy*, February 3: 7.

Osorio, M. (1992) "El crecimiento económico es incompatible con un programa de ajuste," *Economía Hoy*, November 4: 16–17.

Ouellette, A.; Henderson, S.; and Livermore, D. (1992) *Sovereignty, Non-Intervention and the Intrusive International Order*, Policy Planning Staff Paper No. 92/2, Ottawa, Ontario, External Affairs and International Trade Canada.

Oviedo, A. (1993) "Fracaso diplomático," *El Tiempo*, November 13: 4A.

Paez, T. (1992) *Competitividad: Estrategia Nacional?* Caracas, ILDIS/Nueva Sociedad.

Paiva Abreu, M. de (1994) "O NAFTA e as Relações Econômicas Brasil-EUA," paper presented at the VI Fórum Nacional, Instituto Nacional de Altos Estudos, São Paulo.

Paquet, G. (1991) *The Canadian Malaise and Its External Impact*, in F. O. Hampson and C. J. Maule (eds.), *Canada Among Nations 1990–1991: After the Cold War*, Ottawa, Ontario, Carleton University Press: 25–40.

Paradiso, J. (1993) *Debates y trayectoria de la política exterior argentina*, Buenos Aires, Grupo Editor Latinoamericano.

Pardo García-Peña, R. (1990) "La política exterior del Presidente César Gaviria Trujillo," *Colombia Internacional*, 12, October–December: 3–7.

Pardo García-Peña, R. (1993) "Colombia y Venezuela: Integración: La nueva dimensión de las relaciones bilaterales," *Colombia Internacional*, 24, October–December: 3–10.

Pardo García-Peña, R., and Tokatlian, J. G. (1988) *Política exterior: ¿De la subordinación a la autonomía?* Bogotá, Ediciones Uniandes/Tercer Mundo Editores.

Pastor, M., Jr. (1994) "Mexican Trade Liberalization and NAFTA," *Latin American Research Review*, 29 (3): 153–173.

Pastor, R. A. (1991) "The Bush Administration and Latin America: The Pragmatic Style and the Regionalist Option," *Journal of Interamerican Studies and World Affairs*, 33 (3): 1–34.

Pastor, R. A. (1992) "The Latin American Option," *Foreign Policy*, 88, Fall: 107–125.

Payne, A. (1984) *The International Crisis in the Caribbean*, Baltimore, Johns Hopkins University Press.

Payne, A. (1988) *Politics in Jamaica*, London/New York, Christopher Hurst/St. Martin's Press.

Payne, A. (1992) "The 'New' Manley and the New Political Economy of Jamaica," *Third World Quarterly*, 13 (3): 463–474.

Payne, A., and Sutton, P. (1992) "The Commonwealth Caribbean in the New World Order: Between Europe and North America?" *Journal of Interamerican Studies and World Affairs*, 34 (4), Winter: 39–75.

Payne, D. W.; Falcoff, M.; and Purcell, S. K. (1991) *Latin America: U.S. Policy After the Cold War*, New York, Americas Society.

Pentland, C. (1982) "Domestic and External Dimension of Economic Policy: Canada's Third Option," in W. F. Hanrieder (ed.), *Economic Issues and the Atlantic Community*, New York, Praeger: 139–162.

Pentland, C. (1991) "Europe 1992 and the Canadian Response," in F. O. Hampson and C. J. Maule (eds.), *Canada Among Nations 1990–1991: After the Cold War*, Ottawa, Ontario, Carleton University Press: 125–144.

Pereira, L. V. (1993) "O Projeto MERCOSUL: Uma Resposta aos Desafios do Novo Quadro Mundial?" in *MERCOSUL—Integração na América Latina e Relações com a Comunidade Européia*, São Paulo, Instituto Cajamar and Departamento de Estudos Sócio-Econômicos e Políticos da CUT: 11–40.

Poitras, G. (1990) *The Ordeal of Hegemony: The United States and Latin America*, Boulder, Colo., Westview Press.

Poitras, G., and Robinson, R. (1994) "The Politics of NAFTA in Mexico," *Journal of Interamerican Studies and World Affairs*, 36 (1), Spring: 1–36.

Poole, D., and Renique, G. (1992) *Peru: Time of Fear*, London, Latin American Bureau.

Porta, F. (1994) "MERCOSUL: Atualidade e Alternativas," *Nossa América*, 1.

Porter, R. B. (1991) "The Enterprise for the Americas Initiative: A New Approach to Economic Growth," *Journal of Interamerican Studies and World Affairs*, 33 (4): 1–12.

PROMEXPORT (1992) *Evaluación de las exportaciones no-tradicionales 1989–1991*, Caracas, Oficina de Promoción de Exportaciones.

Purroy, M. I. (1993) "Lecciones de 1992," *El Diario de Caracas*, January 23: 17.

"Quais os Objetivos da Viagem de FHC" (1994) *Carta Política*, 42, October 24/30: 1.

Randall, S. J. (1977) "Canadian Policy and the Development of Latin America," in N. Hillmer and G. Stevenson (eds.), *A Foremost Nation: Canadian Foreign Policy and a Changing World*, Toronto, Ontario, McClelland and Stewart: 202–229.

Randall, S. J. (1991) *Hegemony and Interdependence: Colombia and the United States Since the Wars for Independence*, Atlanta, University of Georgia Press.

República Argentina (1991) Decreto 2284/91, *Boletín Oficial*, Buenos Aires, Viernes 1 de Noviembre.

Rico, C. (1986) "Crisis y recomposición de la hegemonía norteamericana: Algunas reflexiones en torno a la coyuntura internacional en la segunda mitad de los ochenta," in L. Maira (ed.), *Una nueva era de la hegemonía norteamericana?* Buenos Aires, Grupo Editor Latinoamericano: 37–58.

Rico, C. (1992) "North-South Relations in a Changing World Order," paper presented at the seminar "The United States and Mexico: Economic Growth and Security in a Changing World Order," University of Miami, Miami, June 10–13.

Ricúpero, R. (1993) "O Brasil, a América Latina e os Estados Unidos desde 1930: 60 Anos de uma Relação Triangular," paper presented at the seminar "Sixty Years of Foreign Policy," organized by the Instituto de Pesquisas de Relações Internacionais (IPRI), Ministério das Relações Exteriores and Programa de Política Internacional e Comparada of the University of São Paulo, Brasília, March: 1–32 (mimeo).

Ricúpero, R., and Amaral, S. (1993) "O NAFTA e o Brasil," *Política Externa*, 2, June/July/August: 91–101.

Rodríguez Gómez, J. C. (1993) *Liderazgo y autonomía: Colombia en el Consejo de Seguridad de las Naciones Unidas, 1989–1990*, Santafé de Bogotá, Centro de Investigaciones y Proyectos Especiales, Universidad Externado.

Rodríguez Mendoza, M. (1993a) "Apertura económica e integración en América Latina: La experiencia de Venezuela," in A. Serbin, A. Stambouli, J. McCoy, and W. Smith, *La democracia bajo presión: Política y mercado en Venezuela*, Caracas, INVESP/Nueva Sociedad.

Rodríguez Mendoza, M. (1993b) Entrevista en *Economía Hoy*, February 1: 14–15.

Roett, R. (1991) "Las alternativas estratégicas de México en un cambiante sistema mundial: Cuatro opciones, cuatro ironías," in R. Roett (ed.), *Relaciones exteriores de México en la década de los noventa*, México, Siglo XXI: 17–41.

Rogers, K. S. (1995) "Rivers of Discontent—Rivers of Peace: Environmental Cooperation and Integration Theory," *International Studies Notes*, 20, 2, Spring: 10–21.

Rojas, L. (1992) "Aspectos económicos de la política exterior de Venezuela," in C. Romero (ed.), *Reforma y política exterior en Venezuela*, Caracas, COPRE/INVESP/Nueva Sociedad.

Rojas, L. (1993) Entrevista en *Economía Hoy*, January 22: 15.

Romero, A. (1987) *La miseria del populismo*, Caracas, Ediciones Centauro.

Romero, A. (1994) *Decadencia y crisis de la democracia*, Caracas, Panapo.

Romero, C. (ed.) (1992) *Reforma y política exterior en Venezuela*, Caracas, COPRE/INVESP/Nueva Sociedad.

Ros, J. (1994) "Beneficios Comerciales y Movilidad de Capital: Estudios Recientes sobre las Consecuencias del TLC," *Comercio Exterior*, 44 (6), June: 498–501.

Rosales, O. (1990) "Escenarios y tendencias en el comercio internacional," in R. Russell (ed.), *La agenda internacional en los años noventa*, Buenos Aires, Grupo Editor Latinoamericano: 97–126.

Rosati, J. A.; Hagan, J. D.; and Sampson III, M. W. (1994) *Foreign Policy Restructuring: How Governments Respond to Global Change*, Columbia, University of South Carolina Press.

Rosecrance, R. (1991) "Regionalism in the Post–Cold War Era," *International Journal*, 46 (3), Summer: 373–393.

Rosenau, J. (1992) *The United Nations in a Turbulent World*, Boulder, Colo., Lynne Rienner.

Rossant, J. (1992) "One Day, Panic. Next Day, Sales. Devalued Currencies Are Bolstering Business in Britain, Italy and Spain," *Business Week*, October 26: 49–50.

Rostow, W. W. (1990) "The Coming Age of Regionalism," *Encounter*, 74 (5), June: 3–7.

Roxborough, I. (1992) "Neo-Liberalism in Latin America: Limits and Alternatives," *Third World Quarterly*, 13 (3): 421–440.

Rozental, A. (1993) *La política exterior de México en la era de la modernidad*, México, Fondo de Cultura Económica.

Rudolph, J. D. (1992) *Peru: Evolution of a Crisis*, Westport, Conn., Praeger Publishers.

Rugman, A. M. (ed.) (1994) *Foreign Investment and NAFTA*, Columbia, University of South Carolina Press.

Russell, R. (1992) *La política exterior argentina en el nuevo orden mundial*, Buenos Aires, FLACSO/GEL.

Russell, R., and Zuvanic, L. (1991) "Argentina: Deepening Alignment with the West," *Journal of Interamerican Studies and World Affairs*, 33 (3): 113–134.

Salazar-Xirinachs, J. M. (1993) "Towards a High Quality International Insertion (HQI) Strategy for Central America and the Caribbean," paper presented at the annual meeting of the International Studies Association, Acapulco, Mexico.

Salinas de Gortari, C. (1990) "Texto Integro del Segundo Informe de Gobierno," *Excélsior*, November 2: 2.

Salinas de Gortari, C. (1991) "Tercer Informe de Gobierno," *La Jornada*, November 2: II.

Santoro, D. (1992) *Operación Condor II: La historia secreta del misil que desmanteló Menem*, Buenos Aires, Ediciones Letra Buena.

Sarti, F., and Furtado, J. (1993) "Os Setores Industriais no MERCOSUL," in *MERCOSUL—Integração na América Latina e Relações com a Comunidade Européia*, São Paulo, Instituto Cajamar and Departamento de Estudos Sócio-Econômicos e Políticos da CUT: 157–194.

Schott, J. J. (1988) "The Free Trade Agreement: A U.S. Assessment," in J. J. Schott and M. G. Smith (eds.), *The Canada–United States Free Trade Agreement: The Global Impact*, Washington, D.C., Institute for International Economics: 1–36.

Schott, J. J., and Hufbauer, G. C. (1992) "Free Trade Areas, the Enterprise for the Americas Initiative, and the Multilateral System," in C. I. Bradford (ed.), *Strategic Options for Latin America in the 1990s*, Paris, OECD: 249–270.

SELA (1991a) *La Iniciativa para las Américas en el contexto de las relaciones de América Latina y el Caribe con los Estados Unidos*, SP/RC-IA/DT 2, April 22–24.

SELA (1991b) *Apertura comercial e integración regional en América Latina: Diagnóstico y escenarios alternativos*, ED/17, July.

Sepúlveda Amor, B. (1994) "Política Exterior y Tratado de Libre Comercio," *Comercio Exterior*, 44 (6), June: 473–476.

Serbin, A. (1989) *El Caribe: zona de paz?* Caracas, Nueva Sociedad/Comisión Sudamericana de Paz.

Serbin, A. (1990) *Caribbean Geopolitics: Toward Security Through Peace?* Boulder, Colo., Lynne Rienner.

Serbin, A. (1991a) "Latin America and the Non-Hispanic Caribbean's European Connection," in P. Sutton (ed.), *Europe and the Caribbean*, Hong Kong, Macmillan: 200–221.

Serbin, A. (1991b) "El Caribe: Mitos, realidades y desafíos para el año 2000," in A. Serbin and A. Bryan (eds.), *El Caribe hacia el año 2000. Desafíos y opciones*, Caracas, INVESP/Nueva Sociedad: 13–33.

Serbin, A. (1992a) "Seguridad ambiental y cooperación regional: Paradigmas, presupuestos, percepciones y obstáculos," in A. Serbin (ed.), *Medio ambiente, seguridad y cooperación regional en el Caribe*, Caracas, INVESP/Nueva Sociedad: 9–26.

Serbin, A. (1992b) "Venezuela y el Grupo de los Tres en el marco de las transformaciones globales y hemisféricas," in A. Serbin et al., *El Grupo de los Tres: Políticas de integración*, Bogotá: FESCOL: 7–23.

Serbin, A. (1992c) "Venezuela: Reversal or Renewal?" *Hemisphere*, 4 (3), Summer: 24–27.

Serbin, A. (1993a) "El G-3 y el proceso de regionalización en la Cuenca del Caribe," *Nueva Sociedad*, 125, May–June: 120–129.

Serbin, A. (1993b) "Las transformaciones globales y hemisféricas y el Grupo de los Tres: Alcances y limitaciones de su proyección subregional," in A. Serbin and C. Romero (eds.), *El Grupo de los Tres: Evolución y perspectivas*, Caracas, INVESP/FESCOL/Nueva Sociedad.

Serbin, A. (1993c) "La política exterior de Venezuela y sus opciones en el marco de los cambios globales y regionales," *Estudios Internacionales*, 26 (104), October–December: 637–681.

Sharp, M. (1972) "Canada-U.S. Relations: Options for the Future," *International Perspectives*, Autumn.

Silva Michelena, H. (1992) Entrevista en *Economía Hoy*, November 4: 16–17.

Skol, M. (1992) "Venezuela no esta lista para ir al libre comercio con U.S.A.," *El Diario de Caracas*, September 14: 29.

Smith, P. H. (ed.) (1994) *The Challenge of Integration: Europe and the Americas*, Miami, University of Miami, North-South Center.

Smith, W.; Acuña, C. H.; and Gamarra, E. (eds.) (1994a) *Democracy, Markets, and Structural Reform in Latin America: Argentina, Bolivia, Brazil, Chile, and Mexico*, Miami, University of Miami, North-South Center.

Smith, W.; Acuña, C. H.; and Gamarra, E. (eds.) (1994b) *Latin American Political Economy in the Age of Neoliberal Reform: Theoretical and Comparative Perspectives for the 1990s*, Miami, University of Miami, North-South Center.

Soares de Lima, M. R. (1992) "Estratégias de Desenvolvimento e Política Externa: O Caso Brasileiro," paper presented at the Conference Estratégias Liberais de Refundação: Dilemas Contemporâneos do Desenvolvimento, IUPERJ/CLACSO/ISA, Rio de Janeiro, August.

Soares de Lima, M. R., and Cheibub, Z. B. (1994) *Elites Estratégicas e Dilemas do Desenvolvimento*, Rio de Janeiro, IUPERJ, October.

Solana, F. (1994) *Cinco Años de Política Exterior*, México, Editorial Porrúa S.A.

Sonntag, H., and Mangón, T. (1992) *Venezuela: 4-F 1992: Un análisis sociopolítico*, Caracas, Nueva Sociedad.

St John, R. B. (1984) "Peru: Democracy Under Siege," *The World Today*, 40 (7), July: 299–306.

St John, R. B. (1992a) "Boundaries, Trade, and Seaports: Power Politics in the Atacama Desert," *Program in Latin American Studies Occasional Paper Series*, 28, Amherst, University of Massachusetts at Amherst.

St John, R. B. (1992b) *The Foreign Policy of Peru*, Boulder, Colo., Lynne Rienner.

St John, R. B. (1994) "Stalemate in the Atacama," *Boundary and Security Bulletin*, 2 (1), April: 64–68.

St John, R. B., and Gorman, S. M. (1982) "Challenges to Peruvian Foreign Policy," in S. M. Gorman (ed.), *Post-Revolutionary Peru: The Politics of Transformation*, Boulder, Colo., Westview Press: 179–196.

Strange, S. (1988) *States and Markets*, New York, Basil Blackwell.

Sukup, V. (1992) *El peronismo y la economía mundial: Modelos de inserción económica internacional del peronismo: 1946–1955, 1973–1976, 1989–?* Buenos Aires, Grupo Editor Latinoamericano.

"Summit Marks Another Major Milestone for the Americas" (1994) *Honduras This Week*, December 17: 5.

Sutton, P. (1993) "The European Community and the Developing World: Past, Present and Future," *The Oxford International Review*, 5 (1), Winter: 32–35.

Tarre, M. (1993) "El impuesto de Clinton," *El Diario de Caracas*, February 10: 4.

Tavares de Araújo, J. (1988) "Os Fundamentos Econômicos do Programa de Integração Argentina-Brasil," *Revista de Economía Política*, 8, July/September: 41–54.

Tavares de Araújo, J. (1990a) "Integração Econômica e Harmonização de Políticas na América do Norte e no Cone Sul," *Texto de discussão n. 32*, Rio de Janeiro, FUNCEX.

Tavares de Araújo, J. (1990b) "El Programa de Integración Argentina-Brasil y las Tendencias Actuales de la Economía Mundial," in M. Hirst (ed.), *Argentina-Brasil: Perspectivas Comparativas y Ejes de Integración*, Buenos Aires, Editorial Tesis: 215–224.

Tavares de Araújo, J. (1991) "A Opção por Soberanias Compartidas na América Latina: O Papel da Economia Brasileira," in P. da Motta Veiga (ed.), *Cone Sul: A Economia Política da Integração*, Rio de Janeiro, Fundação Centro de Estudos do Comércio Exterior: 177–178.

Testimony, August 2, 1994. Ben Nelson, Associate Director for International Affairs, General Accounting Office, House Government Operations/Information, Justice, Transportation, and Agriculture. "New Challenges in Drug Enforcement" (1994), *Federal Document Clearing House Congressional Testimony*, August 2 (mimeo).

This Week in Trade and Foreign Policy (1992) Ottawa, Ontario, Department of External Affairs and International Trade Canada.

Thompson-Flôres Netto, F. (1989) "Integração Brasil-Argentina: Origem, Processo e Perspectiva," in G. Fonseca, Jr., and V. Carneiro Leão (eds.), *Temas de Política Externa Brasileira*, Brasília, Editora Ártica/Fundação Alexandre de Gusmão: 129–134.

Thorstensen, V.; Nakano, Y.; and Lozardo, E. (1994) "São Paulo e Brasil Frente a um Mundo Dividido em Blocos: O Estado em Busca de uma Política de Comércio Exterior," *Política Externa*, 3, June/July/August: 48–83.

El Tiempo (1992) July 22: 1–2B.

Tokatlian, J. G. (1994) "Los componentes políticos de la integración," in J. Acosta Puertas (ed.), *Integración, desarrollo económico y competitividad*, Santafé de Bogotá, Editorial Presencia: 49–58.

Tokatlian, J. G., and Schubert, K. (eds.) (1983) *Relaciones internacionales en la Cuenca del Caribe y la política de Colombia*, Bogotá, Centro de Estudios Internacionales, Universidad de los Andes/FESCOL/Cámara de Comercio de Bogotá.

Tokatlian, J. G.; Cardona, D.; and Reina, M. (1992) *Colombia y el Grupo de los Tres*, Documentos Ocasionales, Centro de Estudios Internacionales, 28, October–December.

Tokatlian, J. G.; Sarmiento, E.; Orjuela, L. J.; and Arrieta, C. G. (1990) *Narcotráfico en Colombia: Dimensiones políticas, económicas, jurídicas e internacionales*, Bogotá, Tercer Mundo Editores/Ediciones Uniandes.

Toro Hardy, A. (1991) *La maldición de Sísifo: 15 años de política externa venezolana*, Caracas, Panapo.

Toro Hardy, J. (1992) *Venezuela: 55 años de política económica 1936–1991. Una utopía keynesiana*, Caracas, Panapo.

Tovar Tamayo, O. (1974) "El Proyecto Bolívariano de Integración Andina," in *Variables Políticas de la Integración Andina*, Santiago, Centro universitario de desarrollo andino, Ediciones Nueva Universidad: 39–42.

"The Trading Game Inside Lobbying for the North American Free Trade Agreement" (1993) Washington, D.C., The Center for Public Integrity (mimeo).

Tulchin, J. (1990) *La Argentina y los Estados Unidos: Historia de una desconfianza*, Buenos Aires, Editorial Planeta.

Tulchin, J. (1992) "La Iniciativa Bush para las Américas," *América Latina Hoy*, 4, July: 39–48.

Tulchin, J. (ed.), with Bland, G. (1993) *Venezuela in the Wake of Radical Reform*, Boulder, Colo., Lynne Rienner.

Turner, F., and Carballo de Cilley, M. (1989) "Argentines' Attitudes Toward the United States," *International Journal of Public Opinion Research*, 1.

Turner, F. C. (1991) "Regional Hegemony and the Case of Brazil," *International Journal*, 46 (3): 475–509.

Tussie, D. (1992) "Las negociaciones comerciales de la Argentina en un contexto de ajuste externo," *Documentos e informes de investigación*, 125, Buenos Aires, FLACSO.

Ulloa Sotomayor, A. (1938) *Congresos Americanos de Lima*, 2 vols., Lima, Imprenta Torres Aguirre.

Ulloa Sotomayor, A. (1941) *Posición internacional del Perú*, Lima, Imprenta Torres Aguirre.

United Nations Economic Commission for Latin America and the Caribbean (1994) *Open Regionalism in Latin America and the Caribbean: Economic Integration as a Contribution to Changing Production Patterns with Social Equity*, Santiago, UN ECLAC.

Urrutia, M. (1993) *Colombia ante la economía mundial*, Santafé de Bogotá, Tercer Mundo Editores/FEDESARROLLO.

U.S. Congress, Joint Economic Committee (1965) *Latin American Development and Western Hemisphere Trade: Hearings Before the Subcommittee on Inter-American Economic Relationships of the Joint Economic Committee*, 89th Cong., 1st sess.

U.S. Department of Commerce, Foreign Broadcast Information Service (1990–1994) *Daily Report: Latin America (FBIS-LAT)*, FBIS-LAT-90-233, 1990, December 4: 66–67; FBIS-LAT-90-217, 1990, November 8: 36; FBIS-LAT-92-170, 1992, September 1: 37; FBIS-LAT-92-168, 1992, August 28: 2.

U.S. Office of the Trade Representative (US-TR) (1991) *Agreement Between the Government of the United States of America and the Caribbean Community (CARICOM) Concerning a United States–ARICOM Council on Trade and Investment*, Washington, D.C., U.S. Office of the Trade Representative.

Uvin, P. (1993) *The International Organization of Hunger*, doctoral dissertation, IUHEI, Geneva.

Vargas de Losada, C. I. (1991) "El derecho y las relaciones internacionales en la nueva Constitución Política de Colombia," *Revista Cancillería de San Carlos*, 10, November: 6–18.

Vargas Llosa, A. (1994) *The Madness of Things Peruvian*, New Brunswick, N.J., Transaction Publishers.

Vargas-Hidalgo, R. (1979) "The Crisis of the Andean Pact: Lessons for Integration Among Developing Countries," *Journal of Common Market Studies*, 17 (3), March: 213–226.

Vázquez Carrizosa, A. (1983) *Las relaciones entre Colombia y Venezuela: La historia atormentada de dos naciones*, Bogotá, Tercer Mundo Editores.

Vega Cánovas, G. (1993) *México, Estados Unidos, Canadá, 1991–1992*, México, El Colegio de México.

Wagner de Reyna, A. (1964) *Historia Diplomática del Perú (1900–1945)*, 2 vols., Lima, Ediciones Peruanas.

Wall Street Journal (1994) April 7.

Weill, R. A. (1993) "Venezuela Versus México, Chile y Argentina," *El Universal*, March 6: 2–3.

Weintraub, S. (1986) "Canada Acts on Free Trade," *Journal of Interamerican Studies and World Affairs*, 28 (2): 103–104.

Weintraub, S. (1994) "El TLC es Sólo el Principio," *Comercio Exterior*, 44 (6), June: 482–485.

West Indian Commission (WIC) (1992) *Time for Action: Report of the West Indian Commission*, Bridgetown, Barbados, West Indian Commission.

Wiarda, H. J. (1992) *American Foreign Policy Toward Latin America in the 80s and 90s: Issues and Controversies from Reagan to Bush*, New York, New York University Press.

Williamson, J. (ed.) (1990) *Latin American Adjustment: How Much Has Happened?* Washington, D.C., Institute for International Economics.

Wood, R. E. (1986) *From Marshall Plan to Debt Crisis: Foreign Aid and Development Choices in the World Economy*, Berkeley, University of California Press.

World Bank (1987) *Argentina: Economic Recovery and Growth*, A World Bank Country Study, Washington, D.C., World Bank.

World Bank (1992) *World Debt Tables 1992/93*, Vol. I: *Analysis and Summary Tables*, Washington, D.C., World Bank.

World Bank (1993) *Argentina: From Insolvency to Growth*, Washington, D.C., World Bank.

World Bank (1995) *World Development Report*, Washington, D.C., World Bank.

Wynia, G. W. (1981) "Illusion and Reality in Argentina," *Current History*, 80: 62–85.

Wynia, G. W. (1992) *Argentina: Illusions and Realities*, 2d ed. New York, Holmes & Meier.

Yopo, B. (1993) "La concertación política en América Latina: Obstáculos y proyecciones," in *Iberoamerica Hacia el Tercer Milenio*, Primer Seminario de la Academia Iberoamericana de Estudios Diplomáticos, Instituto Matías Romero de Estudios Diplomáticos, Editado por la Secretaría de Relaciones Exteriores, México: 39–50.

Zaid, G. (1984) "Pagar la Deuda," *Vuelta*, 89, April: 7.

Zambrano, L. (1992) "Perspectivas macroeconómicas de Venezuela 1992–1996," first workshop on "Libre Comercio e Impacto Ambiental en Venezuela," Caracas, July 8–10.

Zambrano, L. (1993) "Principales problemas y proyectos: Sensibilidad al comercio internacional y al control ambiental," second workshop on "Libre Comercio e Impacto Ambiental en Venezuela," Miami, January 11–14.

Zapata, J. G. (1992) "El G-3: punto intermedio entre el Pacto Andino y la Iniciativa para las Américas," *Documentos del FESCOL*, Bogotá, FESCOL, June.

THE CONTRIBUTORS

◆

W. Andrew Axline is a professor at the Department of Political Science at the University of Ottawa in Ontario. He has written extensively on the Caribbean integration process and on the theory of regional integration in journals such as *International Organization, Journal of Common Market Studies,* and *Political Science* (New Zealand). His most recent publication is entitled *The Political Economy of Regional Cooperation: Comparative Case Studies* (London, Pinter, 1994).

Louis Balthazar is a professor at the Department of Political Science at Laval University in Quebec City. His main areas of interest are U.S. foreign policy, Quebec nationalism, and Quebec-U.S. relations. His numerous publications include *Contemporary Quebec and the United States, 1980–1985* (with Alfred O. Hero; Lanham, University Press of America, 1988) and *Trente ans de politique extérieure du Québec, 1960–1990* (Quebec City/Sillery, Centre québécois de relations internationales/Septentrion, 1993).

Jorge Chabat teaches in the division of International Studies at the Centro de Investigación y Docencia Económicas in Mexico. One of his main research projects deals with Mexico's insertion in the post–Cold War international order. His most recent publications include "Mexico's Foreign Policy in 1990: Electoral Sovereignty and Integration with the United States" (*Journal of Interamerican Studies and World Affairs,* Winter 1991) and "Mexico: So Close to the United States, So Far from Latin America" (*Current History,* February 1993).

Roberto Duran is the deputy director of the Instituto de Ciencia Política of the Universidad Católica de Chile in Santiago. In recent years his main research has focused on regional and global multilateralism. Among his latest publications is "Changing State/Society Perspective on the United Nations System: Some Aspects Concerning the Chilean Case" (Toronto, York University, 1992).

Guadalupe González teaches in the division of International Studies at the Centro de Investigación y Docencia Económicas in Mexico City. She is directing two research projects, one on the role of the

U.S. Congress in U.S.-Mexican relations and the other on the relationship between foreign policy and political transition and economic policy in Mexico. Her recent publications include "La política exterior de México frente al nuevo contexto hemisférico" in *El Grupo de los Tres. Políticas de Integración* (Bogotá, FESCOL, 1992).

Marc Hufty is a lecturer at the Institute of Development Studies in Geneva. He is also completing a doctoral dissertation on Argentina's economic and foreign policies at the Graduate Institute of International Studies. Over the past few years, he has made several research trips in Argentina and in the Southern Cone. Recent publications include "La décennie gagnée de l'Argentine" (in *America and the Americas*, Quebec City, Presses de l'Université Laval, 1992).

Gordon Mace is a professor at the Department of Political Science at Laval University in Quebec City and the director of the Research Group on International Relations at Laval's Graduate Institute of International Studies. A student of regionalism and Canadian foreign policy toward Latin America, he has published in various journals such as the *Journal of Interamerican Studies and World Affairs, International Journal* (Toronto), *Canadian Public Policy,* and *Études internationales* (Quebec City). Recent publications include "Regional Integration in Latin America: A Long and Winding Road" (*International Journal,* 1988) and "Regionalism in the Americas and the Hierarchy of Power" (*Journal of Interamerican Studies and World Affairs,* Summer 1993, with Louis Bélanger and Jean-Philippe Thérien).

Anthony Payne is a professor of politics at the University of Sheffield in Britain. A foremost specialist on Jamaican politics and Caribbean integration, he conducted extensive research in the Caribbean region and was asked to contribute to the West Indian Commission report on the future of the region. His publications include *Politics in Jamaica* (New York, St. Martin's Press, 1988) and "The 'New' Manley and the New Political Economy of Jamaica" (*Third World Quarterly,* 1992).

Andrés Serbin is the director of the Instituto Venezolano de Estudios Sociales y Políticos in Caracas. His main research interests are domestic politics and foreign policy in Venezuela and integration and security matters in the larger Caribbean region. His most recent publications include *Caribbean Geopolitics: Toward Security Through Peace?* (Lynne Rienner, 1990) and (with C. Romero) *El Grupo de los Tres: Evolución y perspectivas* (Caracas, INVESP/FESCOL/Nueva Sociedad, 1993).

Maria Regina Soares de Lima is a professor in the Political Science Graduate Program of the Instituto Universitário de Pesquisas do Rio de Janeiro and teaches also at the Institute of International Relations of the Catholic University of Rio de Janeiro. One of her main research interests is Brazilian foreign policy, about which she has just completed (with M. Hirst) "Between Neo-Alignment and Neo-Autonomy: Is There a Third Way in U.S.-Brazilian Relations?" (Doc. 164, Buenos Aires, FLACSO, 1994).

Ronald Bruce St John received his Ph.D. from the University of Denver's Graduate School of International Studies and now works in the private sector. He has been a student of Peruvian foreign policy since 1968 and has visited the country on many occasions. He has written extensively on Peru and the Andean region in journals such as *American Journal of International Law, Journal of Interamerican Studies and World Affairs, Inter-American Economic Affairs,* and *World Today.* He is also the author of *The Foreign Policy of Peru* (Lynne Rienner, 1992), *The Bolivia-Chile-Peru Dispute in the Atacama Desert* (International Boundaries Research Unit, University of Durham, 1994), and *The Boundary Between Ecuador and Peru* (International Boundaries Research Unit, University of Durham, 1994).

Jean-Philippe Thérien is an associate professor in the Department of Political Science at the Université de Montréal. A student of international organizations, foreign aid, and cooperation processes, he has published in journals such as *International Organization, Journal of Interamerican Studies and World Affairs, International Social Science Journal,* and the *Canadian Journal of Political Science.* Among his publications is *Une voix pour le Sud. Le discours de la CNUCED* (Paris, L'Harmattan, 1990).

Arlene B. Tickner is a research associate and general coordinator at the Centro de Estudios Internacionales of the Universidad de los Andes in Bogotá. A specialist of Latin American studies, she has co-authored *Colombia-Venezuela: ¿Crisis o Negociación?* (Bogotá, CEI/Uniandes/FESCOL, 1992) and *Cultura y Democracia en América Latina* (Bogotá, M and T Editores, 1992).

Juan Gabriel Tokatlian is the academic director of the Diploma Program on Negotiations and International Relations and the director of the Centro de Estudios Internacionales at the Universidad de los Andes in Bogotá. Tokatlian is a foremost specialist of international relations in Latin America, and his main research interests are politics and foreign policy in Colombia, narcotics trafficking, and regional integration in the Caribbean. Among his numerous publications are (with R. Pardo) *Política exterior colombiana: ¿De la subordinación a la autonomía?* (Bogotá, Uniandes, 1988) and (with E. Guhl) *Medio ambiente y relaciones internacionales* (Bogotá, Uniandes, 1992).

INDEX

◆

ABOUT THE BOOK

---◆---

This comparative analysis of foreign policy behavior in the Americas focuses on the emerging trend toward regionalism.

Following a discussion of the phenomenon of regionalism in general, chapters on the countries of North America, the Caribbean, and South America address three questions fundamental to the relationship between national foreign policy and hemispheric cooperation and integration: How has each country been affected by recent changes in its external environment? How has it responded in terms of macroeconomic policies and major foreign policy orientations? And what do these new foreign policy orientations imply in terms of the country's attitudes toward regionalism, whether hemispheric or subregional?

The concluding chapter draws on the themes—the similarities and differences—emerging from the country studies to appraise the prospect for region building in the next decade.

Gordon Mace is professor of political science at Laval University. His publications include *Intégration régionale et pluralisme idéologique au sein du Groupe Andin*. **Jean-Philippe Thérien** is associate professor of political science at the University of Montreal. He is author of *Une voix pour le Sud: Le discours de la CNUCED*.

DATE DUE

GAYLORD